JANE AUSTEN AND THE DRAMA OF WOMAN

JANE AUSTEN AND THE DRAMA OF WOMAN

LeRoy W. Smith

St. Martin's Press   New York   1983

ISBN 0 – 312 – 43991 – 1

Library of Congress Cataloging in Publication Data

Smith, LeRoy W.
    Jane Austen and the drama of woman.
    Bibliography: p.
    Includes index.
    1. Austen, Jane, 1775 – 1817—Criticism and
interpretation.   2. Austen, Jane, 1775 – 1817—
Characters—Women.   3. Women in literature.   4.
Sex role in literature.   I. Title.
PR4038.W6S6 1982 823'.7 82 – 10680
ISBN 0 – 312 – 43991 – 1

For Mary, who bore me; Martha and Dana, who bear me; and especially Phyllis, who bears with me

Contents

Acknowledgements

I am indebted to the College of William and Mary for help with this study through its programme of Faculty Summer Research Grants and Faculty Semester Research Assignments.

My particular thanks go to colleagues Lynn Bloom and Cecil McCulley for their counsel.

Finally, I owe much to the host of Austen scholars who have contributed to the understanding and enjoyment of Jane Austen's matchless novels.

The author and publishers would like to thank Yale University Press for permission to use the extracts from *The Madwoman in the Attic* by Sandra Gilbert and Susan Gubar, copyright © Yale University Press.

Note on Page References

Page references to Jane Austen's works inserted in the text are to

The Novels of Jane Austen, ed. R. W. Chapman, 5 vols, third edition
   (Oxford University Press, 1932–4).
The Works of Jane Austen, ed. R. W. Chapman, vol. VI: *Minor Works*
   (London: Oxford University Press, 1954).

E	*Emma*
MP	*Mansfield Park*
MW	*Minor Works*
NA	*Northanger Abbey*
P	*Persuasion*
PP	*Pride and Prejudice*
SS	*Sense and Sensibility*

After the first citation of a secondary source, if the author's name accompanies a subsequent citation, the page number will appear in the text in lieu of a footnote (unless there is use of more than one work by that author or a duplication of surnames).

. . . they are aware of each other; they live in each other; what else is love, she asked, listening to their laughter.

Virginia Woolf, *The Waves*

1 Introduction: A Subject in Her Own Right

I

The many judgements about Jane Austen's meaning tell how complex is her vision and how unlikely is a single 'reading' of her novels. Does her work show a primary interest in writing as art or in writing as an idea? Is it chiefly concerned with social structure, relationships and roles or with promoting psychological insight and the psychological treatment of the individual? Does she adhere to traditional literary, social and moral models or to a psychological realism close to modern perceptions of the self and of society? Does she accept the structure and values of her community, or is she sharply critical, even 'subversive', in her estimate of that community? Each opinion draws support.

The dominant emphases are a conservative view – Austen is primarily a moral writer, she accepts the structure and values of her society, and she is indebted to the eighteenth century for her beliefs – and a radical view – her fiction exhibits a division within her mind and personality and a conflict with her society. The conservative view has the longer and fuller history.[1] The radical view dates from D. W. Harding's essay, 'Regulated Hatred: An Aspect of the Work of Jane Austen', in 1940, and from Marvin Mudrick's study, *Jane Austen: Irony as Defense and Discovery*, in 1952.[2] Harding argues that Austen is a 'literary classic of the society which attitudes like hers, held widely enough, would undermine' (41), and that her object in writing is the 'desperate one of merely finding some mode of existence for her critical attitudes' (44). Mudrick states that Austen's irony provides a means of avoiding 'a full commitment' to the 'deeply conformist and self-complacent society' in which, willingly or not, she was trapped. Distance – to protect her reserve, to 'put off self-commitment and feeling' – was her first condition for writing (1, 171).

1

Harding and Mudrick challenged a long-popular image of Austen as a complacent, entertaining novelist of manners, conventional and orthodox in her opinions, niggling and aloof in her judgements. In its place they offered a view of Austen as a 'subversive' critic, consciously or unconsciously engaged in a private war with her social environment. Their argument has deeply penetrated subsequent discussion.[3] But in rejecting the image of an Austen without significant incongruities, they pushed to the extreme of grounding her art on apparently irreconcilable incongruities. In Jane Nardin's description, their discovery is one of 'flawed works written by a great ironic artist who was susceptible enough to social pressure to betray her genius in the interests of social acceptability and whose talents could not always conceal the fundamental incoherence of her point of view' (1–2).

In some Austen criticism the conservative view receives extraneous support from a masculine sexual bias. Occasionally sexual prejudice seems obvious, as in H. W. Garrod's concession that she 'comes as near to being judicial as is permitted to the nature of her sex'[4] and in Anthony Burgess's dismissal of her novels as lacking 'a strong male thrust'.[5] Usually, however, the bias appears to be unconscious. Walter Allen, for example, describes Austen's novels as a feminisation of Henry Fielding's, hence marked by a smaller but more intense range of vision (52); for Ian Watt the novels 'dramatize the process whereby feminine and adolescent values are painfully educated in the norms of the mature, rational and educated male world' (218); and Frank Bradbrook finds in *Emma* an approving presentation of traditional sexual stereotypes.[6] Even where bias is not overt, insensitivity to the 'woman problem' and to the likely interests of a female artist may inhibit recognition of Austen's complexity. Linked also to the conservative view is the persistent claim that she endorsed the status quo of women in her society. This argument began at least in 1852 with G. H. Lewes's praise of her 'special quality of womanliness' and her avoidance of any 'trace of woman's "mission"',[7] and it continues in the 1970s in, for example, Patricia Beer's summation that Austen 'not only accepted the limitations of women's scope but seems in her own life to have found happiness within them'.[8]

During the 1970s, in reaction to these perspectives and to the conservative view generally, supporters of the radical view introduced the argument that Austen critically explored the 'woman problem'. A hint of this approach had appeared in 1938 in Mona

Wilson's linking of Austen and Mary Wollstonecraft,[9] and it is anticipated in statements by Lionel Trilling, David Daiches and Patricia Thomson in the 1940s and 1950s.[10] In the 1960s Mary Ellmann noted that Austen is read 'only for her mockery' of domestic ideals, although she also spoke of Austen's frivolity, her acceptance of the social order, and her lack of 'ethical sweep';[11] and Robert Donovan described Austen as concerned with 'feminine heroism', which he defined as 'constancy to whatever ideal of conduct or character . . . [women] profess' in the face of social or practical necessity.[12]

In the early 1970s Austen's interest in the 'woman problem' is formally identified by several commentators, but it is not treated at length.[13] The first important discussion of her as possibly a 'feminist' writer appeared in 1973, in Lloyd Brown's claim that her themes are comparable to those of Wollstonecraft in the questioning of certain masculine assumptions.[14] Other treatments followed. In 1976 Alison Sulloway, with special attention to *Emma*, stressed the common concern of Austen and Wollstonecraft with the influence of sex on wealth and caste and with the importance of training women to think rationally; and she claimed that Austen offered 'a new human archetype, the gentlewoman struggling for responsible autonomy'.[15] In the same year Ellen Moers pointed out that Austen's concern with money reflected a protective interest in women's situation in society.[16] Marian Fowler observed in 1977 that Austen's views on the education of the elegant female and on woman as rational creature closely resembled those of feminist writers of the 1790s. Fowler describes Elizabeth Bennet as 'liberated from the female stereotypes of her society to be herself, a truly delightful model for all feminists, both then and now'.[17] In 1978 Susan MacDonald described the subject of *Pride and Prejudice* as the 'interplay between the individual female character and the conventional social roles into which society tends to force its women'. In her judgement, 'while Jane Austen is perhaps less explicitly a feminist than Charlotte Brontë, George Eliot, or Virginia Woolf . . . she is just as conscious of women's problems'.[18] And in 1979 Warren Roberts argued that in her first three novels Austen took a feminist position, criticising the world of female gentility from a perspective similar to Wollstonecraft's; but that in her last three novels she took a position closer to Hannah More's, defending the traditional assumption of an essential difference between the nature of the two sexes and between their roles in society.[19]

Especially informative are two studies in this period by Patricia Meyer Spacks of the tradition of novels by women. In the first, *The Female Imagination* (1975),[20] Spacks states that Austen operates fully within the setting of what, cautiously, she calls 'a woman's point of view' (4), and she draws these conclusions:

(1) Austen and Ellen Glasgow describe 'the delicate emotional balancing point on which women must poise between commitment to others and preservation of their selves' (106);

(2) Austen shows that a girl may discover 'the positive advantages of maturity over childishness' despite the encouragement of her society to remain immature (121);

(3) A young woman's life and problems are an 'intense microcosm of the adult woman's'. Austen regards female adolescence, despite the discouragement of a girl's sense of worth, as a 'time of development, not of giving up' (133–4);

(4) No more than George Eliot, Elizabeth Gaskell or Fanny Burney can Austen answer the questions about women's lot that she raises. But, although her insistence on self-responsibility and self-development may derive partly from desperation, it produces growth and may 'improve the quality of human relationships' (317); and,

(5) The story of Emma Woodhouse illustrates the point that heroines must 'reconcile themselves to the facts of external experience, which deny the freedom and power they feel in their inner lives . . .' (319–21).

 within the boundaries of social + moral . . . . . .

In the second study, *Imagining a Self: Autobiography and Novel in Eighteenth-Century England* (1976),[21] Spacks identifies as a common property of Austen and eighteenth-century female novelists 'the capacity to convey through conventional structures the private intensity of divided impulse' (63). The strength of Burney and Austen, compared to their predecessors,

 derives from successful exploitation of the dichotomy between public passivity and private energy that weakened those women unable to use their sense of division as material for strong images of female experience. The most successful women writers of the century richly examine what others only imply: the fact that society makes women dwell in a state of internal conflict with necessarily intricate psychic consequences. (89)

The most detailed and assertive analysis of Austen's position in the history of literature by women about women is by Sandra Gilbert and Susan Gubar in *The Madwoman in the Attic: The Woman Writer and the Nineteenth-Century Literary Imagination*, in 1979.[22] In an earlier essay-review, Gubar had declared that Austen 'found female fiction inadequate, even subversive' because 'it helped perpetrate the myths that support female subjugation';[23] and she had made the following observations about Austen's activity as a woman writer:

(1) Austen wrote in order to escape the 'restraints she imposes on her female characters' (255);
(2) Her own self-division is re-enacted in the pairs she describes;
(3) A woman's 'emerging self can survive only with a sustained double vision', with the corollary that 'Austen's heroines can live and flourish *because* of their contradictory projections' (256);
(4) She uses 'imagination or wit or irony as an attribute that defines the assertive independence, the spirited wilfulness of females', which she invariably condemns as 'irresponsible, false to reality, and self destructive', (254);
(5) In *Emma* she confronts the 'inadequacy of fiction and the pain of the "imaginist" who encounters the relentless recalcitrance of the world in which she lives' (254); and,
(6) Emma Woodhouse, by learning 'to relinquish control', is better equipped to live in her patriarchal society (256).

In *The Madwoman in the Attic* Gilbert and Gubar argue that the 'decorous surfaces' of Austen's works conceal an 'explosive anger' (111): 'it *is* shocking how persistently Austen demonstrates her . . . dissatisfaction with the tight place assigned women in patriarchy and her analysis of the economics of sexual exploitation' (112). She knew that because of their vulnerability women must accept confinement (108). But she 'makes a virtue of her own confinement, as her heroines will do also. By exploiting the very conventions she exposes as inadequate, she demonstrates the power of patriarchy as well as the ambivalence and confinement of the female writer. She also discovers an effective subterfuge for a severe critique of her culture' (121). Austen's propriety is seen in the overt lesson she sets out to teach in all of her mature novels – what Gilbert and Gubar label her 'cover story':

she always defers to the economic, social, and political power of men as she dramatizes how and why female survival depends on gaining male approval and protection. . . .

Dramatizing the necessity of female submission for female survival, Austen's story is especially flattering to male readers because it describes the taming . . . of a rebellious, imaginative girl who is amorously mastered by a sensible man. . . . [and] reinforces women's subordinate position in patriarchal culture. (154)

Undoubtedly a useful acknowledgement of her own ladylike submission and her acquiescence to masculine values, this plot also allows Austen to consider her own anxiety about female assertion and expression, to dramatize her doubts about the possibility of being both a woman and a writer. She describes both her own dilemma and, by extension, that of all women who experience themselves as divided, caught in the contradiction between their status as human beings and their vocation as females. (155)

For Gilbert and Gubar Austen herself is 'involved in a contradiction that . . . she approves as the only solution available to her heroines. Just as they manage to survive only by seeming to submit, she succeeds in maintaining her double consciousness in fiction that proclaims its docility and restraint even as it uncovers the delights of assertion and rebellion' (168–9). Thus Austen 'serves as a paradigm of the literary ladies . . . in the mid-nineteenth century . . . who strenuously suppressed awareness of how their own professional work called into question traditional female roles' (169).

The reassessment begun by Harding and Mudrick and by these recent explorers of Austen's interest in the 'woman problem' posits a 'dark side' to her view of the relationship between the individual and society. Tension – from conflict within her own personality, between her ideas of what society is like and what it should be, or between the public and private intentions in her novels – is thought to be a characteristic of her work; and the discovery leads to the uncovering of patterns of concealment and disguise and uses of irony that permit her to retain a double vision without detection, to release her pain and pressure at a minimal risk of public censure, or to soften the consequences of a disclosure of her radical thought. Austen is perceived as critical of her society, rebellious, subversive, even alienated; and her comic treatment is regarded as a mode of accommodation to unalterable circumstances, as an instrument of wishful thinking, or as a means of distancing herself through art from a threatening reality.

Although this argument enhances one's sense of Austen's complexity as artist and person, it encourages a view of her as a victim of her society that seems as narrow as the conservative argument seems in presenting her as its defender. Furthermore, the descriptions thus far of Austen's involvement with the 'woman question' are incomplete and, in some instances, misleading. As an example of the latter, Gilbert and Gubar appear to overstate the problem of division within Austen. They ascribe anxiety and guilt to her because of a contradiction between an overt acquiescence to male domination and a covert activity as a writer,[24] and they base their concept of the 'cover story' on an insolvable conflict between open submission and hidden resistance to male rule. But ascribing to Austen so deep a split with her society and within her own thought and feeling is largely a matter of conjecture. Although Austen very probably did possess a double vision, the novels suggest more plausibly that she reconciled the two modes in her own mind and avoided the deliberate self-blinding, persistent defeat or resort to evasion and the hypocrisy of the subjugated that Gilbert and Gubar, like Harding and Mudrick before them, point to.

One questions Gilbert and Gubar on other points as well, for example their picture of the 'maturity' of Austen's heroines. The novels provide little basis for their assumption that 'Marianne Brandon, Elizabeth Darcy, and Emma Knightley' would have to learn, or practise, 'the intricate gestures of subordination' (163). These ladies accomplish much more than survival by appearing to submit. The arguments that Austen's heroines are engaged in a search for a new and better father, that their happiness depends on their gaining male approval and protection, and that the 'cover story' dramatises the necessity of female submission are equally suspect, especially since Gilbert and Gubar also describe Austen's mature heroines as duplicitous creatures who use 'silence as a means of manipulation, passivity as a tactic to gain power, submission as a means of attaining the only control available to them . . . [and who] *seem* to submit as they get what they both want and need' (163). The description of endings that Gilbert and Gubar offer takes this surprising turn: 'On the one hand, this process and its accompanying sense of doubleness is psychologically and ethically beneficial, even a boon to women who are raised by it to real heroism. On the other hand, it is a painful degradation for heroines immersed or immured in what de Beauvoir would call their own "alterity" ' (163).

In their judgement Austen offers accommodation, acquiescence and development of a double vision, if not a double life, as an optimistic, though qualified, solution to the problems of women. But this remedy, which they describe as 'psychologically and ethically beneficial', resembles the strategy of the conquered or enslaved, not a solution at all but an accommodation long practised though deplored as signifying the acquiescence of the powerless. Gilbert and Gubar acknowledge that such a split has drawn many women to schizophrenia (162); they do not explain how, in the case of Austen's heroines, it can be a tolerable solution. They simply assert that the latter 'live and flourish *because* of their contradictory projections. . . . Self-consciousness liberates them from the self, enabling them to be exquisitely sensitive to the needs and responses of others' (163). This description fits the stereotype of the 'feminine' woman, shaped by her culture to serve, to administer and to survive by pleasing – the angel in the house living an inauthentic life. One is puzzled by both the argument and its application to Austen.

In light of the possibilities and problems uncovered by these discussions, there is a need to look closely at Austen's interest in the 'woman question'.[25] It is a subject that critics often ignore, elide or misinterpret in evaluating the work of a woman writer. In Austen's case, the tendency has been either to deny that her interest went beyond affirming the status quo or to depict her as a victim of repression whose art disguised her frustration. Both treatments, however, appear reductive. Austen could plausibly take a position on the 'woman question' that would be radical in her day and also maintain a conservative outlook in other matters, and her writing suggests that she did look and feel deeply on both sides of a question.

What these recent studies persuasively suggest is that Austen viewed woman as a subject in her own right and gave us a woman's idea of the female rather than a male's. Since the two were radically different, to accomplish the former meant to meet the latter head on; and since the relationship between the sexes was essentially one of male domination and female subjugation, to accomplish it meant to depict woman's sexual inferiority and emotional vulnerability. Such an interest would be consonant with the emerging female consciousness of the late eighteenth century, as well as with that of the generations following and the 'limited revolt' of the feminist campaign of the late nineteenth century. Indeed, so central was the 'woman question' to the lives of Austen and her female contemporaries and so rich were its dramatic possibilities that this interest may be a source of the substantiality of her 'slight fiction'. Many of the competing readings can be reconciled by looking past them to this theme.

An interest in female experience is compatible with one's expectations of the artist, especially of the artist as social critic. The subjugation of women is a major social evil. In treating it, rather than choosing or appearing to choose to support a social order that privately she resists, Austen sets out to improve that order. By reducing or removing the causes of conflict between the individual and society, she wants to affirm the absence of any permanent incompatibility between them. In Austen's handling, woman's quest for freedom and the preservation of her selfhood is an intense version of human experience in general.

Real life informs Austen's art, and the latter gives back a pattern for behaviour, a 'truth of possibility'.[26] Her message is not a negative one – concealment, repression and accommodation – but a positive one – the possibility of personal freedom and happiness. Austen's heroines act out Lee Edwards's description of heroism and the woman-hero: 'The goal of the heroic quest . . . is love and a revised sense of the possibilities of individual relationship'; its purpose is to liberate love from ritual bondage; its success depends 'on the emergence of two fully developed psyches'.[27]

II

Austen lived in an hierarchical society organised on patriarchal principles. As defined by a defender, a patriarchy 'associates authority and leadership primarily with males . . . [who] fill the vast majority of authority and leadership positions'.[28] As defined by an opponent, it is a 'system in which men – by force, direct pressure, or through ritual, tradition, law, and language, customs, etiquette, education, and the division of labor, determine what part women shall or shall not play, and in which the female is everywhere subsumed under the male'.[29] Both proponents and assailants regard patriarchy as an ancient, universal and dominantly masculine society.

Explanations of the origins of patriarchy vary. One traditional but contested claim is that it is the result of biological differences.[30] Engels argued that women's position declined as male-owned private property became an organising principle for society. Domesticating the work of women created a basis for subordinating them to men.[31] Recent explanations ascribe patriarchy to the opposition between the domestic and public orientation of women and men, particularly in the role of the former as mothers; to an assignment of women to a lower order of being than men because they are associated with nature whereas men are identified with culture;[32] and to an obsession by the male with fatherhood and personal continuity, which leads him to assert physical or mental control over the female.

Since patriarchy is widely encountered and deeply rooted in mankind's historical past, its march through the centuries may appear relentless. However, Lawrence Stone, in his impressive study *The Family, Sex and Marriage in England 1550–1800*, points out that such a 'unilinear theory of history . . . ignores the ups and downs of social and intellectual change'.[33] About patriarchalism in England Stone observes that

> in terms of both sexual attitudes and power relationships, [from the sixteenth century to the twentieth] one can dimly begin to discern huge, mysterious, secular swings from repression to permissiveness and back again. In England an era of reinforced patriarchy and discipline lasted from about 1530 to about 1670, with the high point in the 1650s. This in turn gave way to an era of growing individualism and permissiveness which was dominant in the upper middle and upper classes from about 1670 to about 1790. The next stage in the evolution of the family was marked by a strong revival of moral reform, paternal authority and sexual repression, which was gathering strength among the middle classes from about 1770. (666)

Thus Austen grew up during the last years of a period that saw 'greater stress on internal bonding' and a 'marked reversal of the previous trend toward domestic patriarchy', particularly among the gentry and high bourgeoisie, with mate selection based more on free choice than on parental decision and 'as much on expectations of lasting mutual affection as on calculations of an increase in money, status or power' (655–6). This new family type carried 'a much greater load of emotional and sexual commitment'; it 'was more conjugal and less kin and community oriented . . . less patriarchal and authoritarian . . .' (657). Although her fiction appeared during the beginning of a period of reassertion of patriarchal authority in the early nineteenth century, which reached a peak in the middle of the century (667), Austen's sympathy apparently lay with what Stone describes as the 'trends to a more individualistic family type among the middle and upper classes in the eighteenth and the twentieth centuries' rather than with the 'two other centuries of patriarchy during the Puritan and the Victorian periods' (683).[34]

At the heart of patriarchy is a theory of male and female personality, an assignment of sex roles, and a stereotyping of masculine and feminine characteristics. The concept of personality associated with patriarchy is the bipolar, in terms of which the traits of men and women strongly contrast and are characteristic of each sex. Its opposite is the dualistic concept: traits conventionally identified as masculine and feminine may vary more or less independently among individuals of both sexes. Acceptance of the bipolar model encourages the differentiation of sex roles.[35]

In the traditional view differences in genes determine differences in roles and temperament. For women the primary role was childbearing and care of the family, whereas for men it was providing for the family's well-being. This division fostered the development or acquisition of different behaviours and skills. Since the behaviour encouraged in the male induced a dominant physical role and that encouraged in the female induced a submissive one, such a relationship grew between the sexes, with the explanation that it was 'natural'; and it became self-perpetuating. These differences in turn produced a cultural evaluation that the dominant role was superior and the submissive role was inferior.[36]

In addition to the distinction between male and female sex roles, traditional assumptions about biological gender lead to stereotypes of male and female personality. The categories of 'masculine' and 'feminine' are exclusive, contradictory and polar; the sexes are viewed as different in both aptitude and function. The masculine stereotype includes aggressiveness, competitiveness, rationality, analytic ability, objectivity, emotional control, activity, intelligence, independence, confidence and self-sufficiency, linked to consciousness and tending to construct boundaries between the self and the 'other'. The feminine stereotype includes passivity, submissiveness, dependence, subjectivity, intuitiveness, sensitivity, irrationality, emotionality, empathy and adaptability, linked to unconsciousness and tending to reduce boundaries between the self and the 'other'.[37]

The bipolar concept of male and female psychology and the cultural assumption of male superiority produce a formidable sex-role ideology which is inculcated and reinforced by education and training. In patriarchy, from early childhood on, the female is taught that her function is to bear children and to create an atmosphere of support and nurturance for the male. Her education is apt to stress acceptable social behaviour and preparation for the socially defined roles of wife and mother. Since women are taught to desire what men want in a woman, not what is within their natures to be, such training encourages concealment or repression of one's sexual interests and a diminished sense of self. Austen's contemporary Wollstonecraft thought that it could force a woman into a private fantasy life and unfit her for the tasks society assigned to her – the education of children and companionship to men.[38]

The impact of the sex-role ideology of patriarchy on the life of women is far-ranging and deep. Not only does it provide the frame-work in which a young woman develops and to which she has to adjust, but she in turn becomes part of the chain of social continuity and acts in accord with her shaped needs and aspirations. Since those who possess power in patriarchy and who benefit from it most, predominantly males, have little reason to question it, the system seems almost self-perpetuating.[39]

Although the imposition of sex roles restricts the development of both sexes, women are apt to be more aware than men of the limits of their role, because these limits are tighter and opportunities are fewer and less diverse; and they are apt to be more conservative. In patriarchy men compete as individuals and are differentiated in their roles. Women, however, lead similar lives to one another. The society is concerned with them almost exclusively as sisters, wives and mothers. Feeling themselves limited, they distrust action. Although they may not like the place assigned to them, they may doubt their ability to change it and settle instead for what they have. A woman's acceptance of the female role may thus be an expression of submission and resignation. The price she pays to possess security or to avoid the guilt of resisting what society demands may be a crippling self-reduction.[40]

Despite the differences in their worlds men and women in patriarchy generally share the stereotypical notions about what is masculine and feminine, and the latter, in turn, influence their thinking about each other. Thus heterosexual relationships are robbed of candour and marred by fallacies and prejudices. A genuine communication between the sexes requires the breaking down of walls within the male and female psyches as well as within the society, but correction of this situation – achievement of a 'truly open and honest communication, mutual respect', and deep affection – can probably 'only result from interaction among equals'.[41] In this predicament the dualistic concept of male and female personality offers a possible solution. If men and women can look past the traditional sexual stereotypes of personality, they may discover that each possesses traits assigned to the other and in the process become whole persons.[42] + Paubrick chal ? ?.

The primary relationship in patriarchy is one of power, whereby males are dominant and females are subordinate. This imbalance is usually shown by the male's economic hold over the female, her lack of legal status, and the institutionalisation of force to uphold patriarchy's rule. Such an imbalance distorts personal relationships: 'deference or compliance indicates weakness, if not servility, and is accompanied by resentment, conscious or unconscious'.[43] Domination and superiority encourage arrogance and feelings of self-love and are accompanied by favoured access to opportunity, assumptions of the right to make decisions, and expectations of leadership. The effect is corrosive. Often what is considered 'masculine' is something purely egotistic – a 'core of selfish, limited, self-aggrandizing behaviour' that in reality constitutes a disastrous ignorance of self.[44]

To the extent that women agree that they are subordinate, they may project this attitude into the roles they play and build it into the internal structure of their own psyches. In Elizabeth Janeway's summation, because of the loss of direct, personal connection with the public sphere, women lack an objective standard by which to measure themselves and their actions. Their concentration on personal feelings tends to make all judgements personal, private and emotional (168–72). In Adrienne Rich's judgement, women's powerlessness produces, on the one hand, cultivation of feelings of 'lassitude, self-negation, guilt, and depression' and, on the other hand, 'an alert and practical observation of the oppressor' (65). Mary Daly finds in women a psychological paralysis because of their 'general feeling of hopelessness, guilt, and anxiety over social disapproval'; a 'feminine anti-feminism' that 'looks upon a woman who threatens that structure as a threat to herself'; and a false humility that imposes on the self 'a strangely ambivalent fear of success' (51–3).[45]

Driven underground, resentment may seek an outlet in a quest for power. In patriarchy one form that female power may take is the negative power to act as an impediment.[46] Another form is a reversal of roles from docility to dominance. In Janeway's view, the 'bitch' shadows the private, loving woman. The more a woman is prevented from acting for herself in a man's world, the more likely her search for identity and use of her energies will concentrate in her private world. Thus the negative role of bitch may surface in marriage, if this is the only place where a woman can exercise power. Janeway also describes the 'shrew' as a 'negative caricature of the compliant, pleasing woman'. Her behaviour expresses the message that 'pleasing goes with dependence and subordination' (121–7, 205).

The most important casualty of the power imbalance in patriarchy is heterosexual love. The forces of love and power are antithetical, and the struggle between them is always the same. In patriarchy, 'sexual love is imagined as power *over* someone, or the falling *under* someone else's power . . . [and] responsibility toward the other, genuine knowledge of the other as person, is unnecessary'.[47] Love can correct the abuse of power only when one possesses self-knowledge, knowledge of the other person, and knowledge of one's circumstances.[48] Since true heterosexual love involves freedom of choice, a 'high emotional valuation of the other sex', and equality between the loving pair, patriarchy views it as subversive.[49]

In patriarchy, concern for the disposition of property rules the making of marriages. In nineteenth-century England middle- and upper-class women had little choice but to place themselves on the market in hope of attracting a bidder. From her marriage a woman might expect 'freedom from parental authority, social status, and enough pin money . . . to make life tolerably pleasurable'. She might, at the best, 'become a woman in her own right in the eyes of the world' and, depending on her luck, in her own eyes. At the worst, marriage became a form of legalised prostitution.[50]

Transforming a patriarchal society or escaping from it poses a formidable task. Although the dominant male obviously has little incentive to change it, more puzzling is that women themselves have been reluctant to act to free themselves. In explanation, women in patriarchal society not only face substantial psychological barriers to

Surmises ---

altering their situation, but the oppressor also exists within them, producing a self-defeating behaviour. Submerged in roles believed to be pleasing to males, they may fear an alternative freedom. The operation of the patriarchal order itself discourages protest. In Daly's analysis, its 'symbol systems and conceptual apparatuses' tend to falsify women's self-image. The system also acts to disguise women's low estate, first, by sex-role segregation, which makes possible the delusion that women should be 'equal but different'; second, by the fact that women acquire 'various forms of *derivative status*' from their relationship with men, for example as daughters and wives, which divide them against each other; third, by ideologies, such as patriarchal religion, 'that bestow false identities' (7, 2–3, 23–4, 48); and, finally, by provision of a false security, in terms of which a woman who conforms 'need never explore the limits of her abilities' and hence risk failure or take 'responsibility for her own personal identity'.[51] The most important source of women's consent to their own victimisation is the sex-role socialis-ation which begins at birth and continues throughout one's life. In Karen Horney's summation, in a patriarchy 'women have adapted themselves to the wishes of men and felt as if their adaptation were their true nature'.[52]

III

Although, in tracing the history of women, scholars for a long time either largely ignored the eighteenth century or viewed it as a period of unenlightenment, according to recent studies the changing role and increasing importance of women was one of that period's vital events. Without thinking of themselves as feminists in the current sense or developing a political programme, indeed, while often disguising their purposes or apologising for their behaviour, English women of the eighteenth century made concern with the 'woman question' an active issue, especially with respect to a woman's right to choose her husband and her right to an education, that is, her right to knowledge.[53]

Thus Wollstonecraft's *A Vindication of the Rights of Women* (1792), as well as marking the beginning of modern feminism, was the culmination of the increasing female consciousness of the preceding century.[54] Wollstonecraft did not expect a radical reorganisation of society or question the value of marriage or of motherhood; the reforms she proposed were intended to strengthen the family. She argued that women are shaped to be superficial creatures by their environment, not by nature; they are forced into bondage by the false ideal imposed by society. She urged women to assert themselves, to demand equality with men. But first they should develop the intellect and find new activities; they should become judges of their own interest. Wollstonecraft attacked 'woman's helpless position under the marriage laws . . . her exclusion from political life, her effective debarment from respectable employment, and her handicaps if unmarried'.[55] Her principal target was women's education, which failed to develop their capacities or interests. It should be equal to and identical to men's, and it should help women develop the ability to think rationally. Such an education, she thought, would remove the causes of men's prejudices against women. Unfortunately, the outburst of overt feminist statements by Wollstonecraft and her contemporaries fell upon a world in retreat before the heresies of the French Revolution and were eclipsed by the repudiations they prompted.

Women's increasing attention in the eighteenth century to their role and status is reflected in many of the novels written in the period, especially in the latter half.[56] John Richetti observes that by mid-century one can see

> the creation of a distinctively modern kind of heroine and the expression of a new female consciousness, or at least . . . a new awareness of the value of female experience on the part of a male-dominated culture. The transition is perhaps best described this way: woman as moral topic becomes woman as metaphor; from woman as the center of a moral-rhetorical occasion, the literary tradition moves to examining female experience as a revealingly intense version of human experience in general.[57]

Edna Steeves states that although women's writing of the period did not present a 'really serious and practical proposal for bettering woman's condition' (56), it raised the question, especially in the last decades before 1800, of how men should 'feel and act toward women, and how . . . women [should] interest men – within the bounds . . . [of] discretion and security' (49). In Steeves's opinion, the 'seedbed of feminist propaganda was being prepared with patience and care' (57). If, as Lloyd Brown suggests, one may define 'feminism in the novel' as 'a coherent body of opinions held by the novelist on the identity and social functions of women' in accord with a 'liberationist philosophy',[58] then he believes that one may perceive in the 1790s the breaking through of a distinctive liberationist point of view in women's fiction, one generated by pressures of the time (324).

The emergence in the eighteenth century of the novel offered women a means of dramatising the actual circumstances of their existence through the projection of images in a 'fiction'. The most important result of this discovery was a general growth of female self-consciousness. Women novelists wrote not about society but about women's relationship to it, confident of the appeal of this subject to the women readers who were their principal audience. Their success encouraged them to show a 'growing individualism' in their novels – 'a tendency to write as women'.[59]

Samuel Richardson provided the pattern for a 'feminist' novel by focusing on 'internal experience, particularly in the minds of women'. In Katherine Rogers's analysis, he made his 'heroine an independent entity, not one who exists merely in relationship to men'; and he presented 'manners, morals, human relationships as they affect women'.[60] Furthermore, he probed the traditional assumptions about the relationships of men and women. Richardson constantly affirmed women's capacity and desire to be independent. In *Clarissa* he developed 'the tragic conflict between this potential and the patriarchal society which systematically repressed it'.[61]

After Richardson the movement of novels by women towards what Lloyd Brown calls a liberationist point of view was slow, halting and laboured. As Rogers indicates, there was the danger that this pattern 'could degenerate from a model to a set of constrictions', could limit adherents to a subjective world, or could pressure writers to perform contrary to the direction of their own taste and talent.[62] Furthermore, deeply entrenched patriarchal attitudes were difficult to dislodge. Thus many novels, especially near the turn of the century and after, for example Charlotte Lennox's *Euphemia* (1790), Jane West's *The Advantages of Education* (1803), and Hannah More's *Coelebs* (1809), were very conservative in view, describing the proper training of a young woman and acquiescing in women's subordinate position. The note of female self-deprecation continued, as did the assumption of women's susceptibility to a destructive sexuality.[63]

Still, one discerns a growing interest in improving the situation of women, though it is identified in different ways. Edna Steeves notes that even if the traditional social situation itself was not examined closely, issues connected with marriage, as it affected women, were being argued: for example, the inequity involving man's social freedom versus woman's domestic confinement, woman's surrender of control over property both real and personal, and her inability to extricate herself from an unhappy marriage (52–3). B. G. MacCarthy observes that

> Now and then, in these women's novels, a spark leaps up for a moment to throw light on the untouched question of the woman *per se*. Sometimes there is even a tiny blaze. Then we return again to women echoing the masculine ideal of women. . . .
>   Still . . . the current flowed on and gathered force. (43)

And in Spacks's summary, although 'eighteenth-century popular novels reflect the rigid and simplistic morality to which the society paid lip service', the more interesting fact is that 'female novelists . . . find images and actions to express profound ambivalence. They convey the energy of impulse as well as of repression; asserting that women are to be valued for their goodness, they wistfully hint a yearning for other grounds of value.'[64] Spacks discovers in this body of fiction 'deep currents running beneath the placidities of social conformity', 'psychic strategies of survival [that] unconsciously shape their [female novelists'] stories of self and of others' (90). Finally, in Moers's judgement, pre-feminist ideas at the turn of the century were visible and substantial and spurred what she calls 'literary feminism', or 'heroinism', the woman writer's attempt 'to create a heroic structure for the female voice in literature'. Thus the radicalism of Wollstonecraft 'makes only one end of the spectrum of opinion that colors the writing of the self-conscious women of her day. In the 1780s, 1790s, and 1800s, feminism touched them all' (122–5). In Moers's summation, 'when *Pride and Prejudice* finally appeared in 1813, women's literature came of age and with it the English novel' (120).

2 Jane Austen and the 'Drama of Woman'

Little is directly known of Jane Austen's acquaintance with the developing female consciousness in the eighteenth century. That she examines the 'drama of woman' in her novels is a judgement based on the likelihood that she was sensitive to her social and literary environment, on the similarity between her views and those of 'feminist' writers of the 1790s, and, above all, on the evidence of the novels themselves.

The once-popular image of Austen as a 'refined Victorian lady' has generally been discarded. She was a vigorous, vocal member of a large, active family. Even after their protective editing, her letters show that her 'familiar world was, socially and emotionally, much less circumscribed than that of her novels; and that her experience of life was wider, her attitudes to it more various, than some biographical and critical accounts would lead us to imagine'.[1] She jokes about deformity, injury, death, drunkenness, child-bearing and illegitimacy; calls lust and adultery by their proper names; and shows herself to be a caustic and unblinking observer of the realities of women's existence. Similarly, and contrary to the traditional view, Austen does not avoid the subject of sex in her fiction. Although she controls her use to fit her settings, avoid offence and keep attention where she feels it belongs, she is well aware of sexuality's powerful role in human behaviour. In the foreground of her stories it operates as a nearly autonomous influence on the mating manoeuvres of her characters; in the background it may threaten one's social and personal well-being.[2]

By virtually unanimous agreement Austen is a social novelist, focusing on the interaction of individuals and groups within a clearly defined community and hoping to reconcile the demands of self and society. One should expect that she would examine the latter's distinctive characteristics and respond to those questions which affect her by virtue of her age and class; and, despite the tendency to ignore 'the female condition of [her] life',[3] one should not expect that she would rise above a consciousness of gender. Even were the evidence for the strength of social conditioning not overwhelming, she could hardly escape involvement with the dominant sexual ideology of her period – patriarchalism; thus to overlook that fact may be to neglect a significant source of her artistic creation. In Spacks's judgement, 'many of the best women writers have written precisely out of thinking about their sex'.[4]

In Austen's patriarchal society, the life of a young woman of the gentry and upper middle class would likely observe the following pattern:

> She would be encouraged to adapt
> herself to the wishes of men and
> to feel as if her adaptation were
> her true nature.

This adaptation would reduce anxiety about her femininity, whereas resistance would encourage the belief that she was not normal.

Any questioning by her of the accepted body of opinion would have to begin from within and would encounter both social prohibition and an opposing social expectation.

She would be encouraged to define herself by her ability to attract men, with little hope of an alternative definition.

The result of conflict with patriarchal values would be tension, anxiety and anger.

Working within this society a woman writer might well experience ambivalence about her self-image and her relationship to others.[5] More so than now, she would have to struggle through a process of self-recognition. That stage past, as Sheila Rowbotham says of Wollstonecraft, she might well 'only catch vague glimpses of an alternative' and find herself 'fastened in her own dilemma: how to shatter a whole system of domination with no social basis for a movement of the oppressed'.[6] Austen very probably did experience constraints in developing her vision and her art, as Harding and

Mudrick suggest; but the effects of such constraints seem not to have been acquiescence, alienation or a resort to duplicity but commitment, exploration and a positive resolution in the tradition of great art. Her novels portray the possibility of an authentic existence for a woman.

Austen read fiction enthusiastically in a period when women writers, who dominated the field, displayed a growing self-awareness of women's relationship to society. According to Irene Tayler and Gina Luria, women novelists of the 1790s identified four 'rights' of women as the basis of 'a rationale for a novel about women's experience'. All four are prominent in Austen's novels. They are (1) the 'freedom to consider the institution of marriage critically . . . and from a woman's point of view'; (2) the 'freedom to examine with some critical openness the quality of a woman's life after marriage', that is, 'the importance of mature and intelligent choice'; (3) the 'right to appeal . . . to nature as norm at a time when the "law of nature" ' was being redefined along less hierarchical lines, that is, the concept that true nobility is based not on birth but on virtues, a subject that Austen emphasises in *Mansfield Park* and *Persuasion*; and (4) the 'right to open political dissent', that is, criticism of social and legal discrimination on the basis of sex, an undercurrent in Austen's novels with occasional formal notice, as in her comment on the fates of Henry Crawford and Maria Rushworth in *Mansfield Park* (110–13).

These novelists dramatised the actual circumstances of women's existence and probed traditional assumptions about sexual relationships. Fanny Burney, a favourite of Austen, is an important example. Both the older criticism, which tends to treat Burney as a 'feminine' novelist, and more recent discussion, which discovers in her work a slowly surfacing 'feminist' viewpoint, describe her as the first novelist to show life through a woman's eyes and to dramatise her struggle.[7] Evelina, the first and best known of her heroines, lacks self-confidence, despite her beauty, and she experiences acute anxiety as she tries to preserve her delicacy under difficult conditions. As in Burney's other two early novels, the outcome appears to endorse patriarchal attitudes and the status quo. However, by the time of her last novel, *The Wanderer* (1814), Burney's view had changed to a 'repudiation of society and its values'.[8] Previously she had introduced at least 'one woman in whom femininity is a problem rather than a formula'. In *The Wanderer* this character, Elinor Joddrell, is elevated to a role almost equal to that of Juliet Grenville, the traditional Burney heroine, and together they demonstrate the oppressiveness of woman's position.[9]

Other women writers, whose voices Austen could have known, were more direct and forceful in criticising women's condition. Writing primarily when Austen, in her late teens and early twenties, may herself have been most questioning, they protested 'against narrow male definitions of female personality and women's education'.[10] From the number of novels by women in the 1790s that took up the central question of the rights of women, Tayler and Luria infer an 'intense concern for self-exploration and self-determination' (110–15).

Austen was a very literate person.[11] If she turned instinctively to authors who dealt with subjects similar to those which stimulated her own imaginative impulses, she would probably do so not only for realistic accounts of domestic and social life, as critics have suggested, but also for treatments of those women's subjects that fill her pages – for example, women's inner experience in the context of concern with the effects of social forms, the young unmarried girlhood of a woman as the decisive years in her life, the conflict between outward passivity and inner energy, women as interesting in themselves for their intelligence and affective qualities and for the complex, neglected drama of their individual development, women's conventional education as a major cause of their ill preparation for marriage, and so on.

One such novelist was Charlotte Smith (1749–1806), whose novels *Emmeline* (1788) and *Desmond* (1792) 'voice protest against woman's debarment from an independent or even an active life, and blame the debased position of women upon the failure to provide her with a large mental horizon'.[12] In William Magee's judgement, Smith 'influenced . . . [Austen] the most frequently and profoundly of any of her predecessors',[13] especially in treating courtship as a 'profound rather than an automatic view of life' (129) and 'education as a chief concern of heroines' (130).[14] Another member of this group was Elizabeth Inchbald (1753–1821), whose work *A Simple Story* (1791) shows 'how a person [the heroine Miss Milner] who has never been taught to reason or to discover herself will lack serious interests and be unable to see the consequences of her actions'. Bradbrook points to many resemblances among Miss Milner, Isabella, the heroine of Smith's *The Old Manor House* (1793), and Austen's Emma Woodhouse. He observes that Inchbald and Austen are concerned 'not so much to show virtue triumphant as to show what a complicated thing virtue is'. Their heroines 'are subjected to disillusionment and enlightenment about themselves and others, an education in candour. They are trained by experience to be honest about their feelings.'[15]

The best-known member of this group of women novelists was Mary Wollstonecraft. Spacks says of *Mary: A Fiction* (1788) that 'more vividly than any fiction preceding . . . [it] reveals how the novel might lend itself to women's purposes of complaint and opposition';[16] and Moers says of *The Wrongs of Women: or, Maria* (1798) that it contains Wollstonecraft's 'most radical feminism', especially in its attack on marriage laws and in its 'celebration of passion from the point of view of a woman' (150). Although opinion differs on whether Austen read Wollstonecraft's novels or tracts,[17] their views are often so nearly alike as to suggest a similar perception of the problems of women. Both dwell on the influence of sex on wealth and caste, both seem to contend that a woman should be allowed to develop individuality as a human being, both criticise a society that allowed women 'to procreate and rot',[18] both emphasise the importance and difficulty of women's gaining control over their own lives, and both seek not the overturning of society but the attainment of simple, mutual respect between men and women.

One distinctive link between Austen and Wollstonecraft is their questioning of popular assumptions about the 'natural' roles of each sex and about a 'feminine' way of knowing which precedes reason. Each stresses that roles are learned and that 'special' female emotions result from social conditioning. Wollstonecraft is more scornfully direct, but Austen makes the point clearly in *Persuasion* when Anne Elliot suggests to Harville that the circumstances of women's lives account for their capacity for tender and long-lived emotions.[19] Both identify faulty education as the principal source of women's inferiority to men, assumed and real, and they advocate a reform of women's education as the principal hope for redress.[20] The cornerstone of change for both is the subversive idea that women are, or should be, rational beings and can be trained to think rationally.

Although Austen, like Wollstonecraft, regards women's experiences as a subject for serious literary treatment, she is more circumspect in her approach. Every woman writer in Austen's time was subject to what Daly calls 'an invisible tyranny' (11), reflecting that she was a creature of the world she inhabited. Since we cannot think of Austen as somehow protectively isolated from her society, we can expect moderation and ambivalence in her projection of images of women just as they are found, with a few exceptions, such as Wollstonecraft, in those who precede and follow her.

But Austen is not paralysed by restraint, ambivalence or the forms she employs. Working within the range of life explored by many women writers just before her, she developed an authentic voice. In each of her novels, while concentrating on a distinctive aspect of women's problems, she offers a depth of scrutiny previously unknown. In comparison with Burney, for example, she developed a broader, more optimistic answer to the question of how a heroine could protect her selfhood yet avoid passivity, she offered a deeper grasp of the complexities of woman's nature and its fundamental identification with a common human nature, and she replaces Burney's familiar 'dream of female withdrawal' with a dream of the attainment by both sexes of self-knowledge and a mutual respect. Austen created, in Spacks's words, 'strong images of female experience'.[21] She pondered the woman's problems that others only described, and she dramatised the human attainment that others only dreamed of.

Is Austen a 'feminist' writer? Feminism as a movement is almost unknown before the nineteenth century, and the word apparently is not in use before 1850.[22] According to Juliet Mitchell, 'feminism' 'is currently loosely used to indicate anyone who strongly supports the rights of women – to emancipation, liberation or equality'. More carefully defined by Mitchell, ' "feminism" is the belief that women's oppression is first, foremost, and separable from any particular historical context'.[23] The definitions imply a conceptualisation of women's 'rights' and a consciousness of the possibility of deliberate political action that Austen probably did not possess.

One can describe her as a 'pre-feminist', however, in that the views and sense of purpose present in her fiction comprise a 'formative, incipient, or preliminary state' in the development of a feminist perspective (*Webster's Third*). Much of the content of modern feminist thought is there but a full sense of the implications of her position is not. Her situation is like that of many later writers in the nineteenth century. Simone de Beauvoir observes that 'the most intelligent women of the time . . . remained apart from these [women's] movements while fighting their own battles for freedom';[24] and Jenni Calder notes that 'many women, like Charlotte Brontë and George Eliot, were unable to follow unequivocally what instinct and reason suggested' (211). Female protest is latent rather than overt in most prominent fictional representations of women in the nineteenth century.

Austen is engaged in a 'limited' rebellion. She shows as strong a concern about women's problems as Brontë or Eliot, but her dissatisfaction does not cause an open break with her society, nor does she escape such a crisis by repressing a subversive impulse. Rejecting both wishful thinking and a concealed, corrosive despair, she looks for a plausible way to release women from their position of sexual inferiority and emotional vulnerability. She adopts a unifying view that combines the achievement of selfhood by the individual with an accommodation of the legitimate demands of self and society. Although her 'feminist' goals are not distinct from the generalised goals of mankind in the Western democracies for the last three centuries, her interest in achieving them for women was still an unusual one in her society.

Many modern writers believe that 'anger' or 'rage' is an inevitable part of a female's response to her social predicament. Those literary critics who believe that Austen sought to repress, disguise or regulate such a reaction regard the resulting paradoxes as the most striking features of her work. But 'anger' or 'rage' in an artist may serve as a positive and creative influence. Although Austen's forceful treatment of her apparently restricted material may reflect a state of feeling as well as the power of the subject, she distanced herself from the former sufficiently to treat the latter calmly in her art. When the artist's discipline, imagination and sense of form refine and fuse these two sources of energy, the result can be, as it was in Austen's case, artistic achievement of the highest order.

Austen writes about the problems of women in her society with fresh insight, intense but controlled feeling, and commitment to a woman's point of view. Although her interests are certainly not limited to this topic, her deep involvement with it gives substance and dramatic power to her 'slight fiction'. Austen exhibits the 'rising consciousness' of women, if not the fully achieved state; and her rendering may have struck a responsive chord in many readers who were unprepared to identify its source.

II

The principal subject of Austen's fiction is the 'drama of woman', which in de Beauvoir's explanation 'lies in this conflict between the fundamental aspirations of every subject (ego) – who always regards the self as the essential – and the compulsions of a situation in which she is the inessential' (xxviii). With the exception of Emma Woodhouse, Austen's heroines are isolated and economically dependent. They have been educated only for the role of dependent inferior and are threatened by a loss of identity and security. With the exception of Anne Elliot, they are young women at their most mobile in the most crucial period of their lives, the moment of suspension between childish independence and womanly submission. Their fates depend on the disposition they make of themselves in marriage. Apparently they must choose between their vocation as females and an assertion of self, which would increase their worth as human beings but diminish their value in the eyes of men. That Austen ' ''never goes out of the Parlour'' is, hyperbolically at least, true';[25] but women play for high stakes in that arena – the shaping of their destiny.

This emphasis on the 'drama of woman' is compatible with a set of 'givens' established by critical consensus, and it is marked by a set of limitations. The givens include the following:

(1) Because of a lack of information one cannot look to Austen's biography for significant help in understanding the novels;
(2) Austen possessed a high degree of artistic awareness in selecting and shaping her materials;
(3) Her society is patriarchal in character and structure;
(4) Her main characters are young women of intelligence and strong feelings who acquire, or who are supported by, knowledge of their feelings;
(5) For her heroines the problem of self-knowledge matches in importance the problem of adjustment to the social world;
(6) In her characters' complex moral and social environment the best course of action is difficult both to know and to follow when known;
(7) Austen's goal is the 'happiness' of her heroines;
(8) The six novels present quite different heroines and problems but are closely linked; and
(9) Austen is a comic writer.

The last may need some explanation, for the description of Austen as a comic writer may seem incompatible with calling her a 'pre-feminist', distressed, possibly angered, by the plight of women. Her comic approach, however, reflects the nature of her view of women's problems and her strategy in treating them. It suggests, for example, a belief that they are not beyond solution; she avoids a portrayal of the worst possible cases. As the means of exposing both the folly of misdirected sentiment and the hypocrisy and insensitivity of social conventions, Austen's comedy serves as a healing instrument. Though she would increase women's freedom, Austen also looks for a norm of social behaviour, a balance of opposing forces. In place of the exaggerated and ritualised differences between men and women, her comic treatment uncovers, as the basis for accommodation, their remarkable mutual likeness.[26] Thus Austen uses comedy as a means compatible with her hopes rather than as a cover for her dismay or as a sign of her comfort with the status quo.

The limitations of Austen's treatment of the 'drama of woman' include the following:

(1) Although each novel examines a different aspect of the woman problem and there is a continuity of interests and motifs, Austen does not present a unified, comprehensive programme;

(2) Of the issues usually identified with feminism, she takes up education and marriage directly and, less directly, the world of work. She shows little interest in the vote, sexual morality, access to the professions, birth control or legal rights (although the entail is criticised);

(3) Austen seems less interested in women's acquiring 'rights' than in both sexes' acquiring self-knowledge and a sympathetic mutual understanding;

(4) She avoids the most dramatic confrontations between men and women or between women and the patriarchal system. She avoids moments of violence, extremes of behaviour, and the portrayal of irreversible consequences of a tragic nature;

(5) Austen's main characters are fully dramatised and exist within a fully dramatised context. Thus they are not free to stand for a doctrinal point;

(6) Austen does not offer women the alternative of a fulfilled existence outside of marriage. Life for a woman unshared with a man is depicted either as one of neglect and deprivation or as one of self-centred isolation; and,

(7) Austen shows little interest in the direct reform of social institutions. She describes the struggle of individual men and women to attain self-sufficiency and mutual understanding, and

she conveys the conviction that without improved personal relationships changes in economic, social and political patterns are unlikely to occur.

At the heart of Austen's fiction is the quest for freedom: each man or woman's wish to choose his or her own acts and thereby become a person. What she found in the parlour was the drama of woman's subjugation and depersonalisation in a patriarchal society. She describes the moment when, at risk to her security, a woman acts as one who believes that 'she is entitled to an individual life rather than to an impersonal predestination'.[27] Austen shows us what it feels like to be that woman as she explores and forms the values by which she lives. More than any other novelist of her time she presents women who were potentially complete human beings.

A host of problems threaten to hold Austen's women within society's restrictive bounds: for example, the effect of patriarchal culture upon their view of themselves; character neuroses rooted in the social experience of their sex; the narrowness of their vocation as females; confinement within the conjugal sphere; and powerlessness, insecurity and training in dependency and insincerity. Their most difficult tasks are achieving a proper balance within the self and the social environment. Success in both areas is necessary to developing a good life. As Barbara Hardy notes, '*Persuasion* persuades us that someone who achieves the blend of passion and reason is still left with personal and social problems.'[28]

Austen is realistic and practical in treating these problems. She does not promise a general transformation of society, and she avoids idealising her characters. In her view human personality is a mixture of virtues and faults, and human conduct is controlled in large measure by circumstances. When her characters are most confident – for example Elizabeth Bennet and Emma Woodhouse – they are most likely to be in error. They may exhibit moments of heroic courage and steadfastness, for example Fanny Price, but only along with moments of self-doubt and quiet suffering.

Austen understands well the power of social conditioning and the malleability of individual personality. Many of her secondary characters seem almost entirely creations of the patriarchal culture; and either her heroines contend with restrictive social forms and attitudes in an assertion of self, for example Marianne Dashwood, Elizabeth Bennet and Emma Woodhouse, or these influences force them into a defence of their selfhood, for example, Elinor

Dashwood, Fanny Price and Anne Elliot. In every novel her heroines encounter pressures from within and without to conform and only from within to protect their sense of self. However, although men and women are vulnerable to shaping by external forces (Fanny Price moves towards accepting Henry Crawford), this plasticity also offers the possibility that they can affect the direction of their lives. They are not fixed by nature or nurture in a dichotomy of male supremacy and female inferiority.

Since the patriarchal family, in the pattern of ruling husband, submissive wife, favoured sons and dutiful daughters, embodies the false values of the society, Austen duly records its defects. In *Northanger Abbey* Catherine Morland is the victim of the father's unchecked authority. In *Mansfield Park* the behaviour of both parents and children reveals the system's general faults. In *Persuasion* the family structure fails because of the narcissism of its head. In *Sense and Sensibility*, *Pride and Prejudice* and *Emma*, because of the father's death or ineffectuality, Austen's heroines can explore themselves and their circumstances; but outside the family circle they encounter the sexual discrimination of the patriarchal society, and their quest for security, independence and selfhood becomes a struggle for psychological, economic and, for Marianne Dashwood, physical survival.

Parents, themselves products of patriarchy, usually are found wanting: fathers are threatening or incapable; mothers are missing, mean well but cannot act, or are fools. The harshest depictions of the patriarchal father, the brutal General Tilney and the dithering Sir Walter Elliot, expose the workings of a system which fuels self-love and grants power without accountability. The harshest depiction of the patriarchal mother, the nearly inert Lady Bertram, exemplifies the deanimated and thoroughly socialised female. Her daughters, Lady Middleton and Elizabeth Elliot are her spiritual sisters.

Children may escape, survive or overcome the harmful effects of patriarchy; but none, in Austen's depiction, benefits from it. Her pages are filled with its victims: the young men, privileged or dispossessed, in whom it cultivates self-indulgence, sexual aggressiveness and irresponsibility; and the young women who become either its dismal creatures, its quiet victims or its schemers, seeking through guile a place in the sun. Patriarchy inhibits the emotional development of its offspring and encourages an intense egotism in its privileged members by its grant of personal power. They become unfit to recognise the abuses of their society or to discover the cause or cure of their own limitations. When, in *Mansfield Park*, the children rebel against the system, they pursue even greater self-indulgence and irresponsibility.

By presenting parental authority as weak, absent or dangerous, Austen turns attention to the challenges a young woman faces and her need of autonomy. Although the Austen heroines have assimilated the patriarchal ideology in substantial measure, each also resists the social definition of her nature and role. Their troubles show how hard it is to protect oneself or break free, but each has an opportunity, through her parents' absence or failure, to establish her own identity.

In this society, since marriage is a young woman's best chance to gain whatever independence and economic security she may hope to possess, the marriage choice assumes an extraordinary importance. Society wants to create family units for the nurture of children, to channel the sexual drive, and to protect concentrations of wealth and property. A well-bred young woman seeks a quiet equilibrium in life based on social and economic security, fulfilment of her duties to family and society as mother and companion, and, with luck, development of a tender and respectful relationship with her husband, as a means of reducing her sense of subordination and dependence. But true love is rare, and a husband and wife seldom achieve a condition of equality or reciprocity. Since self-interest usually guides both parties, the female hopes to balance her gains with her costs. Mary Crawford, in *Mansfield Park*, sums up her society's view of marriage: it is the transaction in which people expect the most from others and are themselves the least honest; one should marry as soon as it can be done to advantage; it is a manoeuvring business (*MP*, 36). The story of Charlotte Lucas, in *Pride and Prejudice*, illustrates the point. Unfortunately, often the marriage that the female aggressively seeks only perpetuates the practical subjugation to men which is the source of her original anxiety.

Because of the tie between marriage and economic security, the courtship period is a manhunt for most women, the reverse for some men. Mothers train daughters to capture a husband rather than to attain their fullest personal development (and thereby doom them to remaining inferior); and each sex, the female often from desperation and the male with a sense of his freedom from consequences, exploits the vulnerability or susceptibility of the other. Thus John Dashwood openly encourages Elinor to pursue a marriage of convenience:

'A very little trouble on your side secures him. . . . [S]ome of those little attentions and encouragements which ladies can so easily give, will fix him, in spite of himself' (*SS*, 223–4). Since each sex regards the other as property, a woman's beauty is a precious commodity; her body is capital to be exploited. Dashwood regretfully remarks about Marianne: 'She was as handsome a girl last September, as any I ever saw; and as likely to attract the men. . . . [But] I question whether Marianne *now* [wasting away after the slights of Willoughby], will marry a man worth more than five or six hundred a-year, at the utmost . . .' (227).

Although the intensity of the marriage hunt usually reflects an individual's economic need ('Single Women have a dreadful propensity for being poor – which is one very strong argument in favour of Matrimony'[29]), Austen's primary interests are social rather than economic. The 'brutal economic fact', the control of wealth by men, reflects a 'brutal sexism'.[30] In Moers's judgement Austen's 'realism in the matter of money was . . . an essentially female phenomenon, the result of her deep concern with the quality of a woman's life in marriage' (71). But Austen does not tailor or subvert the theme of love to accommodate social or economic realities. Personal integrity, independent of or in conflict with the pursuit of economic security, is championed, vindicated and maintained, especially in *Pride and Prejudice*, *Mansfield Park* and *Persuasion*. In *Emma* the heroine, with independent means, seeks a suitable role in a male-dominated society outside of marriage.

Austen opposes the conventional attitudes of patriarchy: the bipolar concept of male and female personality; feminine and masculine stereotyping; the assignment of sex roles; the assumption of male superiority and female inferiority; and the grant of a privileged status to men, which they assume as a right, and of a secondary status to women, which they cannot completely fail to resent. Her plots bluntly unfold the unfair treatment of the female. Some heroines, for example Marianne Dashwood, Elizabeth Bennet and Emma Woodhouse, contest what they perceive is the system's limited view of the female role; her other heroines, Catherine Morland, Elinor Dashwood, Fanny Price and Anne Elliot, resist an unprovoked threat from the system itself.

The concepts of sex roles and sexual stereotyping, in particular, seem much on Austen's mind. This concern explains her intentions in *Emma* and the actions of its charming, clever, provoking heroine, whom, she said, 'no one but myself will much like'. De Beauvoir sums up the situation which gives rise to the unusual events in Emma Woodhouse's twentieth year:

> It is a strange experience for an individual who feels himself to be an autonomous and transcendent subject, an absolute, to discover inferiority in himself as a fixed and preordained essence. . . . This is what happens to the little girl when, doing her apprenticeship for life in the world, she grasps what it means to be a woman therein. The sphere to which she belongs is everywhere enclosed, limited, dominated, by the male universe. (278)

Each young girl faces this discovery, for example the early histories of Fanny Price, Elinor Dashwood, Anne Elliot and Jane Fairfax; but Emma Woodhouse rejects the role ordained for her sex and attempts to become as men are, a wielder of power, rather than as women are, its victim. Like Lady Susan, Marianne Dashwood and even mouse-like Fanny Price, she becomes or comes near to being a 'role-breaker', an individual who, by moving counter to the function prescribed for her, threatens the society,[31] a negative response to a system of negative role assignment and evaluation. Austen's solution, a point equally applicable to *Pride and Prejudice* and *Persuasion*, is not to expand or mix existing roles but to change the view of them.

By assigning sex roles, society forces women to develop particular modes of behaviour, and then it characterises them as a sex by these modes. Austen treats this problem most fully in *Persuasion*. Captain Wentworth blames Anne Elliot's 'femininity' for her rejection of him, that is, her being flexible rather than single-minded, responsive rather than decisive, and docile and passive in the face of parental authority. Partly in response to her situation, Anne has developed the so-called 'feminine' traits of adaptability and responsiveness, alertness to personal relationships, and intuitiveness and sympathy; but they are not the whole of her personality, as her command of the scene at the Cobb illustrates. Wentworth, however, finds in the sexual stereotype an explanation of Anne's action that relieves him of considering her situation fully and fairly. Anne herself describes the power of sex roles to mould temperament when, in response to Harville's assertion that all differences between the sexes are based on anatomy, she insists that differences in feelings reflect differences in circumstances and experiences. Women's sensibility, she unsentimentally adds, 'is, perhaps, our fate rather than our merit' (*P*, 232).[32]

The oppression of women encourages in Austen's heroines passivity, the 'waiting' role and self-reduction. From her earliest years the female is taught that she must renounce her autonomy and try to please. Thus Elinor Dashwood, Jane Bennet, Fanny Price, Jane Fairfax and Anne Elliot tend to be passive; but, with the possible exception of Jane Bennet, each perceives at some point a conflict between her view of herself and that of the world. The 'waiting' role is imposed upon women by the fact that they live at home, quiet and confined. All of Austen's heroines except Emma Woodhouse assume this role at some point, even Elizabeth Bennet. Anne Elliot's painful vigil lasts nearly the whole of *Persuasion*. Self-reduction offers the possibility of overcoming one's sense of non-being and of acquiring security by denying the self. For example, Charlotte Lucas deliberately limits her expectations in marriage with Mr Collins. In another form, 'a conscious ego makes of itself an object for a being who transcends it'.[33] Circumstances pressure Elinor Dashwood, Jane Bennet, Jane Fairfax and Anne Elliot to accept this kind of self-reduction, and it is repeatedly urged upon Fanny Price.

Frequently the female victims in patriarchy become accomplices of their masters in defending what they perceive are the benefits they have been given, have won or can obtain: for example, the Bingley sisters, the Bertram sisters and the female society at Bath in *Persuasion*. Other women become their rivals, and much of their emotional satisfaction derives from achieving an ascendancy over members of their own sex. Their conduct suggests the self-hatred frequently encountered in an allegedly inferior group, as they pursue the approval of those who possess power and prestige. Lady Susan and Emma Woodhouse, on the other hand, emulate the behaviour of the dominant males. But, like the children of *Mansfield Park*, Emma follows the false directions that the 'rituals' of patriarchy have implanted.

In patriarchy women are encouraged from adolescence to scheme and to dissemble. The feminine role stimulates competition among them; a whole tradition enjoins upon them the art of 'managing' a man. Charlotte Lucas disguises her true feelings; Lady Susan employs her talents hypocritically and exploits convention to protect her independence; her paler counterparts, Lucy Steele, the Watson sisters and Mrs Clay, present false selves for aggressive and protective purposes. Austen is especially alert to role-playing, play-acting and pretence as signs of false being, whether one resorts to imposture to please others or whether, like Henry Crawford and Frank Churchill, one seeks to please oneself. Unfortunately, a woman is rarely regarded 'positively', as she seems to herself to be, but 'negatively', as she appears to men. Fanny Price shrinks from being false; Anne Elliot, apparently unable to shed the spurious image of women, yearns to acquaint Harville and Wentworth, unwittingly her oppressors, with the realities of her nature and life.

Since the cultural definitions of propriety, normality and worthiness become, to a considerable degree, personal definitions, freeing oneself from these standards, however false and arbitrary they may be, becomes a difficult, lengthy and painful ordeal. Such struggles mark the plots of all of Austen's novels, especially *Sense and Sensibility*, *Pride and Prejudice*, *Mansfield Park* and *Persuasion*. Elizabeth Bennet discovers with mortification that her vaunted judgement has been clouded by internalised sexual stereotyping. Fanny Price, stamped as the fully indoctrinated child, preserves her selfhood only at great emotional cost.

But Austen's heroines sense society's threat to their identity, and they possess the strength and courage to resist its moulding. Lady Susan, Emma Woodhouse and Elizabeth Bennet scorn the conventional preoccupations of women of their class and little notice the criticism of their independent conduct. Marianne Dashwood ignores the courtship custom of dignified feminine acquiescence and asks her ex-lover why he has suddenly changed his mind. The meek Fanny Price commits the violent act of refusing to marry Henry Crawford. Each of Austen's heroines retains or acquires a measure of control over her life.

Austen grapples with sexual stereotyping most directly in *Mansfield Park* and *Pride and Prejudice*. In the former, so effectively does she depict the numbing weight of the patriarchal order and the consequent self-effacement of Fanny Price that Fanny's revolt provides the most intense emotional episode in her fiction. In *Pride and Prejudice*, Elizabeth and Darcy, who want to be valued for what they really are, spurn the artificial and demeaning relationships that society imposes. Darcy hopes to find in a woman more than the superficial accomplishments that bait the marriage trap. Elizabeth looks for a man who will value her distinctive personal qualities. But each misjudges the other because of embedded assumptions about gender.

In Austen's presentation two conditions are necessary if the assumption of roles is to follow a natural course. The first is equality between the sexes, as the basis for open communication, mutual respect and deep affection. Rather than sameness, equality means that men and women base their relationships on an assessment of individual worth and on reciprocal respect; hence, openness between individuals is essential. Where equality is absent, genuine love between men and women is impossible.

The second condition is substitution for the bipolar concept of male and female personality of a dualistic concept, that is, the concept that 'masculine' and 'feminine' traits are present in everyone to some degree. Though women pay the higher price, both sexes are hurt by the belief that sexual differences are opposite and exclusive. Thus men who follow the masculine stereotype from fear of not being 'manly' lose the freedom to express their feelings and to be gentle. In the simplest terms, the dualistic concept acknowledges the possibility of rational thought in women and of sensitivity in men.

Austen presents her solution to the problem of artificial sex roles most fully in *Persuasion*. Escaping the evils of sexual stereotyping requires a breaking down of the walls raised by social training within male and female psyches. The dualistic concept offers an answer. If individuals reject the stereotypes, they may discover unexpected traits in the other sex and the traits assigned to it within themselves. Frederick Wentworth follows this course. Achieving a lasting, loving relationship requires a reaching out by both sexes towards completion as human beings, in terms of which each sex may be both assertive and yielding, independent and dependent, strong and gentle – hence, in the eyes of both, equal.

In a patriarchal society the female's subjugation reflects the male's possession of power. Austen explores at length the effect of this imbalance on women's lives. It causes both the problems and the passivity of Elinor Dashwood, Fanny Price and Anne Elliot. Catherine Morland and Elizabeth Bennet feel their seeming lack of power keenly. Emma Woodhouse contests its assignment to men alone. Charlotte Lucas accepts her self-reduction and looks for the most practical arrangement she can manage. Lady Susan and other manipulating females circumvent the system with some success but at the cost of their dehumanisation.

In examining the imbalance of power, Austen shows that the patriarchal family structure encourages its members, especially the favoured young males, to be wilful, overbearing, self-indulgent and selfish. She also shows that where the weak and powerful coexist, the former are strongly pressured and are tempted to resign themselves to forbearance and non-being. Third, as she points out in the cases of Elinor Dashwood, Fanny Price and Anne Elliot, in a world in which a woman is forced to be passive and deferential she is encouraged to look into herself and develop her sympathetic imagination. Finally, Austen indicates that love and power cannot be separated as ruling independently in the private and political orders.[34] The reciprocity of feeling and the equality of status needed for a lasting, mutually satisfying relationship cannot exist without an equilibrium in the power relationships of the sexes.

Austen is especially interested in the effect of power on masculine pride. Egotistical males crowd her pages, products of a culture that provides them with the means and opportunities to rule. In the grip of what Iris Murdoch calls the 'fat relentless ego' each one feels his 'own dazzling particularity' and assents to generalisations about others, especially the other sex;[35] and he pursues his selfish goals in disregard of others' rights and needs. Austen's favourite examples are the flirtatious young men who enjoy immunity from the results of tampering with a woman's affections – Edward Stanley of 'Catharine', John Thorpe and Captain Frederick Tilney, John Willoughby, Charles Bingley, Henry Crawford and Frank Churchill. The women who possess such blindness and arrogance – Mrs Ferrars in *Sense and Sensibility*, Lady Catherine de Bourgh and Mrs Churchill – have found a means of escaping the closed female world and, as proof of their independence, copy male selfishness, lack of feeling for others and fondness of command. However, whereas in the female excessive egotism may bring a reversal from docility to domination, in the male it may bring such an increase in dominance that the possessor appears answerable to no one, for example General Tilney and William Elliot.

In *Mansfield Park*, especially, Austen shows how unchecked power feeds the male's ego, enhances his vanity, clouds his judgement and encourages irresponsibility. Although Sir Thomas Bertram is motivated by principle as well as pride, his failure to perceive how easily the latter subverts the former leads to the near-destruction of his family. At the height of his moral blindness he insists that Fanny Price, despite her personal objection, marry Henry Crawford, a demand that abrogates her rights as a self-determining individual. Angered by her refusal, he inverts the morality of the situation and reprimands her for being selfish, conceited and wilful. In defying him, Fanny becomes in his eyes a threat to the patriarchal order.

Edmund Bertram also misinterprets Fanny's emotions and ignores her insight, because his judgement is clouded by his vanity and his acceptance of the sexual stereotypes. Henry Crawford's insatiable egotism moves him constantly to assert his power over others. He cannot develop a genuine love for Fanny because he cannot fully recognise her reality as 'another'. Fanny Price alone has sufficient objectivity to judge herself. The others, especially the males, are trapped within feelings directed only towards self-satisfaction.

Austen's most absorbing study of the relationship between power and ego appears in *Emma*. Emma Woodhouse is the most egotistical of her heroines; the basis of her energy and style is self-love. Even more than Elizabeth Bennet, she is occupied with her own view of things; more than anything else she seeks to manipulate others. Having enjoyed an unusual degree of independence, Emma rejects the conventional female destiny and aspires to the privileges of power that society accords young men. Like the latter, Emma fancies herself a manager of destinies, rather than one of the managed, and she acts on the masculine assumption that as a consequence of always having one's way one must always be right.

By granting Emma the social freedom of a well-to-do young male, Austen can expose the ill effects of sex-role stereotyping and of behaviour based on the fusion of power and egotism without an imputation of sexual bias. Emma unconsciously but emphatically reduces others to the status of objects without reason for being except as they help to display her talents and virtues. With her, as with Frank Churchill but more strikingly, Austen shows that the ego-centrism that is the product of the fusion of power and pride blinds one to the real nature of things and stimulates an uncontrolled use of the imagination. But Emma cannot sustain her 'illusion of un-checked dominion',[36] because it is false, unnatural and contrary to her genuine needs and wishes, and in her rehabilitation she learns to combine judgement with imagination, with the former in control.[37] This correction of egoism is part of Austen's prescription for coping with the patriarchal social structure, for achieving personal happiness, and for improving the social condition not only of women but of mankind.

Austen does not seek to eliminate egotism and pride, however. The former may be a spur to revolt against external oppression, as one observes in the stories of Lady Susan, Marianne Dashwood, Elizabeth Bennet and Emma Woodhouse. And at the centre of pride is self-regard, which in one direction can become self-admiration and in another, self-respect. What is called for, in David Bakan's phrase, is a 'suspension of judgment, the characteristic of the ego which decides . . . what it will allow and what it will deny'.[38] A healthy egotism recognises the importance of that same sense of self in others. At the close of *Pride and Prejudice*, for example, both Elizabeth Bennet and Darcy have replaced their improper pride, defined as a mode of self-esteem, with a proper pride, defined as an acceptance of responsibility.[39]

III

In contrast to the image of the reduced female widely encountered in her pages, as in her society, Austen describes a potential in women that is substantially modern in character. Her proposals for coping with the problems of being female offer a promise of individual happiness and fulfilment, social harmony and the full development of one's human possibilities.

In David Devlin's words, 'The question of freedom, what it is and how the individual can win it, is at the heart of all Jane Austen's fiction.'[40] She addresses this timeless problem in terms of the specific, immediate and familiar problem of freedom for women. In Austen's view, to be free a woman must possess self-knowledge and self-respect, judge for her self and be true to her self in making judgements, and insist on being judged as an individual and not by a stereotype. Austen defines a woman, as de Beauvoir does, 'as a human being in quest of values in a world of values' (47); she would, like de Beauvoir, give her the power to choose. Both believe that woman has the reasoning power and the potential for learning needed to break free from unreasonable external restraints and to move from ignorance and faulty perception to knowledge.

One of man's deepest psychological needs is a sense of control over his life and surroundings. Each of Austen's novels explores the problems of autonomy; her heroines, who are in a sense parentless, have a chance to be creators of themselves. Lesser characters, for example the Crawfords and the other children of patriarchy of *Mansfield Park*, perceive autonomy as freedom from responsibility and authority beyond the self. Elizabeth Bennet and Emma Woodhouse initially view freedom as a means of escape from the expectations of a restrictive social environment. But like Austen's other principal characters, they learn both the limits of self and the worth of limits imposed by society. Even more important, however, they learn that every human being has an inner life that should be respected by other human beings. Recognition of the personal existence of others is part of the lesson of the inviolability of self.

Attaining one's freedom requires forming a firm and substantial sense of selfhood. Austen's heroines at first are close to the condition that R. D. Laing calls 'ontological insecurity': 'the individual in the ordinary circumstances of living may feel . . . precariously differentiated from the rest of the world, so that his identity and autonomy are always in question'.[41] They move towards acquiring a sense of self that is similar to Laing's model of the 'ontologically secure person': 'A man may have a sense of his presence in the world as a real, alive, whole, and, in a temporal sense, continuous person. As such, he can live out into the world and meet others: a world and others experienced as equally real, alive, whole, and continuous' (40).

Mansfield Park, as Clyde Ryals rightly observes, 'is Jane Austen's examination . . . of what it means to have formed a central core of self, independent of the roles one plays or the masks one wears and of what it means to preserve self-possession against all those pressures hostile to it'.[42] Fanny Price will only be her true self: she will not give up her sense of identity out of gratitude, and she resists assuming false guilt for not being what others want her to be or true guilt for not being true to what she owes to herself.[43] Anne Elliot too and Elinor Dashwood in less distinct outline possess such a core of self. Having achieved a separate sense of being through her years of suffering, Anne understands her own nature and has confidence in her ability to make decisions. Elizabeth Bennet and Emma Woodhouse, however, face a period of mortification before they develop such a capability. The key is self-knowledge (one of Austen's most celebrated themes); they must free themselves from self-deception and improper pride. Darcy, Sir Thomas Bertram, Knightley and Captain Wentworth also acquire this redemptive self-knowledge. Elizabeth Bennet and Darcy contribute to each other's enlightenment, until they stand at the end equal in affection and virtue.

In learning to see the self clearly, Austen's heroines must overcome such powerful obstacles within themselves as social conditioning, the capacity for self-deception, the difficulty of distinguishing between a faulty and a true use of the imagination, and the blinding effects of self-interest and undisciplined emotion. In the climactic scenes of their stories Catherine Morland, Marianne

Dashwood, Elizabeth Bennet and Emma Woodhouse recognise the ambiguity of their own situations.[44] Equally important is achieving a proper balance of the opposing needs of the self and society. Again, her heroines encounter a variety of difficulties, including finding the 'right relation between the individual consciousness and the world outside',[45] overcoming the split between personal and social being and between sexual and personal identity, and accepting both the reality and independence of others and the fact that one's own identity can not be completely abstracted from one's identity-for-others.[46]

Despite the enormous problems that women face, Austen shows a way to overcome them. The first step is to treat a woman as a subject in her own right, that is, to observe the world from her point of view. The next step is to view her positively, as she seems to herself to be, not as she appears to men. A depiction of women's lives based on observation rather than on expectation reveals the conflict between their feelings and aspirations and their condition of subordination and weakness. Then Austen describes the possibility of a woman's developing an authentic self in place of the false self encouraged by sex roles and sexual stereotyping. In her view a psychologically healthy woman possesses a strong, independent ego, influenced by but not wholly dependent on affection from others. In *Pride and Prejudice*, *Emma* and *Persuasion*, the Austen heroine, by becoming responsible in her own eyes, causes the Austen hero to treat her as a responsible person. The most important step is to develop self-awareness and self-knowledge through self-evaluation. Austen's major heroines and several of her heroes have this experience. Although it proves painful, they gain from it the courage and conviction to defend what is owing to the self, the means of discovering and balancing the range of possibilities within one's nature, and the way to a fulfilling, reciprocal relationship with a member of the opposite sex.

In her view of male and female personality Austen follows the concepts of duality and equality rather than the concepts of bi-polarity and complementarity. Duality recognises a spectrum of human traits which exist in some degree in every individual and which may be divided into modalities. Bakan proposes the terms 'agency' and 'communion' for the two fundamental categories. Agency is associated with characteristics of the masculine stereotype, communion with those of the feminine stereotype. Although extremes in either direction are harmful, the gravest danger is that 'overemphasis on the development of the ego', that is, on agency, will repress 'the communion feature of the psyche'.[47] Austen insists on developing the properties identified with communion and restraining the properties identified with agency. In contact between the sexes she insists on the integration of these properties.

Achieving the desired mutuality appears extraordinarily difficult, but it can be accomplished by establishing first a full communication within the divided self. The process that Austen dramatises is like that described later by Daly and others as a movement in members of both sexes towards androgynous being (50); and the concept of androgynous being, despite some ambiguity and 'surplus meaning', provides a useful image for conveying Austen's view of the true psychological nature of men and women, which is at the heart of her unifying vision.[48]

In Carolyn Heilbrun's use of the term in *Toward a Recognition of Androgyny* (1973), 'androgyny'

> defines a condition under which the characteristics of the sexes, and the human impulses expressed by men and women, are not rigidly assigned. . . .
>
> Androgyny . . . suggests, further, a full range of experience open to individuals who may, as women, be aggressive, as men, tender; it suggests a spectrum upon which human beings choose their places without regard to propriety or custom. (x–xi)

Bram Dijkstra describes 'androgyny' as a 'conception of the person as containing within himself both active and passive, "male" and "female" elements'.[49] Elaine Showalter defines 'true androgyny' as a 'full balance and command of an emotional range that includes male and female elements' (263).[50]

Austen believes that individual men and women can develop what Dijkstra calls a balance of 'impulse and motive, of intellectual and emotional structures' that would locate responsibility for actions within the individual (68). Although patriarchal society attempts to divide the psyches of its members, some men – Darcy, Knightley and Wentworth – as well as some women discover the need to 'liberate themselves toward wholeness'.[51] Their becoming whole persons refutes the artificial polarisation of human properties and seems predictive of a radical change in the values of their culture. Austen's belief in the mutual likeness of the sexes and her belief in the possibility of balancing both the opposing forces within the individual and the claims of the individual will and social fact support her underlying optimism.

IV

All of Austen's novels are about getting married. The period of courtship in a woman's life and the meaning of marriage for a woman provide her with a profound subject and a unifying theme, which she treats from a woman's point of view in terms of both the actual and the ideal. She is critical of the way most marriages are made, and most of the marriages in her stories are defective. However, she adheres to an ideal of marriage that offers a resolution of the 'drama of woman', she defines this ideal union in the marriages of her heroines, and she presents it as attainable.

The principal harm of the reduction of marriage to a transaction in Austen's society is the reduction of selfhood that it imposes. All of Austen's heroines, Fanny Price in particular, struggle with the problem of repressing one's real self in favour of a pattern of dissimulation. In severe cases, such as that of Charlotte Lucas, dissembling takes the form in courtship of concealing one's intelligence and pretending ignorance of one's intended and in marriage of constricting one's aspirations to the duties and pleasures of the conjugal sphere. In the actions of Lady Susan, Penelope Watson, Lucy Steele, Isabella Thorpe and Mrs Clay, it takes the more reprehensible form of learning to prey on a man's vanity and weakness. Austen also depicts other forms of flawed selfhood: 'overwrought sensibility' in Marianne Dashwood, the result of an enjoined passivity and the innate need for love; the souring spirit and incipient hysteria discovered in the Watson sisters; and, in Lady Susan, an aggressive masculinisation.

Although de Beauvoir suggests that to reconcile marriage and love in a patriarchal society 'is such a *tour de force* that nothing less than divine intervention is required for success' (412), in Austen's novels happy marriages do occur, the right people do achieve an ideal marriage, and all of her heroines marry for love rather than for expediency.[52] Her ideal marriage fuses passionate and altruistic love in a stable, harmonious and mutually enhancing relationship. Often characterised as overly intellectual and shy of the stronger currents of feeling, it is, in fact, dynamic and forward looking. It offers the balance of cognitive and affective states, the respect for selfhood, and the blending of 'masculine' and 'feminine' qualities within each partner and between them sought by feminist writers since and endorsed by modern psychologists and sociologists.

In granting her heroines success, Austen offers her ideal marriage as a real rather than a fanciful possibility. The key properties, in addition to physical attraction, are mutuality and reciprocity, self-knowledge and knowledge of the other, friendship, esteem, equality and freedom – properties that mark one's escape from patriarchal limitations and one's success in the quest for selfhood. They can be acquired if both parties develop the full range of human responses and if they develop sensitivity to the worth and uniqueness of the other. The initial marital prospects of Austen's heroines would reduce them to subjugation and dependence, but their instinctive movement is towards development, not surrender; and they finally do marry in possession of such a foundation for happiness.

Austen's ideal of love avoids emphasising the sensual, the sentimental or the intellectual at the expense of other qualities. It resembles that of such later nineteenth-century women writers as Charlotte Brontë and Olive Schreiner. As Austen frequently shows – for example, in her letters and in 'Lady Susan', in the characterisations of Willoughby and Marianne Dashwood, in Lydia Bennet's conduct and Darcy's initial attraction to Elizabeth Bennet, and in Maria Bertram's infatuation with Henry Crawford – like Brontë and Schreiner she understood the importance of human sexuality. But these three nineteenth-century women seek to integrate physical passion into a comprehensive affectional relationship. They would agree that the ideal of love fuses the sexual, the affectional and the intellectual. For both Brontë and Austen a true love relationship implies a mutual renunciation of power, a mutual esteem, and submission to the other in the confidence of a common desire to give to the other. In love the impulses for tenderness and sexuality meet in the same object. Austen's heroines embody the love ideal described by Schreiner:

> The one and only ideal is the perfect mental and physical life-long union of one man with one woman. That is the only thing which for highly developed intellectual natures can consolidate marriage. All short of this is more or less a failure, and no legal marriage can make a relationship other than impure in which there isn't this union.[53]

For all three, as well as for the many women for whom they spoke, reaching this ideal form of marriage was a serious problem; however, the difficulty of synthesising the several elements of love was not a basis for rejecting any of them.

Austen does not separate love and money absolutely, and she shows how frequently the latter decides the relationships of individuals. But her heroines will not marry except for love. She reduces or neutralises the far more important requirements of self-knowledge and sympathetic regard for others. Thus Austen rejects a marriage based solely or primarily on either the sensual or the practical. Yet she believes that the best marriages accommodate both, indeed look to satisfy them within reasonable limits. She distinguishes the judicious marriage from the mercenary, just as she separates the marriage based on seasoned affection from the impulsively passionate.

Although Austen fully describes the unfavourable situation of women, she treats their problems in a comic mode from a belief that the division between the sexes is unnecessary and need not be permanent. She concentrates therefore on showing how the effects of patriarchal oppression can be removed from the marriage relationship of individual men and women. The core situation of her heroines is analogous to that of Emma Bovary: a young woman in the process of becoming conscious of herself as an individual seeks a possibility for action or another human being who can comprehend what is happening to her. But whereas Emma Bovary, by her failure, is 'thrown back upon rootless fantasies' and 'becomes a power of destruction',[54] Austen's heroines acquire both a suitably sensitive mate and adequate resources. They achieve the relationship of reciprocal giving and receiving within a loving, caring marriage which is vital to happiness. And these ideal marriages, although they do not represent a general transformation of society, hold out the possibility of broader social change. Her endings, although one may not readily encounter their like in Austen's world, are a statement of what can be.

At the heart of Austen's vision is a belief in the existence of that loving, responsive man whom Emma Bovary failed to find. Does the luck of her heroines imperil our consent? Only if one doubts or rejects her belief. Far from eccentric or new, her vision is universal and ageless and, in her rendering, plausible. With clarity and courage, she insists upon it in the face of the great opposing pressures of her epoch. Far from 'copping-out', acquiescing to an unjust system, adjusting reality to fit her dreams, suppressing her anger in a display of 'regulated hatred', or disguising her mournful knowledge with a 'cover story', Austen faced a major social problem openly, honestly and realistically. She placed herself thereby in the forefront of the unformed movement for its solution.

V

The shadow of the 'drama of woman' falls steadily over the lives of Austen's characters, influencing their acts, their moments of reflection or decision, and their silent passages of feeling. Its presence informs their gestures, language and deeds. Woman's role and place is a subject constantly on Austen's mind, and she attends to it as an end in itself, not a means, an accident or the unintended distillate of an unsuccessful repression. She is moved, as modern feminists are, by dismay and anger over the conditions of woman's existence in a patriarchal society; and her treatment is thoughtful, penetrating and complex. She uses the narrative and dramatic modes in fiction to explore the social problems of woman's place, with astringent clarity and with hope for their resolution; and she does so as a concerned witness who transformed her life's experience into art. This interest provides her novels with a powerful structural and thematic bond. The world of Austen's mature heroines is not a 'fallen world', requiring the continuation of self-division, duplicity and double-talk, but a world of possibility in which the growth of sensitivity and candour points the way to mutual understanding, respect and accommodation between her male and female principals. Austen's vision is not one of an apparently irremediable conflict between female repression and male domination or one of a complacent acquiescence in or endorsement of the status quo. Instead, it is a belief that individual men and women can attain mutual happiness through a discovery of the real self, their own and others' – a knowledge that her principals acquire and that unites them in a true society.

3   Jane Austen's Fiction Before 1810

One encounters the 'drama of woman' at the centre of Jane Austen's fiction from her teens until her death at forty-two. In apprentice work as well as in masterpieces she portrays women's problems in a patriarchal society. Even the farcical pieces of *Volume the First* and *Volume the Second*, written at fifteen and sixteen, exhibit both a lively awareness of the social disadvantages of women and the patriarchal types that reappear in the adult novels: authoritarian fathers; status-conscious mothers, scheming to marry off their daughters; eligible young males, whose insouciance reflects their social superiority; and daughters on display, from elegant ninnies to thwarted young women of sense and sensibility.

In *Volume the First*, 'Jack & Alice' (*MW*, 12–29) and the fragment 'Sir William Montague' (40–2) display a well-developed sense of the male's advantages. In the first, Charles Adams, with such dazzling beauty 'that none but Eagles could look him in the Face' (13), will consider only the woman who like himself is perfect. He subdues the heart of Alice Johnson, who, discovering no return of her attachment, finds relief in the family addiction to drink. Lucy, spurned by Charles in Wales, journeys to his estate but fractures her leg in a poacher's trap. Alice then sums up the social relationships satirised in the story: 'Oh! cruel Charles to wound the hearts & legs of all the fair' (22). 'Sir William Montague' offers an even more absurdly comic picture of the spoiled and privileged male. Having fled from three young ladies with whom he was equally in love, Sir William becomes enamoured of a young widow. When for their wedding she selects a good hunting day, he is enraged and abandons her. In love again within a few weeks, he shoots the favourite of his intended – who 'had then no reason to refuse him' (42). When the dead man's sister begs some reparation, Sir William offers himself. For a fort-night he is completely happy until he falls violently in love with a young lady whom he sees entering a chariot.

In 'The Three Sisters', also from *Volume the First* (*MW*, 57–71), Austen satirises the obsession of many women with material and social gain in marriage. Miss Mary Stanhope leans towards accept-ing the despised Mr Watts because of the promise of a new carriage, the superior status that marriage confers, and fear that if she refuses him a younger sister will not. She balances the asset of his great wealth against the liability of his good health. Mr Watts, who cares little which pretty sister he acquires, assumes that his wealth assures his success. To the mother he is a valuable property that must not escape her family. In the end the two younger sisters manipulate the tormented Mary into a loveless marriage as revenge for her selfish-ness.

In *Volume the Second*, 'Lesley Castle' (*MW*, 110–39) follows the fortunes in courtship and marriage of several young women who display the unnatural behaviours often associated with those activities: obsession with appearance, place and fortune; disguise of one's natural disposition; excessive sensibility; and even cultivation of eccentricity, which, ironically, gives the possessor the appearance of equanimity and common sense. In a 'Collection of Letters' (*MW*, 150–70), Austen touches on the humiliation of the economically disadvantaged female who is forced to become a fortune-hunter, the distortion of personal relationships created by inequality of fortune, and the economic dependence of the young on the old.

'Catharine', from *Volume the Third* (*MW*, 192–240), is an astonishing effort for Austen at sixteen: her 'first full-scale attempt to place a heroine in a completely realistic social situation and probe her reactions to the complex (and often contradictory) demands of conventional morality and social custom' in the course of which she slowly awakens 'to a sense of her own identity and the world's demands upon her'.[1] Catharine, an intelligent, lively girl of good family who is looking for friendship and is open to love, is trapped between two dehumanising pressures: the excessive sexual prudery of her guardian and the obsession of her society with wealth, power and status. In both cases Catharine's modesty, openness and exuberance are more a handicap than a help. In the background, in the story of her friends the Wynne sisters, one observes the harsh fate awaiting females cast upon the mercies of a patriarchal society. Abruptly deprived of their parents, the elder is forced into an unhappy marriage and the younger into a demoralising dependence on patronising relatives. In her first ambitious effort at serious fiction, Austen shows a mature perception of woman's role and place in a man's world.

Catharine discovers that her new friend Camilla Stanley, a product of conventional female education, is vacuous and fatuous. Subjected to the audacious flirtation of Camilla's attractive brother, she is led by her natural unreserve and vivacity and the pressure to marry to excuse his faults. Then Stanley's abrupt departure brings an embarrassing recognition that a young woman should not expect seriousness from a socially privileged young man. So great, however, is the pressure to believe what sense will not support that Catharine is persuaded by Camilla that his 'Gaiety and Inattention' may yet disguise a serious love.

The young author vigorously criticises the conventions and attitudes that cause her heroine distress. First, the narrator attributes Camilla's shortcomings to the patriarchal view that a female's education should develop only her ornamental capacities (*MW*, 198). Then, in response to Camilla's endorsement of society's treatment of the Wynne sisters, Catharine indicts the system which subjects the undeserving to humiliation:

> 'But do you call it lucky, for a Girl of Genius & Feeling to be sent in quest of a Husband to Bengal, to be married there to a Man of whose Disposition she has no opportunity of judging till her Judgement is of no use to her, who may be a Tyrant, or a Fool or both for what she knows to the Contrary. Do you call *that* fortunate?'

> 'But at least you will not defend her Sister's situation? Dependant even for her Cloathes on the bounty of others, who of course do not pity her, as by your own account, they consider her as very fortunate.' (205–6)

Finally, after discovering that Stanley's greater freedom and privilege unfairly relieve him of a concern for consequences, Catharine deplores the double standard in courtship:

> She could not help feeling both surprised & offended at the ease & Indifference with which he owned that all his intentions had been to frighten her Aunt by pretending an affection for *her*, a design

so very incompatible with that partiality which she had at one time been almost convinced of his feeling for her. (234)

'And this [Stanley's abrupt departure] . . . is the affection for me of which I was so certain. Oh! what a silly Thing is Woman! How vain, how unreasonable! To suppose that a young Man would be seriously attached in the course of four & twenty hours, to a Girl who has nothing to recommend her but a good pair of eyes! . . . But it is just like a Young Man, governed by the whim of the moment, or actuated merely by the love of doing anything oddly! Unaccountable Beings indeed! And Young Women are equally ridiculous.' (236)

These titles, including 'Catharine', comprise approximately half of the three volumes of juvenilia. Although the general mode is genial satire of individual behaviour, the female's life is much more difficult than the male's, and often the disparity inspires the sketch. Austen already understood how individuals are affected by patriarchal values. In 'Catharine', the last in composition, the tone becomes serious; both narrator and main character, the latter the first of Austen's deserving but unappreciated heroines, criticise the patriarchal system, despite an implied hope for accommodation.

II

In 'Lady Susan' and *Northanger Abbey*,[2] two longer works from the period immediately following, Austen offers contrasting wish fulfilment or 'fantasy' treatments of the same concern.

Critics disagree widely about 'Lady Susan': its importance, the view to take of its heroine, and its relationship to Austen's other work. To some, it is a surprising anomaly;[3] to others, it is in the main line of her work or a landmark in her artistic development.[4] Several characterise the piece as a 'literary product' that points to eighteenth-century influences on Austen's developing skills;[5] but it is also said to present one of a series of 'dangerous women' who pursue 'the modern creed of self'.[6] Lady Susan is labelled 'a female monster', Austen's attempt at an 'unrelievedly evil character', or a 'cruising shark';[7] but she is also perceived as a 'tragic victim' or a victim of her world.[8] Some writers find little to like or to praise: for example, Lady Susan is totally immoral and learns nothing, and the story is unsuccessful because Austen is working outside her experience or because it lacks high spirits and serious moral impulse or a 'presiding moral vision'.[9] Yet one critic finds the title character portrayed with 'satiric polish scarcely surpassed in any other of Miss Austen's works', another finds the story 'the most fiercely exuberant and critical' of her pictures of London society, and a third describes the heroine as an exhilarating figure and the work as a *tour de force* of which Austen was justly proud.[10]

Four critics, in particular, treat 'Lady Susan' as a work of importance. Mudrick makes the strongest claim: 'It holds in steady focus, for the only time in Jane Austen's work, her essential subject, that complex of hard, avoidable [*sic*] social facts which is always at the center of her awareness.'[11] Lady Susan's 'world is negative and anti-personal'; 'the individual exists to use and be used'; 'she is skilled and active enough to be the user and not the used' (137). But her victories are hollow after all: 'Energy, in her immobile bounded conventional world, turns upon and devours itself. The world defeats Lady Susan, not because it recognizes her vices, but because her virtues have no room in it.' Mudrick concludes that 'Lady Susan' 'is a quintessence of Jane Austen's most characteristic qualities and interests; and it is her first completed masterpiece' (138).

A. Walton Litz replies that Mudrick inflates the importance of 'Lady Susan'. However, Litz believes that the piece is 'central to Jane Austen's artistic evolution in the 1790s' and that it points to an eighteenth-century literary origin, especially in the 'thoroughgoing *hypocrisy*' of Lady Susan. She is also unique in her freedom from 'self-deception and illusion'. Most interestingly, Litz observes that

> Lady Susan's success is the direct result of her consummate talents as an actress. She can seldom be faulted because she has perfected herself at the art of simulation, and she can disguise her basic self-interest because she has mastered, through shrewd observations, the roles society assigns to its women. (40–2)

Subsequently, Louis Kronenberger describes Lady Susan as 'a coldly self-seeking, self-indulging woman', an 'intrigante in a society that is hers by birth, rather than a mere adventuress'. She 'opposes her *own* values, however indefensible they may seem, to those of the world she preys upon' and is 'determined to succeed at the social level that was hers by birth'. However, she is a victim of her world because 'she is so unalterably its product' (133–9). Lloyd Brown, however, argues that the dominant theme of the book is

> the ambiguities of Self. For while the ego becomes a destructive and antisocial force in Lady Susan's character, it is also pre-requisite to any concept of experience or personality. Hence if Lady Susan's ego is disruptive, it is also true that Frederica's personality suffers from an extreme repression of Self. While she may resist the projected marriage with Sir James, Frederica seems always available, and vulnerable, as the unwitting tool of intrigue by her mother or by Mrs. Vernon.[12]

Despite their diversity, these critiques offer a basis for a unified view of the story. Five related points are discernible:

(1) Lady Susan's society is harsh and exploitative;
(2) To avoid victimisation, one must be free of illusions about one's self and one's society;
(3) One can use the latter's own weapons of egotistic self-assertion and manipulation to resist its encroachments;
(4) By self-masking and skilful acting, one may use the roles assigned by society to one's advantage; and
(5) A waste of energy and talents, a coarsening of sensibilities, and a corruption of values are the price paid to rule rather than to be ruled.

In 'Lady Susan' Austen depicts a woman who, possessing spirit and will, a strong sense of survival, and an inextinguishable sense of selfhood, prospers within a patriarchal society by turning its rules and practices to her advantage. Lady Susan is not a tragic figure, as Mudrick claims; she is, however, more solidly conceived and controlled than others acknowledge. Austen dramatises the harsh social facts of her world, as Mudrick observes; but the story is unique because of her unusual treatment, not because she later avoids the topic. She returns to it constantly, with increased breadth and depth of purpose.

The hard truth about Austen's world is the fact of male domination. Women, characteristically, are devalued, as are the things they do. Their social status is narrowly and rigidly defined; passivity is their expected state. Any attempt by them to acquire or exercise power is viewed by men as 'manipulative, disruptive, illegitimate, or unimportant'.[13] But the female's craving for power is as deeply rooted as the male's, and in the absence of freedom it becomes the goal of both. The quest also represents an attempt by strong spirits 'to transcend social and personal limitations through the power of the individual will'.[14] Finally, it represents a source of psychological survival, which is as important for a woman as her economic and social survival.

Being a woman in a patriarchal culture means being inferior, restricted, in the control of someone else; but some women, instead of acceding to dependency, sustain their self-esteem by a compensatory striving for power that takes the form of imitation of the dominant male.[15] Lady Susan, by assuming male values and denigrating femaleness, follows this course. She attempts to turn masculine morality to her own advantage and to acquire the sexual and social power that it embodies. She becomes, indeed, the 'cruising shark', the female counterpart of the male seducer.

In addition to the issue of power between the sexes, women engage in a constant competition to capture the best available man. As a result, in Spacks's analysis,

> The passivity implicit in a social condition of 'belonging to' the other sex, the powerlessness of existence as a 'prize' merge strangely into the activity and power of 'conquering' and 'extortionating' – alternative definitions of the identical social condition. From the women's world of 'walls and fortifications' the battle of the sexes is waged.[16]

In this equivocal situation women learn to conceal their true feelings and purposes and act a part. Lady Susan and her less jaunty sisters, Lucy Steele and Penelope Clay, resemble such male dissemblers as George Wickham, Frank Churchill and William Elliot. Behind her mask, however, the 'prudent' female, like Lady Susan, may cold-bloodedly employ both sensibility and sexual charm to improve her social and economic position.

Lady Susan, like Becky Sharp, is a moral freebooter in female shape.[17] She is potentially a victim, but she achieves both means and satisfaction by beating her society at its own game. Unlike Lucy Steele and Penelope Clay, Lady Susan towers over the other characters by the force of her personality and her bold control over events. What appears to be her defeat, in the exposure of her liaison with Manwaring and the collapse of her engagement to Reginald

De Courcy, leaves her with apparently no consciousness of guilt or embarrassment, and she promptly recovers by marrying the rich and foolish Sir James Martin.

Lady Susan possesses intelligence, a strong self-image, determination, a contempt for weakness in others and the pragmatism of the underdog. Lacking funds but having wit, beauty and charm, she seeks the excitement of power, the satisfaction of independence and the vindication of proving her superiority. She plays the power game of sex and money astutely and with zest, with the weapons available to her gender; and she delights in success more for the pleasure of triumph than for its material rewards. She prefers her freedom of spirit (*MW*, 299) to wealth and security. She rejoices in maintaining an independent situation even at the price of the blowing up of her plans (307). Her dominant trait is her refusal to submit her will to the will of others.

Lady Susan is a hypocrite; in a society which forces demeaning roles upon women she uses role-playing to manipulate others. Her hypocrisy is a weapon suited to the contours of the battlefield and the circumstances of the combatants. It is the dissembling of the rogue who knows the game and plays it to win, using her wit and craft to exploit the society's greed, snobbery and moral confusion. Although her description of her behaviour contains an element of ironic self-disclosure, Lady Susan is remarkably self-knowing. The 'vicious' inclinations beneath her charming surface are those commonly identified with the sexually dominating male; she cultivates and prizes them. Her 'masculinisation' is the necessary condition of her survival as well as of her success. She accepts it, feeling only scorn for the innocence, good nature, trusting affections and artlessness of her daughter, qualities that others praise as feminine but that in Lady Susan's eyes expose her to men's ridicule and despising.

Perhaps Lady Susan's behaviour is most disturbing because she imitates the male. Her treatment of her daughter is like that of a patriarchal father. Her reluctance to surrender her freedom by marrying parodies the male's view of matrimony. She uses the argument of the world to delay the marriage that Reginald is eager to consummate: the need to guard against a precipitous surrender to feeling; the right of Reginald's father to expect him to marry to advantage; and the indelicacy of an early re-marriage on her part. Finally, Lady Susan possesses an egotism identified with the male. Her love of power and of conquest where she believes she is scorned, her incapability of loving another as much as herself, and her fondness for manipulating others as a proof of her superiority bring Robert Lovelace to mind. Like Lovelace with Clarissa Harlowe, Lady Susan views her encounter with Reginald as a contest of wills, and she is driven by the need to subdue his pride. To her old friend and ally, Mrs Johnson, she writes:

> This Reginald has a proud spirit of his own! – a spirit too, resulting from a fancied sense of superior Integrity which is peculiarly insolent. I shall not easily forgive him I assure you. . . . It would have been trifling with my reputation, to allow of his departing with such an impression in my disfavour; in this light, condescension was necessary. (292)

After describing how she beguiled him into altering his opinion, she gloats:

> Oh! how delightful it was, to watch the variations of his Countenance while I spoke, to see the struggle between returning Tenderness & the remains of Displeasure. There is something agreeable in feelings so easily worked on. . . .
>
> Humbled as he now is, I cannot forgive him such an instance of Pride; & am doubtful whether I ought not to punish him, by dismissing him at once after this our reconciliation, or by marrying & teizing him for ever. (293)

As with Lovelace, the satisfaction of her own goals and the vindication of her own purposes are sufficient grounds for any action. When she defeats Reginald, she will be pleased to be on good terms with him (294).

The behaviour that readers most blame Lady Susan for is her manipulation of her daughter Frederica. They view her not only as a predatory female but also as a tyrannical parent or scheming mother who seeks to force her daughter into an unwanted marriage. But Lady Susan's treatment of Frederica may also be seen as practical. She regards her daughter's naïvety and complaisance as increasing her vulnerability. By forcing Frederica to marry Sir James, she expects to protect her. Unfeeling as such behaviour appears today, it was then a course imposed by mothers and fathers, evidence of a prudent parent's concern. Lady Susan may have been less practical about herself. Although Mrs Johnson urges that she secure Reginald de Courcy, she prefers her freedom.

Lady Susan is a threat to the patriarchal order. Sir Reginald de Courcy regards her as a kind of female buccaneer who pursues his son as a prize. In expressing his dismay at the prospect of their marriage, he summarises the patriarchal attitude towards marriage, which emphasises the acquisition of property and its transfer through the male heir as the controlling principle of family organis- ation: 'as an only son & the representative of an ancient Family, your conduct in Life is most interesting to your connections. In the very important concern of Marriage especially, there is everything at stake.' He assumes that Reginald would not marry without his parents' approval, and he offers as the vital qualification in a wife that 'her family & character must be equally unexceptionable'. Lady Susan is a disturbing, alien figure, an unwelcome intruder into an established, comfortable family order (260–1).

Lady Susan rejects the role assigned to her and triumphs over the society that would victimise her. As a female who circumvents society's repressive conventions, maintains her independence and asserts her selfhood, she embodies an idea of great dramatic power which must have strongly appealed to the spirited, perceptive young author. Since merit in a woman is unlikely ever to be valued sufficiently in a patriarchal society and since one could not envision a radical change in the society itself, Austen ascribes this triumph to the female's turning the system to her advantage. But Lady Susan pays a price for her satisfaction. She has the pleasure of retaining her independence, the excitement of exercising power and the vindic- ation of asserting her superiority; but she undergoes a serious contracting of her personality.

Is the story one of defeat for Lady Susan? So it may appear to her enemies, who believe that they have turned aside her foray and exposed her character, but it is not viewed so by her or the narrator. She sees herself as having preserved her freedom and, in her prompt marriage to the adoring Sir James, as having assured its continu- ation. When the narrator refers to her husband and her conscience as the only handicaps to her happiness, the reader knows that neither poses a serious obstacle. Moreover, the narrator's 'Conclusion' is notably free of moralising or support for conventional social values. Reginald and Frederica will probably marry, but of Lady Susan's other victims the narrator extends sympathy only to Miss Manwaring, who, 'putting herself to an expence in Cloathes, which impoverished her for two years, on purpose to secure him [Sir James], was defrauded of her due by a Woman ten years older than

herself' (313). Is Lady Susan evil? Only if the society itself is evil, or
if by a perverse logic the conduct condoned in the male and
surreptitiously followed by the practical female can be reprehensible
when the latter follows it openly and successfully.

At the close Lady Susan feels no defeat but finds satisfaction in
being again free from the need to submit her 'will to the Caprices of
others – of resigning . . . [her] own Judgement in deference to those,
to whom I owe no Duty, & for whom I feel no respect' (308). Austen
neither idealises nor condemns her, neither extols nor demeans her,
but develops the character in her strengths and weaknesses as the
product of the society with which she contends. In the absence of
moral judgement, the figure of Lady Susan gains attention and
respect by virtue of her powers of mind and spirit and her domination of events. Austen's zest in the representation, coupled with
her apparent moral neutrality, suggests that the character had a
special appeal to her. She may have viewed Lady Susan simply as a
dramatically exciting figure or as an amusing experiment. But the
sense of satisfaction, of vindication, which Lady Susan enjoys, may
have offered Austen, at least briefly, a vicarious pleasure.

'Catharine', a creation of Austen's adolescence, anticipated the
mature novels by offering a prototype of the Austen heroine and a
view of society's demands upon women in a patriarchal society.
'Lady Susan', a product of her very early twenties, approached the
same problem very differently. Both are incomplete; both were
experiments. Like the later fragment, 'The Watsons' (1804–5),
'Lady Susan' was a response – narrow, abstract and possibly more
'modern' than anything else Austen was to write – that she would
not repeat. When she returned to the subject after 1805, she followed
the approach of 'Catharine' rather than that of 'Lady Susan' (and
'The Watsons'), treating the 'drama of woman' with a view to
reconciling conflicting demands rather than to engaging in covert
hostilities, an approach better suited to the task she had chosen of
mediating the claims of self and society.

III

In *Northanger Abbey*, apparently written shortly after 'Lady Susan',
Austen combines satire of romances and burlesque of the Gothic
novel with imitation of the novel of initiation. The emphasis on the
former, however, has inhibited recognition that the novel shares the

serious interest that had replaced the impulse towards burlesque in her other early fiction, at the heart of which is concern with the problems of women, an interest which also connects the novel with the later major works.[18]

Contrary to the persistent view that Catherine Morland is a product of the reading of romances, she is unheroic in her origin, in her childhood activities and in her adolescence, an unconventional heroine because she is so natural and normal. As she begins her Bath adventure, the narrator contrasts her 'moderation and composure' with the 'refined susceptibilities, the tender emotions which the first separation of a heroine from her family ought always to excite' (*NA*, 19). Although she shares with Isabella Thorpe an enthusiasm for 'horrid' novels, their interest is not obsessive, and the thoughts of both girls flit between books and beaux.

Except for the brief Gothic episode, Catherine is modest, sensible and restrained in her behaviour. From innate good taste she doubts the propriety of John Thorpe's offer to drive her out daily (47), and her good sense leads her to question whether he is altogether agreeable, despite being Isabella's brother (66). Attracted by the idea of exploring a castle, she would rather give up that happiness than be thought ill of by the Tilneys (88). She is dejected and humbled by her unintended rudeness to them (93). Soon after, Catherine faces either displeasing her brother and the Thorpes or breaking a second engagement with Miss Tilney. The narrator assures the reader that she acts from what she felt 'was due to others, and to her own character in their opinion' (101).

Throughout Catherine's developing acquaintance with the Tilneys she appears as a nice girl of modest beauty and attainment and little experience of the world. She is honest, open and spontaneous. She is not sentimental, nor is her imagination turned by her reading. Henry Tilney describes Catherine's basic disposition: 'You feel, as you always do, what is most to the credit of human nature' (207). At her first ball her prospects are limited – she hopes to pass uncensured; and her disappointment is restrained – boredom and awkwardness from having no acquaintance. A single overheard compliment contents her 'humble vanity' (24). Not Catherine's but the narrator's voice cites how real life fails to meet the expectations fostered by romances.

That *Northanger Abbey* is an attempt at serious social fiction is obscured by the attention given to Catherine's presumed Gothic fantasising, which ranges from viewing the work as a simple

burlesque of the Gothic novel to regarding it as a dramatisation of
the conflict between the 'real world' and the imagined world of a
headstrong young lady.[19] However, until Catherine's mis-
adventure at Northanger Abbey, references to the Gothic appear
only in connection with her enthusiasm for Gothic novels, an interest
that does not control her imagination (see 37–41, 48–9, 51, 85–6,
88, 196–7). The episode itself provides the major point of interest in
only six of thirty-one chapters. Once Catherine conceives her
strange opinion that General Tilney may have murdered his wife, it
persists until just before she is surprised by Henry in Mrs Tilney's
room. Having already recognised her folly, she feels acute
embarrassment (199). Remarkably, however, within little more than
a day 'her spirits became absolutely comfortable'. Having determined always to judge and act 'in future with the greatest good
sense, she had nothing to do but to forgive herself and be happier
than ever' (201). The episode is hardly alluded to again in the novel.

The extraordinary event is the episode itself, not Catherine's
rapid recovery. Her previous behaviour displays a clear sense of
right and wrong grounded in common sense and reflecting
conventional moral and social standards. Not being acquainted with
the variety of human behaviour, she expects of others what she
expects of herself; and when she misjudges others or is surprised by
events, the cause is ignorance of the world, not a delusion nurtured
by reading. Except in this instance, she does not attempt to interpret
the world according to an image supplied by her imagination, nor
does such an image cause her to resist the lessons of experience. She
is not harmed by her folly or fundamentally changed by it. Henry's
proposal at the end issues from admiration of the same qualities as
attracted him at the beginning. In fact, the Gothic episode seems
little more than an amusing interlude, largely unaccounted for by
what precedes and soon forgotten.[20]

Catherine Morland's briefly deviant behaviour does contribute to
her education in the ways of the world. As one of several instances of
her making judgements from a limited and subjective view of reality,
it shows her learning from the clash between what she assumes and
what is real. It suggests, however, a stage of adolescence already
effectively behind her, when fantasy might well affect one's sense of
the world. Now that sense is being shaped by her encounter with it,
and of greater consequence is a more dangerous kind of illusion:
Catherine was little 'in the habit of judging for her self, and unfixed
. . . [in] her general notions of what men ought

to be' (*NA*, 66). Ignorant of the 'laws of worldly politeness' (92), she ascribes others' behaviour to good nature because of her own superior good nature (133). Whereas the first kind of illusion creates a monster that does not exist, the second obscures a threat that strikes at her hopes of personal happiness.

Although Catherine's fear that her brief delusion has driven off Henry Tilney proves false, in short order she is dismissed from the Abbey by General Tilney, whose genuine rudeness proves much more disturbing than his imagined villainy (227). For the first time Catherine directly experiences ill-feelings in others and encounters the apparently arbitrary and unfair standards of the patriarchal society. The real-life General Tilney is the epitome of the patriarchal father, exercising power based on arbitrary distinctions and grounded in differences in class, wealth and sex. While the narrator contrasts Catherine's return home with that of a heroine of romance (232), Catherine's thoughts are taken up with more real and immediate concerns:

> It was not three months ago since, wild with joyful expectation, she had there run backwards and forwards some ten times a-day, with an heart light, gay, and independent; looking forward to pleasures untasted and unalloyed, and free from the apprehension of evil as from the knowledge of it. Three months ago had seen her all this; and now, how altered a being did she return! (237)

However, the qualities that have attracted Henry Tilney to Catherine from the first – spontaneity of feeling and expression, honesty and openness, natural taste – are unchanged by her disillusioning experience. They move Henry to propose in spite of his father's objections: 'he felt and delighted in all the excellencies of her character and truly loved her society' (243).

Catherine Morland's success occurs in the same apparently repressive environment as Lady Susan's. The same stereotypes appear, the same display of the advantages of being male and the disadvantages of being female. For example, Captain Frederick Tilney possesses such confident freedom that he may play the courtship game for purely mischievous reasons (219), and the bumptious John Thorpe is shielded by his maleness from exposure of his ignorance, bad manners and meddling. General Tilney's male sense of superiority is so strong that with perfect equanimity he acts to control the lives of others. Thus Catherine's entry into society is an entry into a masculine world. She already possesses the 'civility and deference of the youthful female mind, fearful of hazarding an opinion of its own in opposition to that of a self-assured man' (48); she hears from Henry Tilney how in both a dance and a marriage the man has the advantage of choice, the woman only the power of refusal (77); she experiences in Henry's treatment the assumption of the inferiority of the female's understanding; and she discovers that a woman's fate may depend on the possession of property, even though property is largely in the male's control (208). No wonder that Catherine on her return home is amazed at 'her own change of feelings and spirits' (237).

In such a society one of the debasing roles into which women are forced is that of the fortune-hunter. Isabella Thorpe's goals are not different from Lady Susan's: independence and a humbling of the opposite sex. Lady Susan, however, is more intelligent, appreciates the game's larger dimensions, and plays it for excitement as well as for survival on the most favourable terms; she is always superior to the forces with which she must contend. Isabella is only vain, selfish, insensitive and materialistic; her shallowness contrasts with the soft ideal provided by Elizabeth Tilney, who 'had more real elegance' and who 'seemed capable of being young, attractive, and at a ball, without wanting to fix the attention of every man near her' (56). Catherine rejects Isabella's values: '. . . to marry for money I think the wickedest thing in existence' (124). Learning that all of Isabella's behaviour is due to ambition (206–7) is the first of her two great lessons about the world.

The second lesson is that the society apparently cares little for the qualities she brings to it. It bases rank and values on the possession of property and encourages viciousness and venality in personal and social relations. It gives power to the male through the laws of property and inheritance, and it encourages an aggressive ego-centrism in both its favoured members and its designated victims. From Henry Tilney's assumption that his father would object to a marriage between Frederick Tilney and Isabella because of her poverty, Catherine learns to worry about being 'insignificant' and 'portionless' (208). Her lack of property, she discovers, accounts for her rude dismissal from Northanger Abbey (244). She realises that the hobgoblins of reality are more substantial and dangerous than those of the imagination. Catherine's initial reaction to General Tilney is awe; her final one is indignation. She returns home depressed and apparently defeated.

Despite this rebuff, however, Catherine achieves both recognition and happiness within the patriarchal order. Although Austen's depiction of Catherine and Henry Tilney avoids a complete polarisation of 'feminine' and 'masculine' traits, the basis of their union is a tacit assumption by each that it is fit and natural that Henry play the dominant role. Each partially escapes the 'prison of gender', but their pleasure in each other's company and Catherine's final happiness result from her almost worshipful regard for his superior understanding and rationality and his timely exercise of 'masculine' self-command and self-assertion.

Their relationship develops as one of mentor and pupil. Although Darrel Mansell regards the shift from an ironic Henry Tilney to a 'mentor-Henry' as a sign of some confusion (36–7), both Henry's irony and the role of mentor are natural to him and appropriate to his relationship with Catherine. His ironic manner protects him against others' foolishness and eases Catherine's discovery of the true dimensions of folly and evil in the world. As his regard for the naïve and idealistic young woman grows, he assumes in a way gratifying to both the roles of confidant, protector and teacher.

In their first meetings Henry behaves like a mildly superior 'quiz'. Since his purpose is to entertain, by his banter he avoids wounding her ego while pleasing his own. On their third meeting the foundations of their relationship are clearly established. Henry is 'very much amused' by the simplicity and directness of her replies, the 'fresh feelings' she brings to the exchange. Her response is one of 'attention to his words, and perfect reliance on their truth' (*NA*, 79–80).

Subsequent encounters reinforce the appreciation each has for these qualities of the other: Henry's worldly charm and his knowledge; Catherine's beauty, her affectionate heart and her integrity. Henry's teasing becomes instruction, to which Catherine assents because of his superior knowledge. At one point she feels 'heartily ashamed of her ignorance', but, as the narrator comments wryly,

> Catherine did not know her own advantages – did not know that a good-looking girl, with an affectionate heart and a very ignorant mind, cannot fail of attracting a clever young man. . . . In the present instance, she confessed and lamented her want of knowledge . . . and a lecture on the picturesque immediately followed, in which his instructions were so clear that she soon

began to see beauty in every thing admired by him, and her attention was so earnest, that he became perfectly satisfied of her having a great deal of natural taste. (110–11)

Henry opens Catherine's eyes to the cynicism of Isabella Thorpe and Frederick Tilney. The remark cited by Mansell as evidence that the mentor-Henry emerges accompanied by 'a nervous, girlish giggle – or leer' (39) is, rather, a gentle correction of Catherine's naïve assertion that 'a woman in love with one man cannot flirt with another' (*NA*, 151); and the remark that Mansell cites as smacking of Pandarus (40) is a tactful suggestion that the flirtation will end with little harm done. Henry wants to acquaint her with a broader range of possibilities than her inexperienced judgement can credit but to spare her pain in the discovery. He gently hints at the contradictions between her assumption and the performance of Isabella and Frederick Tilney, avoids the direct but disturbing answers she demands, and offers a scenario for the future of the flirtation which she gratefully accepts: 'Catherine would contend no longer against comfort. . . . Henry Tilney must know best' (*NA*, 151–3).

However, when Henry discovers that Catherine erroneously suspects that his father may have murdered his mother, his rebuttal is direct and sharp (197–8). Catherine fears that 'he must despise her for ever' (199). Her return to good spirits is immeasurably aided by Henry's greatest act of consideration, his 'astonishing generosity and nobleness of conduct, in never alluding [again] in the slightest way to what had passed' (201). His awareness of the difference in their understanding and experience of the world and his pleasure in her enthusiasm and naïvety, to which her folly in this case is greatly owing, explain his restraint. One must add that Henry is partly responsible for Catherine's error. On the trip to the Abbey he had amused himself by playing with his power over her imagination, and Catherine was too apt a pupil (157–60). She observes herself that her folly was 'in a great measure his own doing' (173). Soon after Isabella's jilting of Catherine's brother, Henry praises Catherine as possessing a mind 'warped by an innate principle of general integrity, and therefore not accessible to the cool reasonings of family partiality, or a desire of revenge' (219). When Henry declares his love, the pain for her of General Tilney's rude dismissal quickly passes.

In the comfortableness of both with Henry's role as mentor lies the key to the novel's apparent acquiescence to the social conventions of sexual discrimination. The relation of mentor and pupil reflects the society's assumptions of male superiority, arises naturally from the roles which each has learned to play, and defines the relation that will characterise their married life: 'her spirits became absolutely comfortable, and capable, as heretofore, of continual improvement by any thing he said' (201).

Catherine's success thus occurs within the existing order. An unspoiled and portionless Catherine marries well for love, an accommodation that occurs without defeminisation or dehumanisation. Indeed, the society's threatening actions, ironically and unexpectedly, may even have worked to the couple's advantage:

> . . . the General's unjust interference, so far from being really injurious to their felicity, was perhaps rather conducive to it, by improving their knowledge of each other, and adding strength to their attachment. I leave it to be settled by whomsoever it may concern, whether the tendency of this work be altogether to recommend parental tyranny, or reward filial disobedience. (252)

Northanger Abbey and 'Lady Susan' offer opposing fantasy solutions to the 'drama of woman'. Catherine Morland is the antithesis of Lady Susan in every respect. Although her story recalls Catharine Percival's, she is a seeming incarnation of Lady Susan's daughter, Frederica, whose 'weaknesses' become Catherine Morland's 'strengths'. The key to Catherine's success is that these qualities attract a man able to appreciate them as signs of personal distinction in the female. 'Lady Susan' offers the fantasy of successful combat, of a wily female guerrilla triumphing over patriarchalism. It is naïve because it proposes the ascendancy of the female through self-assertion in a continuing confrontation. *Northanger Abbey* offers the fantasy of successful accommodation, of a female winning a place within the system through its recognising and rewarding her inherent virtues and intrinsic merit, an equally naïve solution.

Lady Susan and Catherine stand alone among Austen's heroines. The heroines following Lady Susan solve the problems of identity, achievement of selfhood and acquisition of a suitable mate by means both more desirable and less disturbing to the existing order. In contrast to later heroines, Catherine Morland more closely fits the feminine stereotype, and she escapes a difficult period of self-adjustment, a period of alienation, or a prolonged clash with an unsympathetic society. Catherine's success is uniquely achieved within the society without alteration of her personality or character. Within the decade Austen perceived the distortion of personality and social experience implicit in each work. Lady Susan is reduced to the subordinate and distasteful Watson sisters, Lucy Steele and Mrs Clay. Catherine Morland is replaced by the more problematic Elizabeth Bennet, Emma Woodhouse and Anne Elliot.

IV

The fragment 'The Watsons' (1804–5; *MW*, 314–63), which followed 'Lady Susan', *Northanger Abbey* and the first versions of *Sense and Sensibility* and *Pride and Prejudice*, represents a transition stage between 'Catharine' and the mature novels in its direct engagement with the problems of women. One meets again the prototypic Austen heroine of the sketch – an intelligent, lively, sensible and deserving young woman who is looking for friendship and is open to love. Like Catharine also, Emma Watson is in the uncomfortable position of being without effective parents and adequate financial means, and she must cope with the attentions of a male flirt. However, she does not face the other pressure weighing upon Catharine, her aunt's inflamed sexual prudery; and, unlike Catharine, she recognises the behaviour of the male flirt from the beginning as conceited and contemptible. Emma faces two additional possible suitors, an aristocrat and a clergyman; and the crueller possibilities of the fate of the female in a patriarchal society, confined in 'Catharine' to the summary account of the Wynne sisters, come to the fore. In its treatment of Emma Watson's relationships with Tom Musgrave and Lord Osborne and with her eldest sister Elizabeth, 'The Watsons' resembles *Pride and Prejudice*, a similarity which may help to explain Austen's abandoning the fragment. In the isolation of the heroine it looks forward to *Mansfield Park*, *Emma* and *Persuasion*.[21]

'The Watsons', like *Pride and Prejudice*, concentrates on the problems of marriage. It describes the past, present and future marital prospects of the four Watson sisters, with glances at the situation of one married and one unmarried brother. The circumstances of the four sisters represent three stages in the careers of young unmarried women, and their differences in temperament show the effects of their prospects on their personalities. The result is an almost clinical concentration on the practical and emotional difficulties encountered by women in search of husbands. In contrast, in *Pride and Prejudice* the treatment is softened by the depiction of an estimable hero and heroine moving towards an ideal marriage through a maturation of personality and attainment of the freedom to be, and to assert, one's self.

Like the Bennet sisters, the four Watson sisters are portionless girls of good family. The eldest, Elizabeth, in her late twenties, is nearly resigned to spinsterhood as a situation she apparently cannot avoid; her disclaimer of interest in marriage reveals her fear of growing old alone: she would be satisfied with 'A little Company, & a pleasant Ball now & then . . . if one could be young for ever'. Her resignation is further qualified by her plaint: 'you know we must marry' (*MW*, 317). Shocked at the idea of marrying a man 'merely for the sake of situation', Emma replies that she would rather be a teacher than marry a man she did not like. Miss Watson's response, however, reflects the pressure on a woman to make the best of a poor thing: '*I* have been at school, Emma, & know what a Life they lead; *you* never have. – I should not like marrying a disagreable Man any more than yourself, – but I do not think there *are* many very disagreable Men; – I think I could like any good humoured Man with a comfortable Income' (318).

The two middle sisters, Penelope and Margaret, are active in the marriage market, but their lack of success has scarred their personalities. Penelope has become recklessly aggressive. 'There is nothing she w^d not do to get married – she would as good as tell you so yourself' (316–17). Her sense of desperation leads her finally to desperate measures: 'And since then, she has been trying to make some match at Chichester; she wont tell us with whom, but I believe it is a rich old Dr Harding, Uncle to the friend she goes to see; – & she has taken a vast deal of trouble about him & given up a great deal of Time to no purpose as yet. – When she went away the other day she said it should be the last time' (317–18).

One meets the type of Penelope Watson in Isabella Thorpe of *Northanger Abbey* and Lucy Steele of *Sense and Sensibility*. Penelope's sister Margaret is another example, but Austen gives Margaret a neurotic edge unmatched in her other female hunters. While Penelope acts out her frustration in reckless public behaviour and speech, Margaret exhibits a growing split between the pleasing public face that she assumes for pursuit and a shrewish private face that reflects her increasing anxiety. Emma quickly notes the difference between the 'languishing tone' and fulsome praise of Margaret's public expression and the 'sharp quick accent' of her inquiry about Penelope. She fears that the latter 'would be Margaret's common voice, when the novelty of her own appearance were over' (351).

The well-being of all the Watson children depends on practical marriages. Emma's brother Sam is thwarted in his attachment to Miss Edwards because he is only a surgeon and she is an only child with ten thousand pounds whose parents look much higher. In contrast, Emma's other brother Robert has been 'lucky' in securing a 'good wife & six thousand pounds' (321), and the latter eyes Emma with 'Triumphant Compassion' (349). Robert, like John Dashwood of *Sense and Sensibility*, places regard for property above even family feelings. His attitude sums up the patriarchal tie between marriage and property. His first words alone to Emma are a complaint that her Aunt Turner's incompetence with money has sent Emma back to her family a liability rather than an heiress: 'A woman should never be trusted with money' (351). Then he heartlessly stresses the pressure on the impecunious female to marry, a circumstance which has distorted his sisters' lives (353).

Inexperienced Emma Watson enters a world of portionless women who are frantic or defeated in their search for security through marriage. From her aunt and uncle she has formed notions of behaviour based on a sense of what is owing to an individual and to the self. On returning to her family, she quickly discovers the pecking order of the society and experiences unpleasant feelings about her own sisters from Miss Watson's account of their efforts to marry. Emma attracts the attention of three young men: the male flirt Tom Musgrave, for whom she has already conceived a dislike; the shy and obtuse young Lord Osborne; and Mr Howard, rector of the parish. They represent a partial categorisation of male personalities which Austen frequently uses: Musgrave recalls young Stanley of 'Catharine', John Thorpe of *Northanger Abbey*, Philip Elton of *Emma*, and their darker cousins Willoughby, Wickham and Henry Crawford; Osborne is a foreshadowing of Darcy; Howard an embryonic Henry Tilney or Mr Knightley. At the winter assembly Emma is very taken with Mr Howard's quietly cheerful, gentleman-like air, she is pleased to overhear Lord Osborne ask Musgrave to introduce her, and she takes satisfaction in refusing Musgrave, to his surprise and discomfort.

To the amazement of all, on the next day Lord Osborne pays a call. Although Emma accepts it as a compliment, she does not enjoy it because she perceives that such an acquaintance is inconsistent with her humble manner of living. When Lord Osborne awkwardly initiates a conversation on the weather and the opportunities for a woman to present herself advantageously walking or riding, Emma refuses to play the coquette. In exasperation she proclaims the reality of female economic dependence in contrast to the myth of feminine rule. Lord Osborne is shaken from his masculine complacency and condescension (346). The scene anticipates Anne Elliot's restrained but firm critique of the feminine stereotype in *Persuasion* and Fanny Price's even more restrained but equally firm protest in *Mansfield Park*. It anticipates both *Pride and Prejudice* and *Persuasion* in its disturbance of the young male's facile assumptions.

Fresh from her introduction to the problems and frustrations of mate selection, Emma encounters in her brother's obsession with property as the measure of personal worth the social standard that forces the female to engage in the demeaning marriage game. No wonder that she finally seeks her father's chamber to escape 'the immediate endurance of Hard-hearted prosperity, low-minded Conceit, & wrong-headed folly'. There she contemplates the evils that the abrupt alteration of her situation has brought: 'from being . . . the expected Heiress of an easy Independance, she was become of importance to no one, a burden on those, whose affection she c^d not expect, an addition in an House, already overstocked' (361–2).

Courtship and marriage occupy the principal characters in 'The Watsons'. Consciousness of match-making or match-breaking permeates the most casual conversations. The pressure to marry divides the four Watson girls, and it induces in the middle sisters a frantic and even neurotic response. They face strongly opposing pressures and very limited alternatives. In Emma's case the result is a distressful clash between her emerging self-image, with its basis in self-determination and in the concept of a society of equals, and the repressive stereotypes of feminine nature and feminine conduct. Each girl faces the charge of unfeminine behaviour if she seeks to control her destiny. Each is forced to engage in role-playing, which she resists, as shown by Margaret's violent reversal of behaviour when she can drop the mask and Emma's abrupt, although controlled, contradiction of Lord Osborne. Austen's theme in 'The Watsons' is the clash between the spirit of nascent womanhood and the forms of the patriarchal system that are most repressive of the female. In this transition piece, midway between the youthful experiments of the 1790s and her mature work, Austen's depiction of the obsession of the Watson sisters with marriage and security epitomises the general social predicament of the female in her society.

4 *Sense and Sensibility:*
The Risk of Being Female

In the traditional view *Sense and Sensibility* juxtaposes ethical or moral opposites and satirises the novel of sensibility by showing that feeling is a dangerous guide to conduct.[1] As a chapter in Jane Austen's treatment of the 'drama of woman', the novel concentrates on the sexual and emotional vulnerability of women in a patriarchal society.

Disagreement about Austen's view of the desirable relationship between feeling and reason[2] has led to doubts about the clarity of her intention in *Sense and Sensibility* and about her artistic success. They centre on two points: the shifts in mode in the novel and uncertainty about who is the true heroine. In the first instance, although the novel begins as a comedy and returns to comedy, for many readers it projects a 'dark view'.[3] In one explanation, its grim social order makes oppressive demands on its members and threatens their survival. In another, it bares the precarious situation of single women in this society and the inadequacy, except for economic satisfaction, of most marriages. In a third, the suffering of the character of sensibility, Marianne Dashwood, who escapes the mould of allegoric or didactic representation, stimulates an emotional response like that of a character of tragedy.

In the second instance, in the opinion of some readers Marianne, not her sister Elinor, is the true heroine of *Sense and Sensibility*. In Alistair Duckworth's summary, 'For some she is a heroic nonconformist resisting the hypocritical conventions of society, an insurgent but finally betrayed part of Jane Austen herself.'[4] Mudrick vigorously argues for this position:

> Against her own moral will and conscious artistic purpose, the
> creator makes her creature wholly sympathetic – because, one
> must conclude, Marianne represents an unacknowledged depth

of her author's spirit. Still, because it is an aspect which, even outside herself, Jane Austen will not acknowledge to be good, Marianne must be humiliated and destroyed.

He claims that 'What the novel goes on to prove beyond a doubt, over the author's protests, is that sense . . . is mean and deadly, but sensibility . . . is generous, responsive, frank, loyal, loving, passionate, tragically open to the torment of rejected love.'[5] Henrietta Ten Harmsel echoes this view, and other critics have suggested that Austen may be at least as much on Marianne's side as on Elinor's.[6]

Critics also have often described *Sense and Sensibility* as Austen's most flawed novel: the moral case, we are told, is unmade; it fails to win us to the side of sense. One also hears that Austen's own deepest feelings are compromised by the formal design, that she has not really made her mind up about the issues, or that her failure is artistic, for example an inability to get us to read with the necessary ethical detachment, to provide Marianne's learning experience with 'any substantial meaning', to subordinate sensibility adequately to sense in the total pattern, or to 'integrate the inherited novelistic antitheses'.[7]

One persistent comment is that, despite its inception in parody, the novel deals seriously with serious issues, the most prominent of which is the relationship of the individual, especially the female, to society.[8] What begins as a literary joke ends with the lesson that a wrong view of life or, more to the point, a wrong view of how to conduct oneself in society can lead a woman to appalling results, such as death, dishonour or mental illness.[9] According to Robert Garis, of the two chief meanings of the word 'sense' – 'seeing well' and 'behaving well' – the emphasis in *Sense and Sensibility* is on ' "behaving well" – actually on "behaving cautiously" ' (61), and Christopher Gillie argues that Marianne must

> learn to distinguish between the appearances which repel because they express bad or trivial qualities in human nature, and those which overlie good qualities . . . because the prevailing vulgarity and moral unscrupulousness of those whose values are purely worldly force on the others a disguise induced by frustration, fastidiousness, or scruple, or a mixture of the three. Elinor . . . already has this sort of discernment, but it is a gift which forces on her the static attributes of patience, endurance, and detachment.[10]

Although Austen makes all well for her heroines finally, the emphasis does fall differently in this novel than in the others. The plot swings closer to potentially tragic action; the tone at times approaches the melodramatic; the dominant subjects of her other major novels – the search for self-knowledge and a suitable husband – are tempered by an emphasis on the single woman's vulnerability and need for prudence. Nowhere else in Austen's novels are the facts of life for unmarried females so baldly stated, the selfishness and love of power of patriarchy's privileged few so starkly shown, the pressures for self-reduction so burdensome, the possibilities for disgrace so clear. As Austen's most pessimistic rendering of the 'drama of woman', *Sense and Sensibility* comes nearest to exhibiting what Harding and Mudrick describe as an irreconcilable discrepancy in Austen's life and work between 'social pretense and moral actuality' and what Gilbert and Gubar describe as her 'cover story', the call for accommodation, acquiescence and the development of a double vision of life.

To understand Austen's plan in this novel, one must look closely at its treatment of the 'drama of woman'. Social behaviour and events are regulated by patriarchal principles; social values are based on the possession of property; the female is subordinated to the male in the family and in society. The widow of Henry Dashwood and her three daughters are economically disadvantaged by the practice of transferring property between generations through a male heir. Of immediate influence in their lives is the power that property-holders have over those who are dependent upon them or whose expectations depend upon their favour. Thus the sisters vainly look to their half-brother John Dashwood for relief. The female's unfavourable position encourages the view that entrapment is her motive in courtship and barter of her beauty for financial security her purpose in marriage: 'It would be an excellent match, for *he* was rich and *she* was handsome' (*SS*, 36). The 'cold-hearted and rather selfish' John Dashwood bluntly advises Elinor that with some little exercise of a woman's coquetry she can 'fix' Colonel Brandon in spite of himself and her own small fortune (223–4). On the other hand, Marianne's illness blights her prospects: 'I question whether Marianne *now*, will marry a man worth more than five or six hundred a-year, at the utmost . . .' (227). Although John Dashwood is a fool, his views are typical of his society; his sisters face a severer form of his own dehumanisation.

In *Sense and Sensibility*, Austen emphasises women's vulnerability by stressing the sexual dangers that confront the young female, especially seduction and rape, considerable hazards in a world in which she is prized for her physical beauty yet is at a serious social disadvantage. Two seductions in the background darken the relationship of Marianne and Willoughby, the first by the resemblance in temperament between Marianne and the victim and the second by the fact that Willoughby himself is the seducer, so that Marianne is moved to wonder what her own sexual nature might contribute to a 'fall' and, along with others, what Willoughby's intentions towards her may have been. One of the lessons of the book is that for a woman surrender even to normal heterosexual emotion may prove a fatal error.

Except for the unions that Elinor and Marianne finally achieve, the marriages in *Sense and Sensibility*, existing and proposed, illustrate the destructive working of the patriarchal order. Willoughby's marriage to the heiress Miss Grey completes his failure to avoid the system's corruption of his spirit. In finally overcoming the pressure to marry first Miss Morton and later Lucy Steele, Edward Ferrars narrowly escapes a comparable fate. The worthy marriages of Elinor and Marianne occur only after great suffering and, in the latter's case, after the threat of social disgrace.

In the background three other marriages show how patriarchal values can vitiate personal relationships. Sir John and Lady Middleton are models of sex-role indoctrination, without feeling or sense of mutuality of interest, though foolish rather than vicious in their behaviour:

> however dissimilar in temper and outward behaviour, they strongly resembled each other in that total want of talent and taste which confined their employments, unconnected with such as society produced, within a very narrow compass. Sir John was a sportsman, Lady Middleton a mother. He hunted and shot, and she humoured her children; and these were their only resources. (32)

Like Lady Bertram of *Mansfield Park*, Lady Middleton is an example of the reduction of the female to near non-being. The Palmers, like the Bennets of *Pride and Prejudice*, discover how limited is the happiness of a marriage based on a regard for beauty as a woman's most valuable attribute. Mrs Palmer is a ninny, the product of her society's cultivation of passivity and dependence in the female.

Her buoyancy in the face of her husband's 'studied indifference, insolence, and discontent' is explained by her delight in thinking that he can not get rid of her. Elinor concludes that Mr Palmer's 'temper might perhaps be a little soured by finding, like many others of his sex, that through some unaccountable bias in favour of beauty, he was the husband of a very silly woman . . .' (112). Finally, Mr and Mrs John Dashwood are well matched in selfishness, meanness of spirit and devotion to the acquisition and improvement of property at the expense of personal relationships. In describing their dinner party, Austen shows how rigid sex roles and obsession with wealth and status dull personality and social intercourse:

> no poverty of any kind, except of conversation, appeared – but there, the deficiency was considerable. . . .
>
> When the ladies withdrew to the drawing-room after dinner, this poverty [of conversation] was particularly evident, for the gentleman *had* supplied the discourse with some variety – the variety of politics, inclosing land, and breaking horses – but then it was all over; and one subject only engaged the ladies till coffee came in, which was the comparative heights of Harry Dashwood, and Lady Middleton's second son William, who were nearly of the same age. (233)

In *Sense and Sensibility*, in addition to the quests of her heroines for self-knowledge and for the worthy man, Austen stresses their vulnerability and need for prudence. She warns against a foolish and dangerous indulgence of feeling and a marriage of convenience, showing an understanding of the temptations of each; and she explores the common source of prudential and hypocritical self-cloaking. With unusual bluntness she depicts the social and sexual hazards that confront her heroines: unreason and patriarchal norms are seemingly invincible foes. Nowhere else does her final reconciliation of love and marriage seem such a *tour de force*.

To emphasise the power of patriarchy over individual lives, Austen also describes its nearly ruinous influence on Edward Ferrars and John Willoughby. Austen's other pairs of males offer opposing types of conduct and are contending figures in the plot; and one or both, with relative success, withstand the demands of the society. But Willoughby and Edward Ferrars, although they contrast in temperament and as models of 'principled' and 'unprincipled' behaviour, are not rivals; and they are alike in situation in that the social order forces difficult and unpleasant personal decisions upon them and, by its prior shaping of their personality and circumstances, limits their ability to act.

Like the women they love, Edward and Willoughby appear trapped by the system. Edward's predicament began with his acquiescence at eighteen to a career of idleness, and Willoughby's stemmed from 'too early an independence and its consequent habits of idleness, dissipation, and luxury' (331). Each is under the restraint of dependence upon the will of a wealthy widow and is forced to act a part contrary to his wishes and genuine welfare. To support his style of living Willoughby must either marry a woman of fortune or please his elderly cousin, whose property he expects to inherit; and Edward's mother threatens to withhold current income and to disinherit him unless he weds her choice.

Furthermore, the antitheses of personality and motive that mark Austen's other male pairs are softened by a more sympathetic rendering of Willoughby's nature and predicament than she provides her other 'villains' or 'anti-heroes', despite what is also a more specific 'crime': his seduction and abandonment of Eliza Williams. Elinor comes to regard Willoughby as 'a man who, to every advantage of person and talents, united a disposition naturally open and honest, and a feeling, affectionate temper. The world had made him extravagant and vain – Extravagance and vanity had made him cold-hearted and selfish' (331). Thus the influence of external forces partially excuses Willoughby's 'unprincipled' behaviour. In *Sense and Sensibility* Austen stresses that the system is more the enemy than either the self or others, that men as well as women are victims, or potential victims, and that distinctions among individuals are more likely to reflect differences in vulnerability or degree of victimisation than in ability or accomplishment.

Edward Ferrars is often described as unprepossessing: he 'was not handsome, and his manners required intimacy to make them pleasing. He was too diffident to do justice to himself; but when his natural shyness was overcome, his behaviour gave every indication of an open affectionate heart.' His own 'wishes centered in domestic comfort and the quiet of private life'. He is completely a man of honour and conscience (15–16), the opposite of Willoughby in personality and behaviour. One of Austen's 'principled' men – like Henry Tilney, Edmund Bertram, George Knightley and Frederick Wentworth – Edward is unlike the others in two respects: Austen limits his attractiveness in order to stress his predicament, and he is much more inhibited by the patriarchal order in his ability to act. Edward is obviously a man in conflict, his spirits dampened by his dilemma, his reserve a reflection of his discouragement. He is well aware of his problem and its cause: 'It has been, and is, and probably will always be a heavy misfortune to me, that I have had no necessary business to engage me, no profession to give me employment, or afford me any thing like independence. But unfortunately my own nicety, and the nicety of my friends, have made me what I am, an idle, helpless being' (102). His sons will be brought up, he promises, 'to be as unlike myself as is possible. In feeling, in action, in condition, in every thing' (103).

So serious is Edward Ferrars's plight that the integrity which usually protects the Austen hero threatens to perpetuate his capture. In giving Lucy Steele the option of continuing their engagement, without regard for his own feelings or the loss of friends and fortune, Edward defies the system; but his 'principled' action promises to keep him subject to it, since Lucy would use his offer to acquire the place which society denies her (367). In holding unselfishly to his word, in deferring to what is owing to another, in implicitly recognising the unequal position of women in society, and in subordinating his own welfare to Lucy's, he acts as a 'principled' man should by scrupulously observing the forms which almost alone shield the individual, especially the female, from injury. But he is in danger of becoming another Mr Palmer or Mr Bennet, an estimable man beguiled in youth by beauty and apparent good humour into a marriage of incompatible and unequal natures. Elinor wonders: 'Could he ever be tolerably happy with Lucy Steele; could he . . . with his integrity, his delicacy, and well-informed mind, be satisfied with a wife like her – illiterate, artful, and selfish?' (140).

There is less distance between villain and hero in *Sense and Sensibility* than in Austen's other novels. Although one's moral choice may be obvious between the 'cad who loves and leaves and the man of honour who will not forsake Lucy Steele whom he has grown to hate',[11] equally important is that Willoughby and Edward face similar problems, set by the same forces and apparently beyond their control. Both Willoughby's social gyrations and Edward's silence and inaction arise from their financial dependence, which inhibits their ability to act decisively in their own behalf in an honourable manner. The former's 'villainous' acts are no more certain signs of a natural propensity to evil than the latter's immobility and depression are certain signs of an innate morbidity or timidity. The same environmental forces that have curtailed Edward's ability to act have corrupted Willoughby's personality.

The natural personalities of Willoughby and Edward Ferrars correspond, respectively, to those of Marianne and Elinor Dashwood. In contrast to the sensible, sober and controlled Elinor and Edward, Marianne and Willoughby possess quick imaginations, lively spirits and open, affectionate manners. Both display a natural ardour of mind, a want of caution and a tendency to make light of propriety when their enthusiasm (and in his case self-interest) so directs. Austen makes two points. First, although all four characters are vulnerable, the pair whose acts are guided by feeling are more easily victimised than the pair whose acts are guided by thought, and they are more likely to contribute by their imprudence to their disappointment and are more susceptible to corruption or exploitation. Second, although both men and women may suffer in a patriarchal society, the social inequality of the sexes makes women more vulnerable and less able to cope with the dangers. Although Willoughby's selfish acts render Eliza Williams an outcast and bring Marianne to the point of emotional collapse, because of society's favourable bias he can escape the consequences. Here lies the great lesson of the novel. Nowhere else does Austen place such stress on the risk of being female in a patriarchal society. She may not let a heroine fall from virtue, but she insists on the danger of a surrender to sexual impulse. In her reckless flirtation with the sexually aggressive Willoughby, an immoderate and imprudent Marianne skirts sexual 'ruin' and social disgrace.

The Dashwood sisters live in a harsh, demanding, often antagonistic society. Its temptations are numerous, its pressures onerous, its evils disguised and insidious. Their choices are restricted and seldom simple or clearcut. They encounter similar problems: patriarchal practices constrict their lives; each is separated from the man she loves; each faces the danger that her behaviour may contribute to her victimisation. In addition to the traditional legal and social barriers to freedom, equality and full personal development, the sisters struggle with two special problems: understanding the behaviour of oneself and others, the latter a problem of others' concealment and disguise as well as of one's own perception; and coping with human sexuality in a society in which a woman's fall means her ruin. How can a young woman best preserve her integrity, selfhood and chance for happiness? Three possibilities are described: pursuing one's desires in defiance of social				attitudes and customs; collaboration with a dehumanising social order; or judicious adjustment to its insistent social pressures. The main problem for the sisters is to discover on what basis in this society one can exist.

The first possibility is described in the stories of the two Elizas. Although both mother and daughter suffer from male sexual aggression, each contributes to her downfall by the warmth and liveliness of her passions. The first Eliza was forced to marry Colonel Brandon's brother because her fortune was large and the Brandon estate much encumbered. Her misery and her husband's unkindness had an effect on 'a mind so young, so lively, so inexperienced . . . [that] was but too natural'. Without a friend to advise her (Colonel Brandon being in service abroad), she fell to a seducer. Following disgrace and a divorce, she sank into a life of sin and died from consumption (*SS*, 206–7). Her history shows how a woman may be corrupted and how that danger is increased if she possesses an undirected and unrestrained 'eagerness of fancy and spirits' and 'warmth of heart'. Impressed by how strongly Marianne resembles her in mind as well as person (205), Colonel Brandon fears a repetition of her fate (208).

The second Eliza, illegitimate daughter of the first, is seduced at sixteen by Willoughby, who abandons her 'in a situation of the utmost distress' (209). Consequently, after Willoughby dishonourably breaks off with Marianne, Colonel Brandon questions what may have been his designs. Marianne, he believes, can regard her present state with gratitude 'when she considers the wretched and hopeless situation of this poor girl' (210). Willoughby offers no defence for his treatment of the second Eliza but points to 'the violence of her passions, the weakness of her understanding' (322) as contributing to her misfortune.

The story of the two Elizas specifies the disaster that Marianne foolishly risks. Although he insists that his love for her was honourable, Willoughby is a practised seducer, the most sexually attractive of Austen's males. On his first appearance in the Dashwood household, his impact is almost overpowering:

> . . . while the eyes of both [Elinor and her mother] were fixed on him with an evident wonder and a secret admiration which equally sprung from his appearance, he apologized for his intrusion by relating its cause, in a manner so frank and so graceful, that his person, which was uncommonly handsome,

received additional charms from his voice and expression. . . .
[T]he influence of youth, beauty, and elegance, gave an interest
to the action which came home to her [Mrs Dashwood's] feelings.

His manly beauty and more than common gracefulness were
instantly the theme of general admiration. (42–3)

Elinor Dashwood later responds with unmistakable sexual feeling as
Willoughby explains his treatment of Marianne (333).

As one critic observes, *Sense and Sensibility* is 'very much a book
about sexual wiles and entanglements'.[12] Willoughby's sexual
magnetism draws women's interest, but their danger comes from
their sexual response as well as from his appeal. Unrestrained
sexuality can destroy women by its influence from within as well as
from without. Colonel Brandon and Elinor question Willoughby's
designs on Marianne, but Marianne comes to wonder whether her
own impulses may not have contributed, as they did with the two
Elizas, to make her vulnerable: 'My peace of mind is doubly
involved in it [the question of Willoughby's duplicity]; – for not only
is it horrible to suspect a person, who has been what *he* has been to
me, of such designs, – but what must it make me appear to
myself? – What in a situation like mine, but a most shamefully
unguarded affection could expose me to – ' (*SS*, 345).

Like the two Elizas, Marianne possesses traits which add to a
woman's vulnerability, and she is a near victim. The point is not
whether Willoughby approached Marianne with seduction in mind
or whether he was led only by his ruling passion of pursuing his own
pleasure (351), but whether Marianne, like the younger Eliza,
increased the possibility of seduction by her response. Furthermore,
since her nature and Willoughby's are so very similar, Marianne
seems appalled that her vulnerability, as he suggests about Eliza
Williams, may have been increased by the activity of her own
impulses.[13] Marianne discovers something of the danger of
passion. She learns that the sexual trap may be sprung from within
as well as from without and that prudence is needed to protect one
from self-betrayal as well as from betrayal by another. She learns
that 'to submit to passion means to abandon the controls by which
women even more than men – given their social condition – must
live'.[14]

The story of Lucy Steele describes the second possibility, collaboration with the patriarchal order. Lucy Steele possesses spirit,

will and a strong sense of survival, she has imbibed the society's materialistic values, but she lacks education, position and wealth. She is one of several examples in Austen's novels of women who work within the society and with its weapons in an effort to acquire the place denied them, but whose performance is crass and demeaning. The precarious situation of the single woman helps one to understand their actions. Like other oppressed people they learn to dissemble, to scheme and to act to achieve their ends. Prudence for them involves both calculation and self-concern. Some, such as Lucy Steele, use sexual attraction cold-bloodedly. As an example of the type, Lady Susan engaged Austen's sympathy, but her other examples – Isabella Thorpe, Lucy Steele and Penelope Clay – are mean-spirited creatures for whom she shows little regard.

Lucy Steele is also a victim of patriarchalism, as Elinor Dashwood acknowledges. Elinor describes Lucy as being superior in person and understanding to half her sex (*SS*, 263). She was

> naturally clever; her remarks were often just and amusing; and as a companion for half an hour Elinor frequently found her agreeable; but her powers had received no aid from education, she was ignorant and illiterate, and her deficiency of all mental improvement . . . could not be concealed . . . in spite of her constant endeavour to appear to advantage. Elinor saw, and pitied her for, the neglect of abilities which education might have rendered so respectable. (127)

However, Lucy, like Mrs Clay, is a woman without a place who wishes to be noticed. Elinor sees 'with less tenderness of feeling, the thorough want of delicacy, of rectitude, and integrity of mind, which her attentions, her assiduities, her flatteries at the Park betrayed . . .' (127).

Like Willoughby, Lucy is guided by self-interest. Both are adventurers, as Gillie points out, 'in the sense that they aim at wealth without scruple as to means'. They are also alike in an initial social insecurity, though of a different kind: Lucy is trying to raise herself from the lower middle class and Willoughby is trying to find support for his aristocratic tastes. Both manage rich marriages. For Gillie both are merely selfish creatures who have elected Mammon (8–9). Their basic affinity, however, is that both are products of the patriarchal order. Although their behaviours differ, as Gillie points out, in that Lucy is 'almost ludicrously single-minded in . . . [her]

unscrupulous ingenuity' whereas Willoughby agonises over the choice between his love and his interest (8), this difference reflects the difference in their initial social position (Lucy has farther to go and starts with greater handicaps) and the fact that the path of the dispossessed female is more difficult than that of her male counterpart. Lucy cannot afford Willoughby's agonising. Austen criticises both the individuals in whom self-interest rules (*SS*, 376) and the social environment that produces such dedicated spirits.

The third possibility, a judicious adjustment to society's pressures, is described in the story of the Dashwood sisters. The view that Elinor and Marianne are simple opposites has largely been abandoned. 'Sense' is not all-powerful, and Elinor has strong feelings; Marianne's instincts are often right, but she must keep her emotions under control. Austen is specific on the point that each girl is a mixture of qualities and is meant to be attractive to the reader:

> Elinor . . . possessed a strength of understanding, and coolness of judgment. . . . She had an excellent heart; – her disposition was affectionate, and her feelings were strong; but she knew how to govern them. . . .
>
> Marianne's abilities were, in many respects, quite equal to Elinor's. She was sensible and clever; but eager in every thing; her sorrows, her joys could have no moderation. She was generous, amiable, interesting: she was every thing but prudent. (6)

The crucial difference between the sisters is the contrast between Elinor's self-control and prudence and Marianne's impulsiveness. Austen assesses the suitability of their contrasting modes of behaviour in a threatening environment.

For some readers much of the novel's interest derives from viewing Marianne as the true heroine. One does find her personality appealing – she is enthusiastic, energetic, idealistic and uninhibited; and one does find her situation appalling – she seemingly must surrender her idealised vision of reality and her autonomy in order to assume her vocation as a female. But in her materialistic, manipulative, phallocentric world, the kind of resistance that Marianne offers is potentially self-destructive rather than liberating. Her intense sensibility and subjectivity magnify the tensions of adjustment to the social order; and her indulgence of feeling, lack of self-command and disregard of civility increase her vulnerability to its snares.

By stopping short of actual seduction and betrayal in her case, Austen keeps our attention on the interaction of forces that contribute to such events. Watt rightly observes that Austen 'thought that in life sensibility would founder if it were not directed by sense, because its course would take no account of what she thought were the actual . . . configurations of society' (one should not agree that she thought they were unalterable). The central problem is not one of choice between isolated and antithetical modes – sense or sensibility – but, as Watt observes, 'how far one can afford to be either intellectually or emotionally sincere, and under what conditions'.[15] Marianne learns that her mode of behaviour is incompatible with achieving such happiness as may realistically be hoped for. She comes to regard it as

> nothing but a series of imprudence towards myself, and want of kindness to others. I saw that my own feelings had prepared my sufferings, and that my want of fortitude under them had almost led me to the grave. My illness, I well knew, had been entirely brought on by myself. . . . Had I died, – it would have been self-destruction. (*SS*, 345)

She comes 'to discover the falsehood of her own opinions, and to counteract, by her conduct, her most favourite maxims' (378). As an example of a woman revolting against the 'convention of dignified acquiescence',[16] her revolt is isolated and unplanned, she fails to disturb the hostile world, and she contributes to her own near-victimisation before she recognises what she describes as her folly.

Marianne, in effect, is reborn at nineteen. Like Catherine Morland, Elizabeth Bennet and Emma Woodhouse, she undergoes a process of re-education. Two basic changes in her view of herself and of the world give this event significance: the discovery that one's well-being may be threatened from within as well as from without and the discovery of the value of social forms. The significant advance of *Sense and Sensibility* over Austen's earlier treatment of the 'drama of woman' is that she adds to one's awareness of the threat of the society the idea of the importance of self-restraint and self-knowledge as part of a prescription for survival.

The interplay between individual character and social behaviour is always on Austen's mind. The connection cannot be safely broken, rejected or ignored. Self-knowledge and knowledge of the world are both essential (*SS*, 56). Marianne is the first of her heroines to discover that selfishness and vanity may augment the threat to selfhood of the social order. She discovers that the preservation of individual integrity requires knowledge and control of one's emotional impulses as well as a circumspect response to external pressures or events: the possibility for self-betrayal that she discovers in another may exist in herself. She discovers that trusting one's intuition or feelings in forming judgements may be as unreliable as trusting the social stereotypes. Mistaken judgements of others result both from their disguises and from the limits of one's perception. Like Frank Churchill with Emma Woodhouse, Willoughby plays the part that Marianne gives him.[17] Like Emma, she discovers that one cannot dwell long or safely in an imaginary world, however gratifying. Extreme subjectivity may appear attractive as a refuge or defence, but the self, detached from the forms of social interaction, soon finds itself estranged.

Marianne acquires a 'new character of candour', which Alan McKillop connects with the eighteenth-century balanced view of human nature – 'justly appraising faults and virtues and giving judgment accordingly'.[18] Such candour, by tempering moral idealism with a view of social actualities and by balancing the desire of the will to assert its uniqueness against the identity of the self as a social fact, is a vital first step in the preservation of selfhood. It represents a major ingredient of Austen's solution of the 'problem of woman'. Austen recognises the malleability of personality under the pressure of circumstances, and she describes the experience of living as a continuous process of adaptation. In *Sense and Sensibility* she argues that since the social world will present no sudden change of heart, a woman's hope of achieving happiness depends upon her maintaining self-discipline within the world as she finds it.

As the second basic change in Marianne's view of herself and of the world, she acknowledges the importance of social forms. Initially, as Duckworth says, Marianne has substituted 'emotional laws for social laws'.[19] One sees this difference between the sisters in their behaviour towards their lovers. Elinor is reluctant to believe or to have the world believe that she feels more towards Edward Ferrars than a high regard until 'his sentiments are fully known' (*SS*, 21). Marianne, however, is indifferent to how the world assesses her relationship with Willoughby. The 'inconveniences attending such feelings as Marianne's' (56) take two serious forms. The first is personal compromise. By ignoring social forms, Marianne risks the disaster that befell Eliza Williams; with slight alteration Willoughby's characterisation of the latter – 'the violence of her passions, the weakness of her understanding' (322) – could apply to Marianne. The second 'inconvenience' is social compromise. Since women are vulnerable to exploitation yet are obliged to secure husbands, society has developed an elaborate courtship ritual. Each stage offers formal guarantees of the male's regard and his intention to marry. If, in her personal relationship with a potential mate, a woman ignores these guarantees, she risks her reputation and welfare.

Initially, Marianne scorns any view of marriage as other than a union of kindred spirits through the pull of feeling. Because she believes that Willoughby is a kindred spirit, she engages in indiscreet acts – accepting the gift of a horse, inspecting with him the house he may inherit, using first names, and giving him a lock of hair – with the explanation that 'if there had been any real impropriety in what I did, I should have been sensible of it at the time, for we always know when we are acting wrong' (68). In her heedlessness Marianne assumes that Willoughby is committed to her without his providing any of the formal guarantees (186).

Willoughby's abrupt termination of their acquaintance causes Marianne both a public and a personal humiliation. Elinor's reaction upon reading his 'impudently cruel' letter is one of shock at his 'breach of faith'; behind her judgement of his character one detects her sense of the female's vulnerability:

> nor could she have supposed Willoughby capable of departing so far from the appearance of every honourable and delicate feeling – so far from the common decorum of a gentleman . . . [It was] a letter of which every line was an insult, and which proclaimed its writer to be deep in hardened villany.
>
>   . . . [S]o bitter were her feelings against him, that she dared not trust herself to speak, lest she might wound Marianne still deeper by treating their disengagement, not as a loss to her of any possible good but as an escape from the worst and most irremediable of all evils, a connection, for life, with an unprincipled man. . . . (184)

As much as Marianne should be concerned about her own imprudence in slighting the forms, she should be equally concerned about Willoughby's indifference to them. Social conventions help to control or reduce the male's advantages. (In the background are the two Elizas.) The man who honours them and thus voluntarily limits his freedom, whether from a concept of right and wrong or from a code of behaviour appropriate to his nature or his social position, is Austen's 'principled' man. Elinor calls Willoughby 'unprincipled' and rejoices at Marianne's escape. By contrast, the behaviour of Edward Ferrars reflects a sense of duty, a respect for forms and a belief in the sacredness of one's promises. His reserve with Elinor (what Marianne calls his lack of fire) partly derives from a commitment to Lucy Steele which he regrets but feels bound to honour. So great is his sense of duty that briefly he is in defiance of the patriarchal system itself by accepting disinheritance rather than break his promise. Only the Dashwood sisters recognise Edward's true merit (270).

As Robert Heilman observes, sense and sensibility are options to be explored (124). Marianne's story shows how an unfettered sensibility can contribute to a woman's defeat in a hostile environment; Elinor's story shows how a woman can survive through a judicious restraint of feeling and impulse. Although Elinor possesses the 'true . . . unpretentious and valuable' sensibility found also in Henry Tilney, George Knightley, Fanny Price, Jane Fairfax and Anne Elliot – 'a feeling recognition of the rightful claims of others and of one's own responsibilities', marked by 'a heightened perception of feelings in a complex social moment' and 'accompanied by a moral response, an increase in life'[20] – she is still vulnerable to neglect and mistreatment. Indeed, as the stable member of a family given to emotional self-indulgence, she carries an increased burden. But, like Fanny Price, she protects her integrity by exertion of her will to control her emotions, by occupation as a means of distraction, by devotion to a clearly defined sense of duty, and by adherence to the forms of civility. Above all, she avoids her sister's solipsism.

Elinor at times appears in danger of attempting to avoid non-being by denying the self. She conceals her true wishes and feelings, substitutes self-denial for self-assertion (*SS*, 240), and provides the lies required for politeness. At times the difference between her discretion and prudence and Lucy Steele's hypocrisy and calculation may seem more one of degree than of kind. But there is a difference. Lucy Steele dissembles for consciously exploitative purposes, whereas Elinor disguises her wishes and feelings the better to 'fulfill her obligations as a daughter, a sister, and member of society'.[21] Elinor and Marianne are both champions of individual integrity. But the latter's assertion of self brings only frustration, disappointment and severe illness of body and spirit. Elinor's prudent steering past the reefs of defiance, capitulation and collaboration permits her to live within the patriarchal world with greater ease of spirit and body, if not with greater hope of a fulfilling happiness.

Consistent with the 'dark view' that *Sense and Sensibility* projects, one perceives that Elinor's 'sense' encourages 'realistic behaviour'. As Heinz Hartmann defines 'realistic behavior', 'its means are chosen according to its goals in the light of correctly appraised external (and internal) conditions'.[22] Actions are realistic 'which fit into the conditions of the external world so that they actually further the reality relations of the individual' (87). Such a definition well describes the difference between Elinor's behaviour and Marianne's. The programme that 'sense' prescribes for Elinor includes an understanding of the ways of the world, an avoidance of extremes of behaviour which would intensify sexual conflict or increase woman's vulnerability, and devotion to social forms, which, as a way of regularising conduct, appear to offer the disadvantaged female a degree of protection.[23] In Hartmann's view, the ability to take actions that are realistic is evidence of one's 'adaptation' to one's environment, a conception based on the assumptions that a reciprocal relationship exists between the organism and its environment and that there is no absolute incompatibility between them, assumptions that Austen consistently makes. Such an adaptation appears complete in Elinor and underway in Marianne.

One is well adapted when one's productivity, ability to enjoy life and mental equilibrium are undisturbed. In her other novels (except perhaps for *Mansfield Park*), Austen's hero and heroine appear to achieve this desirable state after a struggle which emphasises more the recognition of their own strengths and the removal of their personal differences than a significant alteration of social circumstances. But in the 'dark' *Sense and Sensibility*, Edward and Elinor, the 'principled' man and the woman of sense, are so severely handicapped by circumstances that they appear unlikely to attain this personal satisfaction without Austen's *coup de théâtre* – Lucy Steele's surprise elopement with Robert Ferrars.

What Austen found in the parlour was the drama of woman's subjugation and depersonalisation. Behind her urging of self-knowledge, self-command and respect for social forms in *Sense and Sensibility* was her perception of woman's vulnerability in a society in which she occupies a position of sexual inferiority; and she depicts the hazards for women from within and without with a scepticism and candour unmatched in her other novels. Elinor Dashwood lacks the initial optimism of Elizabeth Bennet in affirming her integrity; she is not allowed Fanny Price's dramatic insistence on her right to choose for herself in marriage; she is given little opportunity, as Anne Elliot is, to show the superiority of her judgement over conventional social wisdom; the final reconciliation of love and marriage occurs as a stroke of luck rather than as the sign of a prospective reconstitution of the social order. In *Sense and Sensibility* Austen examines and rejects two responses to the dehumanising pressures of the patriarchal order – a foolish and dangerous indulgence of feeling, walking the edge of the sexual abyss; and the marriage of convenience, sex for sale or barter – in favour of a programme of realistic adjustment to the existing terms of the 'drama of woman'. Although the two sisters and Edward Ferrars do not satisfy their personal wishes for self-fulfilment by their own means, they survive with their integrity intact and remain worthy of their creator's generous final dispensation.

5 *Pride and Prejudice:* No Improper Pride

I

Although Jane Austen, in her probing of the 'drama of woman', constantly explores the making of marriages, she examines the process of courtship most closely and defines the bases for an ideal marriage most fully in *Pride and Prejudice*. This concentration of interest is anticipated in 'The Watsons' and in *Sense and Sensibility*. However, the former so stresses the endemic difficulties of single women in search of husbands that the reader is occupied more with the problems of the society and the Watson household than with those of the heroine. Similarly, in *Sense and Sensibility*, although the opportunities and hazards of courtship impel the plot, the novel emphasises the social and sexual dangers that young women face because of sexual discrimination and their emotional vulnerability. In *Pride and Prejudice*, however, Austen concentrates on the threat to selfhood of the marriage-making process. The engagement of her hero and heroine signals their overcoming that threat, achieving their own potential and acquiring a sensitivity to the worth of the other. Elizabeth Bennet in her marriage appears to have resolved the conflicts at the heart of the 'drama of woman'.

In Austen's society, wedlock was the expected means for single young women to gain or retain social and economic security. Indeed, since their chief alternatives were remaining a spinster or becoming a governess, they may have thought of little else. Thus a woman's unmarried girlhood was often the decisive period of her life, and her decision about marriage might be the most important one she would make. No wonder that to win a husband often seems the only aim of Austen's female characters, or that they appear to be in constant competition with their own sex. Their plight, if they fail, is constantly on their mind.

The centre of activity in *Pride and Prejudice* is the operation of the marriage market, where a woman's beauty is a precious commodity, bait for the marriage trap, and her body is capital to be exploited. The male's sexual susceptibility offers the female a point of attack. Mrs Bennet touts Jane's beauty to Bingley (*PP*, 44), and he succumbs. Darcy, more aware, avoids the trap at the price of the charge of rudeness, only later to fall to the 'charms' of Elizabeth Bennet against his will. Since young women were encouraged to use sexual attraction cold-bloodedly, the relation between the sexes was in danger of reduction to that of the interchangeability of beauty and status. Some women – Lady Susan, Penelope Watson, Isabella Thorpe and Mrs Clay – wage deliberately predatory campaigns.

Events like the balls at Meryton and the party at Sir William Lucas's provide showcases for eligible young women.[1] Thus when Jane dances twice with the naïve Bingley, Mrs Bennet believes that she will soon be happily settled at Netherfield. The warier Darcy at first refuses to participate in the game in which he would be the prize. At the Lucas's party, however, Elizabeth is offered to him as a partner a second time: 'You cannot refuse to dance, I am sure', says Sir William, 'when so much beauty is before you.' Since Elizabeth has caught his eye, Darcy now is 'not unwilling to receive [her hand]' (*PP*, 26). The dance, earlier a metaphor of courtship, becomes one of sexual encounter. Though Elizabeth refuses Darcy lest he think that she was looking for a partner, her love of dancing suggests her capacity for sexual love, just as Collins's ineptness predicts her sexual unhappiness if she marries him:

> The two first dances . . . [with Collins] were dances of mortifi-
> cation. Mr. Collins, awkward and solemn, apologising instead of
> attending, and often moving wrong without being aware of it,
> gave her all the shame and misery which a disagreeable partner
> for a couple of dances can give. The moment of her release from
> him was exstacy. (90)

In the marriage market the male also is a commodity. After a girl has attracted a man's attention, she should play the game of pleasing, as described by Charlotte Lucas, in order to 'fix' him. 'When she is secure of him, there will be leisure for falling in love as much as she chuses.' Thus deception begins: at first the means of male entrapment (for example, in the making of Mr Bennet's unsuitable marriage), and later the means of managing a husband.

Elizabeth acknowledges the practicality of such a plan, 'where nothing is in question but the desire of being well married' (22).

In the light of this harsh reality, Mrs Bennet's frantic behaviour, though exaggerated, acquires a considerable plausibility. Self-centred and boorish as she is, she tends to 'tell the truth about the economic objectives pursued by members of her class'.[2] She is beset by the very real problem of providing with little income for five genteel daughters in a self-aggrandising society heavily weighted against the female. Their only plausible path to security is the church aisle:

> . . . I tell you what, Miss Lizzy, if you take it into your head to go on refusing every offer of marriage in this way, you will never get a husband at all – and I am sure I do not know who is to maintain you when your father is dead. (*PP*, 113)

It is not absurd that Mrs Bennet should 'rail bitterly against the cruelty of settling an estate away from a family of five daughters' (62), that she should be thrown into ill-humour upon hearing that Charlotte Lucas has replaced Elizabeth as Collins's intended, or that she should fall into a fit of joy upon hearing of Elizabeth's engagement to Darcy (378). Her loud assault on the marriage problem is quietly seconded by the sensible Mrs Gardiner, who cautions Elizabeth about the imprudence of an attachment to the penniless Wickham.

Although marriage often appeared to offer women their best means of integration into the community and their nearest approach to freedom, a preoccupation with matrimony could lead to an inconsequential life. As one sees in the stories of the Bingley sisters, Lady Bertram and Mary Crawford, Mrs Elton and Elizabeth Elliot, it encourages a repudiation of selfhood, as women become the accomplices of their masters because of the advantages they anticipate. It encourages self-repression in favour of a pattern of dissimulation, a problem Austen's heroines struggle with continually; and, except for Emma Woodhouse, it forces them into a passive, waiting role. In the most extreme case Charlotte Lucas conceals her intelligence and her indifference to her intended; she sacrifices 'every better feeling to worldly advantage' (125). Finally, preoccupation with marrying encourages the separation of sex from love, the exploitation of the sexual for non-sexual purposes.

Paradoxically, the marriage that women pursued very frequently continuance of the subordination that produced their original anxiety. Balance and reciprocity in marriage seemed impossible; the female continued to be subservient to the male. Not only does Charlotte Lucas begin her marriage in bad faith, but she sharply limits her aspirations; confined within the conjugal sphere, she exemplifies the woman restricted by traditional marriage, in de Beauvoir's phrase, to the status of the Other.

Each of Austen's heroines learns that in the eyes of the world she is inferior, as a condition of her existence; that is, she discovers what it means in her society to be a woman. But each, in a way suited to her personality, temperament and circumstances, resists society's expectations in order to preserve her integrity. Elizabeth Bennet, who appears to some a new kind of heroine,[3] is only the most captivating of Austen's valiant women, all of whom represent potentially complete human beings, with the power of mind and spirit to guide their own destinies. Each heroine, by her response to the problem of marriage, shows her regard for self-respect above expediency, the sincerity of her personal code, and her independent spirit. Each one aspires to speak from the self; their actions are based on genuine feeling, not on form. Each one is also steadily developing, steadily increasing her self-knowledge, and by her acts increasing her influence on events in her life. Austen sanctions the same essential concepts in each story: the inviolability of the self, the need for self-knowledge, the richness of one's full human nature, and the importance of mutual regard and reciprocity in human love and marriage.

II

Against the background of the marriage market Elizabeth Bennet acts out the 'drama of woman', the 'conflict between the fundamental aspirations of every subject (ego) – who always regards the self as the essential – and the compulsions of a situation in which she is the inessential'.[4] She is expected to subordinate her will, needs and interests to those of the superior male sex, to accept a life of passivity and dependency, and to welcome an unloving and unequal marriage. But Elizabeth rejects both the feminine stereotype and the feminine role. She can think for herself and intends to make her own decisions. She insists that she be treated and judged as an individual. Like Fanny Price, she insists on her right to choose in marriage;

like Emma Woodhouse and Anne Elliot, she insists on equal commitment, mutual affection and mutual choice as the bases for marriage.

But Elizabeth does not defend those views without risk to her social well-being and to her emotional health. Her behaviour appears wilful, proud and perverse to other members of her society (6); and the humiliation and frustration she undergoes bring tension and an increasing restlessness, discouragement and sense of isolation. Many of her difficulties, however, result from the clash between her strength and a society that tries to curb strength in a woman, and her distress is partly a result of her tenacity in preserving and expressing a deep-seated sense of self.

Elizabeth's resistance is complicated by her upbringing. In general, daughters in a patriarchal society have been raised to live in that world. Since the patriarchal culture thus already exists in each subject, it may influence the direction of revolt. Elizabeth risks following a false direction in attempting to escape its control.

Elizabeth's assertion of personal freedom takes two related forms: an assertion of superiority and an assertion of invulnerability through non-involvement. In the first instance, as Litz observes, she is tempted by the dream of total freedom – of being self-reliant and contemptuous of convention (104–5). Like Emma Woodhouse, Elizabeth initially is an egotist, preoccupied with her own view of things and unable to see accurately very far beyond herself. Like Emma, she wishes to prove the superiority of her own judgement in order to feel a sense of power. Although she lacks Emma's delight in manipulating others, she perceives that with power one may please where one chooses. However, Elizabeth risks acquiring an exaggerated self-esteem, an improper pride and a false freedom in which individuation runs wild – of becoming a shrew, the caricatured opposite of the compliant woman. There is justice in Darcy's accusation that she has a propensity 'wilfully to misunderstand' others (*PP*, 58) and in Jane's quiet reproof that 'it is very often nothing but our own vanity that deceives us' (136). Elizabeth risks becoming like Lady Catherine de Bourgh, whose behaviour expresses the message that the independent woman need not please at all.

Elizabeth also protects her personal freedom by striving to avoid involvement. She thinks of herself as an observer. She tries to keep the world at a distance by suppressing her feelings and emphasising her wit and the satirical eye that she attributes to Darcy. They provide the defence of distancing through laughter. However, the characterisation of wit by the conduct books as a dangerous talent, flattering to one's vanity and thus encouraging a loss of self-command, is not without validity. Although Darcy admires Elizabeth's cleverness and vivacity and much of the reader's delight stems from her buoyancy and keen intelligence, her reliance on wit as a defence distracts her from a real solution to her difficulties. Elizabeth runs the risk both of an aggressive dogmatism – a sub-ordination of awareness to self-assertion, which she shares with Darcy and Emma Woodhouse – and of alienation – separation from the mutual social activity which is distinctively human.

The obstacles that prevent an ideal marriage are thus individual as well as social. Elizabeth must set her own emotional house in order to avoid a fall into isolation and eccentricity. She must avoid irrational reactions to environmental pressures. She must learn that she cannot gain her precious freedom by imposing a construction of the imagination on reality (a lesson also learned by Emma Wood-house), with the risk of a disconnection from others and from a part of her own being. She must free herself from a crippling prejudice against the male sex and find a satisfactory outlet for her own sexual tension. Finally, she must learn that personal freedom depends not on the absence of restraints but on clarity of vision, openness and self-control. From *Pride and Prejudice* on, Austen's focus is always on the struggle within the self, as well as that between the self and society, and on the need to balance the claims and needs of both.

Elizabeth undergoes a significant growth and change. Like other Austen heroines she learns through suffering; she and Emma Woodhouse undergo a similar emotional and moral education. As a result of a misjudgement of their powers of understanding and an injudicious self-assertion, both are led into errors, Elizabeth into a misanthropic estimate of her fellow beings and Emma into a mis-directed attempt to escape the artificial restrictions on her sex. Very much like Emma, Elizabeth discovers that she cannot escape involvement, that her defences of wit, satire and imagination cannot withstand 'the solvent of strong feeling',[5] that unchecked individuation is destructive, and that love alone sets people free.

Pride and Prejudice marks an advance over *Sense and Sensibility* because Austen explores more fully the problem of self-knowledge – understanding the contribution of internal elements to one's problems with the world. In the later novel the happiness of the 'woman of sense and the civilized moral man', who are apparently less vulnerable to external dangers, appears to depend more on their recognising their own strengths and ironing out their own differences. Thus Darcy and Elizabeth are separated in part by the conflict within Elizabeth and her lack of knowledge of herself. Once these handicaps are removed, she can perceive Darcy's true nature and worth. But until she gains in self-knowledge and self-control, she is in danger of slipping into a sour misanthropy.

Her most embittering experiences are the insulting proposals from Collins and Darcy and the self-betrayal of Charlotte Lucas. The former epitomise the potential for arrogance and self-deception of the patriarchal male. Having now a good house and a very sufficient income, Collins intends to marry, and he means to choose one of the Bennet sisters if they are as handsome and amiable as reported (*PP*, 70). Picking out Elizabeth, he 'made his declaration in form. . . . with all the observances which he supposed a regular part of the business' of love-making (104). If the only basis of marriage is mutual convenience, his sentiments appear generous; he expects that by lessening the impact of the entail he will rise in her esteem (106). Indeed, he cannot conceive that she could refuse: the establishment he offers is highly desirable, and she cannot be certain of another offer because of her small fortune. Elizabeth reacts, however, with mingled incredulity and mortification. At Hunsford Darcy makes the same assumption about a female's dependence and limited choice (189). Elizabeth's rejection of his proposal is the most courageous act of her independent spirit and her boldest challenge of the view of marriage in her society.

In her debate with Charlotte Lucas, Elizabeth meets the argument for acceding to the marriage practices of the society; their discussion defines the basic difference for Austen between a good marriage and merely being well married. Charlotte argues that marriage is a practical matter, that a woman should do everything within her power to bring a suitable and interested man to a proposal, and that happiness afterwards is 'entirely a matter of chance'. In fact, 'it is better to know as little as possible of the defects of the person with whom you are to pass your life'. Elizabeth cannot believe that she is serious and insists that each party must fully understand the other's character (21–3).

But Charlotte does mean what she says. She secures Collins for herself 'from the pure and disinterested desire of an establishment':

Without thinking highly either of men or of matrimony, marriage had always been her object; it was the only honourable provision

for well-educated young women of small fortune, and however
uncertain of giving happiness, must be their pleasantest preservative from want. This preservative she had now obtained; and at
the age of twenty-seven, without having ever been handsome, she
felt all the good luck of it. (122–3)

Elizabeth is astonished and horrified by the news:

> . . . she could not have supposed it possible that when called into
> action . . . [Charlotte] would have sacrificed every better feeling
> to worldly advantage. Charlotte the wife of Mr. Collins, was a
> most humiliating picture! – And to the pang of a friend disgracing
> herself and sunk in her esteem, was added the distressing convic-
> tion that it was impossible for that friend to be tolerably happy in
> the lot she had chosen. (125)

Elizabeth's dismay springs not only from the sexual indignity of
the event but also from its compromise of personal values and the
impossibility of compatibility. Charlotte's act denotes the evil of the
system. She has succumbed to the pressure to forsake liberty and
become a thing.

Elizabeth receives other lessons in the influence of economic and
social pressures on personal relationships. When Mrs Gardiner
cautions her that she should avoid an affection for Wickham, 'which
the want of fortune would make so very imprudent' (144), her reply
reveals her conflicting feelings. She will try to prevent Wickham's
falling in love with her, yet he is the most agreeable man she has ever
met. She can see the imprudence of an attachment, yet how can she
promise to be wiser than so many other young people if she is
tempted (144–5)? Since she escapes humiliation in this instance,
Elizabeth views the outcome with ironic detachment as well as
chagrin. Later, she declines to distinguish between the actions of
men and women who, in the absence of adequate personal security,
must manipulate the marriage market: '. . . what is the difference in
matrimonial affairs, between the mercenary and the prudent
motive? Where does discretion end, and avarice begin?' Her
description of Wickham's courting of Miss King – '*He* shall be
mercenary, and *she* shall be foolish' (153) – with a shift of pronouns
would fit Charlotte Lucas's accommodation with Collins as well.

In the main Elizabeth's reaction to the marriage market is one of
disbelief, frustration and brief alienation. She cannot comprehend

Charlotte's sacrifice. She welcomes the trip to Hunsford, where she will not run the risk of falling in love and facing disappointment (154). Dismayed by Bingley's neglect of Jane, she exclaims,

> The more I see of the world, the more am I dissatisfied with it; and every day confirms my belief of the inconsistency of all human characters, and of the little dependence that can be placed on the appearance of either merit or sense. I have met with two instances lately; one I will not mention; the other is Charlotte's marriage. It is unaccountable! in every view it is unaccountable! (135)

In this environment Elizabeth struggles to hold on to self-respect. She rejects Charlotte's decision to avoid economic risk by accepting depersonalisation, and she deplores the passivity that is forced on Jane (although it may be natural to her as well) (133–4). She insists that Collins regard her not 'as an elegant female' but 'as a rational creature speaking the truth from her heart' (109). She replies to Mrs Gardiner: 'I will try to do what I think to be wisest' (145). In her most vigorous assertion of self, she counters Lady Catherine's attempt to bully her out of hope of an alliance with Darcy: 'I am only resolved to act in that manner, which will, in my own opinion, constitute my happiness, without reference to *you*, or to any person so wholly unconnected with me' (358).

But she finds the struggle wearing. Collins forces her to an unpleasant bluntness, and Charlotte's prospects pain her. She is, she believes, patronised and insulted by Darcy, and she is attacked by Lady Catherine as an upstart 'lost to every feeling of propriety and delicacy' (355). Believing that she is alone in resisting the patriarchal standard, she cannot believe that Darcy could act from any other: 'A man who has once been refused! . . . Is there one among the sex, who would not protest against such a weakness as a second proposal to the same woman?' (341). Her sense of her singularity increases her frustration. Nervous distress produces 'agitation and tears' and 'a headache'. In anger at the apparent necessity of masking her independent spirit and critical intelligence, Elizabeth resorts often to surprisingly aggressive language and behaviour. Mrs Gardiner warns that her speech 'savours strongly of disappointment' (154). The sense of superiority and detachment that she prizes threatens to produce a painful estrangement.

III

In the course of her struggle, Elizabeth cautiously assesses the nature and forms of love, including sexual love. To reunite sex, love and marriage, separated within the individual psyche and in relationships between men and women by society's low evaluation of wedlock, is one of Austen's major purposes in *Pride and Prejudice*.

Austen was coolly cognisant of the role of sexuality in human behaviour. Her characters' sexual natures – for example, the sexual charm of Willoughby, Wickham and Henry Crawford, Lydia's sexual exuberance, and the susceptibility of Marianne Dashwood and Maria Bertram – often direct the action in her novels. In *Mansfield Park* sexual interest dominates the activities of the young adults; in *Sense and Sensibility* Austen describes 'the very nature of seduction itself'.[6] In her discriminating treatment of 'rakes' and 'seducers', she shows a subtle knowledge of the interplay of sexual and social forces; and she uses figurative representations of sexual motive and behaviour as a means of advancing her stories.[7] Specific sexual events, although kept offstage, may substantially influence the plots.

The power of erotic attraction to blur one's vision or dull one's sense is well illustrated in *Pride and Prejudice*. It actively contributes to the mutual interest of Jane Bennet and Bingley. At one point Darcy's 'powerful feeling towards' Elizabeth prompts him to excuse her behaviour and direct his anger elsewhere (94). Later he is impelled by his sexual interest to make her an offer of marriage in spite of the objections of experience and training. Elizabeth's 'excessive reaction when Darcy slights her beauty and the strong feeling in their early verbal sparring' suggest a sexual attraction.[8] Darcy's sister is barely kept from eloping with Wickham. The connection between Lydia and Wickham, of course, is openly sexual and is dealt with frankly. Elizabeth thinks that Wickham simply wants a 'companion', and Lydia apparently is well satisfied with such a relationship.

Austen depicts the distorted forms that sexual behaviour may take when society slights its affective role and assumes the superiority of the male, and she depicts the dangers to society and the individual that arise from a lack of sexual restraint. Her novels also show how practical and prudential views of marriage encourage the separation from marriage of both love and sex. Such a separation increases the difficulty of self-control and the possibility of abuse of the sexual drive by opening it to selfish and exploitative treatment. These effects in turn lead to a mistrust of the sexual because of its association with the impulsive and irresponsible, and they encourage its relegation to the unlawful.

Austen wished to heal the division between the sexes. First, she reduced the prominence given to sexual activity by its identification with the irregular, the unlawful or the sinful. Thus she refrains from presenting Wickham as a 'moral monster' (as also the more culpable Willoughby in *Sense and Sensibility*); there is no outcry about ruined maids or loss of virtue. Wickham is not an evil man, only a cad. Elizabeth is shocked socially but not sexually by the elopement. Austen can consider her principal characters apart from the hazards of sexuality, and she removes the latter from a position of central concern. Second, Austen looks for a mode of accommodation for the sexual drive that avoids the evils of either a lack of control or sexual manipulation. Her answer is to include the sexual life within a relationship between two individuals that encourages development of the full range of sexual, affective and social responses. In the contrast between Elizabeth's cautious exploration of the sexual and Lydia's defiant indulgence, Austen provides a basis for regularising attitudes towards one's sexual nature and for defining its boundaries. Her position in the main is sensible, practical and modern.

In both *Pride and Prejudice* and *Sense and Sensibility* two sisters, with apparently very dissimilar personalities, experience the sexual magnetism of the same young male. When Marianne Dashwood discovers Willoughby's inability to resist sexual temptation, she wonders if that 'wickedness' is not present within herself as well. She discovers how dangerous uncontrolled passion can be, especially for young women. Mansell describes Austen's cautious handling of this question:

> Marianne's potential wickedness has been shunted off onto her counterpart Eliza, who has the 'same warmth of heart, the same eagerness of fancy and spirits' (p. 205). Eliza goes astray, and her own daughter Eliza is then seduced by [Willoughby]. . . . In these Elizas Jane Austen has indirectly revealed what may indeed lie beneath the romantic yearnings of the early Marianne. (52)

But the erotic inclination is generic, not individual. Elinor Dashwood also responds to Willoughby's sexual charm:

She felt that his influence over her mind was heightened by circumstances which ought not in reason to have weight; by that person of uncommon attraction, that open, affectionate, and lively manner which it was no merit to possess; and by that still ardent love for Marianne, which it was not even innocent to indulge. But she felt that it was so, long, long before she could feel his influence less. (*SS*, 333)[9]

Elizabeth Bennet exhibits both Elinor's susceptibility to sexual charm and a restrained form of Marianne's overt response. When Wickham appears at Mrs Phillips's party, Elizabeth is as ready to admire him as the others (*PP*, 85). In fact, sexual interest so dulls her vaunted discernment that she judges his character by his manner and appearance: 'A young man too, like *you*, whose very countenance may vouch for your being amiable' (80–1); 'there was truth in his looks' (86). When she hears that Wickham has been abused by Darcy, admiration and prejudice reinforce each other: she honoured him for his feelings and 'thought him handsomer than ever as he expressed them' (80). At the end of the evening Elizabeth 'could think of nothing but of Mr. Wickham, and of what he had told her, all the way home' (84). She dresses for the Netherfield Ball 'prepared in the highest spirits for the conquest of all that remained unsubdued of his heart' (89).

Elizabeth is pleased by the thought of Wickham's becoming 'really attached' to her. Briefly temptation collides with prudence; she perceives how possible is the behaviour that Lydia later heedlessly displays (44–5). Not until Darcy's letter does she realise how she has been beguiled by Wickham's 'countenance, voice, and manner' (206). Unwittingly, she cites the cause of her folly: 'Had I been in love, I could not have been more wretchedly blind' (208). The discovery of her sexual vulnerability is humiliating.

In Mansell's view, Elizabeth's realisation of her self-deception holds the same implication for her character that it did for Marianne's, that is, that the 'wickedness . . . discovered in the man for whom she felt such an attraction is also potentially in herself as well'; but in *Pride and Prejudice* it is 'shunted only as far as . . . [Elizabeth's] own sister Lydia' (52–3). What Elizabeth glimpses is the erotic drive itself, the dark power that can be ignored or stifled or indulged only at great risk to selfhood. However, in *Pride and Prejudice* Austen ignores the stock judgement of a woman's sexual delinquency. Lydia not only survives her folly; by her own lights she prospers. Instead of dramatising the potential for tragedy of the female's sexual vulnerability, a theme of *Sense and Sensibility*, Austen explores the problem of mediating between the extremes of self-repression and self-indulgence, as shown on the one hand by society's insistence that marriage is the be-all and end-all of a woman's life and on the other hand by Lydia's willingness to subordinate her interest in marriage to her sexual inclination.

Elizabeth is as opposed to Lydia's 'way of getting husbands' (*PP*, 317) as she is to Charlotte's. However, the difference between her course of action and Lydia's is not one of libidinal potential but of age, experience and the development of judgement and self-control:

> . . . [Lydia] is very young; she has never been taught to think on serious subjects. . . . Since the ——shire were first quartered in Meryton, nothing but love, flirtation, and officers, have been in her head. She has been doing every thing in her power by think-ing and talking on the subject, to give greater – what shall I call it? susceptibility to her feelings; which are naturally lively enough. And we all know that Wickham has every charm of person and address that can captivate a woman. (283–4)

In the last instance Elizabeth is speaking from personal experience. She has discovered both her own vulnerability and the ill conse-quence of allowing erotic inclination to sway her judgement:

> His countenance, voice, and manner, had established him [Wickham] at once in the possession of every virtue. . . . She could see him instantly before her, in every charm of air and address; but she could remember no more substantial good than the general approbation of the neighbourhood, and the regard which his social powers had gained him in the mess . . . (206)

The narrator carefully summarises Elizabeth's final choice between opposing sources of 'love':

> If gratitude and esteem are good foundations of affection, Elizabeth's change of sentiment will be neither improbable nor faulty. But if otherwise, if the regard springing from such sources is unreasonable or unnatural, in comparison of what is so often described as arising on a first interview with its object, and even before two words have been exchanged, nothing can be said in

her defence, except that she had given somewhat of a trial to the latter method, in her partiality for Wickham, and that its ill-success might perhaps authorise her to seek the other less interesting mode of attachment. (279)

IV

To escape the consequences of her society's separation of sex, love and marriage and of its low opinion of women, Elizabeth will pay the price, if unavoidable, of spinsterhood. However, as Hardy observes, Austen chose 'to write about the Elizabeths who *do* get their Darcys'; although they live in a world where few are so fortunate, she 'doesn't put the wilderness at the centre'.[10] Austen's purpose in *Pride and Prejudice* was to reconcile sex, love and marriage. She wished to describe an alternative to the dominant – submissive model for marriage by bringing men and women together in a partnership based on mutual respect and affection and shared emotion. The means of bringing Elizabeth's participation in the 'drama of woman' to a successful close is Fitzwilliam Darcy, the principal stimulus and target of her misanthropy.

Initially, Elizabeth and Darcy square off as types of the female struggling for freedom and the conventional male oppressor.[11] Each is deeply influenced by the concept of roles, which leads one individual to judge another primarily as society thinks that person ought to be. Its companion is the concept of stereotypes, which, by stressing the differences between masculine and feminine identity, restricts one's hopes of finding in the opposite sex those qualities that would minister to one's own human needs. Roles and stereotypes are learned. They are internalised and become part of 'the fabric of one's psyche and personal relationships'.[12]

Darcy appears at Meryton as a refined product of the patriarchal order: handsome, self-assured, cultivated and apparently confident of his superiority. Elizabeth is annoyed by the scrutiny of 'so great a man', who she assumes dislikes her (*PP*, 51). She accuses him of being proud, in the sense of possessing an overweening self-regard and love of rule, in the manner of Lady Catherine de Bourgh. As a reflection of the 'rituals of patriarchy', she assumes that Darcy's attitudes can be predicted by Lady Catherine's (337–8).

Patriarchal patterns of thought do control Darcy's performance until well after his proposal at Hunsford. Like a patriarchal father who seeks to prevent a child's imprudent marriage, he interferes with the friendship of Jane Bennet and Bingley (84–7). When he finds himself strongly attracted to Elizabeth, he resolves, because of 'the inferiority of her connections' (52), 'to be particularly careful that no sign of admiration should *now* escape him, nothing that could elevate her with the hope of influencing his felicity' (60). He informs her, finally, that because of his irrepressible feelings he has decided to overlook 'his sense of her inferiority – of its being a degradation – of the family obstacles which judgment had always opposed to inclination' (189) – and to make her an offer of marriage. Darcy's proposal is as tasteless as Collins's: he makes the same assumption that he will not be refused; he is as tactless, or more so, in telling her that he likes her against his will, his reason and even his character; and he receives her refusal with greater resentment (189–90). Elizabeth informs Darcy that no proposal from him would have tempted her. Despite an initial sense of gratification at having 'inspired unconsciously so strong an affection', anger at Darcy's 'pride, his abominable pride', soon rules her thoughts (193).

Elizabeth describes the proposal as 'almost incredible', but her declaration of independence – 'You could not have made me the offer of your hand in any possible way that would have tempted me to accept it' (192–3) – is an unthinkable response by a young woman in her circumstances. Darcy's astonishment and his mortification are obvious. The impasse that follows marks a fundamental clash on the issue of male social and sexual superiority. Both parties appear hopelessly bound by the stereotyped view each holds of the other, an attitude that is intensified by their blows to each other's self-regard. Elizabeth's 'flattened interpretation' of Darcy[13] is nourished by her resistance to the masculine domination of the world that he appears to embody and to the operation of the marriage market as she has observed it. Although she believes that she is free of prejudice, her anger and frustration influence her reasoning. Long before her humiliation at Hunsford, she has reacted to Darcy's apparently improper pride by resolving to give him no opportunity to despise her, by attempting, like Emma Woodhouse in her relationship with the Knightley brothers, to prove the superiority of her judgement, and by making him the butt of her mischievous and occasionally sarcastic wit.

Hunsford, however, marks the turning point in their relationship. At Hunsford their expectations are shaped by their assumptions about masculine and feminine behaviour. Both disdain the marriage market and insist on something better than practicality as a basis for marriage, but each mistakenly identifies the other with the general view. At Hunsford both experience the frustration and pain of being judged by a stereotype rather than as an individual, and both are mortified by the result. Darcy is startled by Elizabeth's stern reproof of his conduct, and she learns from his subsequent letter that her behaviour has been 'grounded in a prejudice that distorts reason'.[14] They discover how stereotyping has inhibited their ability to achieve their personal goals.

Both have been wrong about the other, but they have also been in the dark about themselves: they give each other 'severe lessons of liberality'.[15] Darcy experiences the greater shock, since, as a beneficiary of the system, he is less sensitive to the restrictions that sex roles impose. Elizabeth's internal conflict, however, seems the greater, and she is slower to recover because, as victim, she has to overcome both the habit of stereotyping and the warping of her judgement by resentment at being the oppressed.

During this period feeling clouds Elizabeth's judgement. Her sensitivity to affront and her spirited nature have encouraged an overly aggressive defence of her selfhood. Hence she falsely judges Darcy's behaviour and exaggerates his role. Her scorn reflects resentment at the circumstances that decree their apparent inequality. Since she seems to cultivate her dislike at every opportunity, her reaction may be a mode of ego-gratification at the expense of the 'enemy'.[16] (By contrast, in the relative absence of such reason for conflict, her liking for Wickham flourishes.) Her emotional response to Darcy seemingly helps to keep her from the self-knowledge and self-restraint that mark the self as a social creature. When she finally recognises how 'blind, partial, prejudiced, absurd' (*PP*, 208) she has been in judging both Darcy and Wickham, Elizabeth senses how close she has come to slipping into a false existence.

Both Darcy and Elizabeth demand that they be judged as individuals, both discover how difficult it is to shake off conventional modes of thought in judging others, and both come to realise that correct judgement depends upon a knowledge of both oneself and the other, an attitude inherently at odds with entrenched sexual assumptions. But instead of blaming the other, they begin the difficult task of removing the imprint of sexual stereotyping on their own behaviour. On their success rests their chance of discovering their individual human potential and of arriving at an intimate personal relationship.

Like Anne Elliot and Frederick Wentworth, Elizabeth and Darcy draw together because recognition of their own needs replaces a faulty social pattern as the monitor of their behaviour. As his discussion with Elizabeth and the Bingley sisters shows, Darcy hopes to find in a woman more than the superficial accomplishments that bait the marriage trap or mark the 'genteel' woman as decorative and unsuited for serious activity or intellectual enterprise: to the list of ornamental accomplishments 'she must yet add something more substantial, in the improvement of her mind by extensive reading' (39). Although Elizabeth's beauty first stimulates his interest (23), he is soon drawn by the discovery that she is different from other women of her age. Later he distinguishes her by assuming that she reads books and can discuss ideas (93). When Elizabeth asks him why he fell in love with her, he stipulates that it was 'for the liveliness' of her mind (380).

Elizabeth also appears different to Darcy because she does not pretend an interest in him as a possible husband. During the time that she is indifferent or hostile, he comes to admire her for her own sake, when evidence of a design on her part to attract his attention would have repelled him. Elizabeth describes how this interest began:

> . . . you were sick of civility, of deference, of officious attention. You were disgusted with the women who were always speaking and looking, and thinking for *your* approbation alone. . . . [I]n spite of the pains you took to disguise yourself, your feelings were always noble and just; and in your heart, you thoroughly despised the persons who so assiduously courted you. (380)

Thus the attachment he develops is spontaneous. Darcy seems to be falling into the trap that he has warned Bingley against, but he is saved by the distinction in Elizabeth that he prizes, in that she scorns to adopt the response of a Charlotte Lucas. When his mind is cleared of patriarchal bias, Darcy will no longer have to excuse his action on the grounds of irrepressible feelings.

Both Elizabeth and Darcy believe that for a happy marriage each party must fully understand the reasonableness of his or her 'regard', an achievement which in turn requires understanding the other's character. Elizabeth expresses this view directly to Charlotte (22); Darcy does so indirectly, in the metaphor of the dance, in his comment that he detests dancing unless he is particularly acquainted with his partner (11). They uphold a standard of openness for relationships among individuals, especially between the sexes, which though not endorsed by their society, in Austen's view is needed for clarity in one's thinking and in one's understanding and appreciation of others. This emphasis is a major theme in Austen's novels. In *Emma*, for example, Frank Churchill employs disguise and deception in order to gratify his vanity at the expense of women, Knightley calls for 'truth and sincerity' between individuals (*E*, 446), and Emma, at the end, expresses her relief that the 'disguise, equivocation, mystery so hateful to her to practise, might soon be over' and be replaced by 'that full and perfect confidence which her disposition was most ready to welcome as a duty' (475).

At Hunsford Darcy and Elizabeth begin the double movement of hero and heroine that one also finds in *Emma*. They speak to each other directly and unambiguously. On the basis of this candour and the response it provokes – Darcy's expression of interest in why Elizabeth spurned him 'with so little *endeavor* at civility' and her interest in why he told her that he liked her against his will, his reason and even his character – the door to accommodation begins to open. Because each favours candour and finds it in the other and because they are basically compatible, they discover signs of unexpected traits in each other and grope towards revising their assumptions.

Both undergo a process of education. Darcy, no less than Elizabeth, wants to arrive at 'the merits of the particular case'.[17] But first, like Elizabeth, he must free himself of the biases generated by the patriarchal society. Each redefines freedom as liberation from the artificial and restrictive roles that obscure one's vision rather than as escape from emotional and social involvement, as initially both seem to desire. In her presentation of Darcy, Austen advances the idea that, despite the obvious advantages of supporting the status quo, some men will accept the invitation to liberate themselves from the restrictions of sex-role stereotyping. Three of her male principals – Darcy, Knightley and Wentworth – overcome its effects, with the difference that Austen's heroines accompany the first two in this deep change of mind and heart, whereas Wentworth does so alone, since Anne Elliot has already made the transformation.

The key to this event is that each places a premium on the value of experience in making judgements. In a threatening world Austen believes that the relationship between individuals is paramount.[18] Although one person may treat another as though the latter were not a person and although one can become alienated even from oneself, unaware of what has happened, genuine encounters between individuals can happen. In such meetings one's experience and one's actions occur in relation to some one other than the self. The last point describes the source of the forward movement in *Pride and Prejudice*. After Hunsford the relationship of Darcy and Elizabeth follows the principle that personal experience can transform attitudes and behaviour. Moving from disputes about beliefs to concern about misunderstanding, Elizabeth and Darcy begin to evaluate their experience of themselves and of each other. They begin to pare away what stands between them and thus place themselves in position to regain the ground lost.

Austen recognises that within a social system what others attribute to one implicitly or explicitly plays a decisive part in forming one's sense of one's identity. Initially, Elizabeth experiences the pain of being aware of a discrepancy between her self-identity and how others perceive her. When Collins proposes, she experiences the shame of perceiving herself condemned to an identity as the complement of one whom she wishes to repudiate but cannot. She solves her problem, however, when she acquires a stable identity in the eyes of another, Darcy, that is consistent with her view of herself. Austen describes how both Elizabeth and Darcy replace their initial identity – the concept of self based on socially defined and imposed stereotypes – with an identity based on the mutual and reciprocal knowledge that two open and right-minded people gain.

In Austen's view, every human being requires a place in another's world where what one does bears significance for someone else. In order to acquire this significance, Elizabeth and Darcy must alter the way in which they present themselves, which others perceive as exhibiting a sense of superiority and excessive self-regard. This behaviour may protect them against the incursions of society, but it lacks the balancing influence of a sufficient regard for the selfhood of others. In particular, they need to detach their own sense of self from a sense of sexual differentiation lest they become 'locked into a defensive-aggressive stance that forbids growth'.[19]

The growth of both is marked by a 'humbling' by the other. Elizabeth first 'humbles' Darcy, who learns to appreciate her merit as a female and as a person:

> I have been a selfish being all my life, in practice, though not in principle. . . . I was given good principles, but left to follow them

in pride and conceit. . . . [I was] allowed, encouraged, almost
taught . . . to care for none beyond my own family circle, to think
meanly of all the rest of the world. . . . [S]uch I might still have
been but for you, dearest, loveliest Elizabeth! What do I not owe
you? You taught me a lesson, hard indeed at first, but most
advantageous. By you, I was properly humbled. I came to you
without a doubt of my reception. You shewed me how insufficient
were all my pretensions to please a woman worthy of being
pleased. (*PP*, 369)

In turn she is 'humbled', that is, turned away from an aggressive,
defensive reduction of self prompted by frustration and fear of loss
of selfhood:

> Of neither Darcy nor Wickham could she think, without feeling
> that she had been blind, partial, prejudiced, absurd.
> 'How despicably have I acted!' she cried. – 'I, who have prided
> myself on my discernment! – I, who have valued myself on my
> abilities! who have often disdained the generous candour of my
> sister, and gratified my vanity, in useless or blameable distrust.
> . . . Had I been in love, I could not have been more wretchedly
> blind. But vanity, not love, has been my folly. . . . I have courted
> prepossession and ignorance, and driven reason away, where
> either were concerned. Till this moment, I never knew myself.'
> (208)

Each discovers that the other is not the enemy but the one with
whom one can be free. In the flush of mutual appreciation each
acknowledges responsibility for the near-failure in accord:

> [Darcy] 'What did you say of me, that I did not deserve? . . .
> [M]y behaviour to you at the time, had merited the severest
> reproof. It was unpardonable. I cannot think of it without
> abhorrence.'
> 'We will not quarrel for the greater share of blame annexed to
> that evening,' said Elizabeth. 'The conduct of neither, if strictly
> examined, will be irreproachable; but since then, we have both,
> I hope, improved in civility.'
> 'I cannot be so easily reconciled to myself. The recollection of
> what I then said . . . is now, and has been many months,
> inexpressibly painful to me.'

[Elizabeth] 'Oh! do not repeat what I then said. These recollections will not do at all. I assure you, that I have long been most heartily ashamed of it.' (367–8)

In the healing process described in *Pride and Prejudice*, like that in *Emma* and *Persuasion*, Austen provides a model for the overcoming of all other separations. Each party accepts the reality and independence of the other and approaches the other in a spirit of mutual regard, cooperation and dependence.

V

Elizabeth's rejection of Darcy 'substantiates her claim to selfrespect, [and] proves the sincerity of her passionately held personal code'.[20] The effect on Darcy is dramatic. It prompts the self-examination that results in his rescue. He no longer assumes the female's availability; he learns to place the same value on another person, even a woman, that he does on himself (*PP*, 369). Elizabeth's independence, moreover, encourages him to believe that she may be receptive to a renewal of his suit.

As a result of the 'proofs of time and crisis',[21] Elizabeth 'began now to comprehend that he [Darcy] was exactly the man, who, in disposition and talents, would most suit her' (*PP*, 312). Her shift of feeling is encouraged by gratitude that Darcy does not judge her by the stereotype and react to her rejection with the anger of outraged masculine egotism, that he loves 'her still well enough, to forgive all the petulance and acrimony of her manner in rejecting him' (265), and that he appears to value her for herself. As a result, not surprisingly,

> she respected, she esteemed, she was grateful to him, she felt a real interest in his welfare; and she only wanted to know how far she wished that welfare to depend upon herself, and how far it would be for the happiness of both that she should employ the power, which her fancy told her she still possessed, of bringing on the renewal of his addresses. (266)

Austen is describing in Elizabeth the birth of love. In Theodore Reik's definition, love is a relationship which permits a giving and taking by both parties without fear of loss of selfhood or self-control.

The love need is an emotional craving for tenderness and consideration and for release from self-defensive mistrust. 'To love satisfies a craving, a desire to give tenderness; being loved fulfills another need, the individual wish to be wanted and appreciated. . . . To love means to long for someone. To be loved means to belong to someone.'[22] In Austen's view a loving relationship is neither predominately sexual nor based solely on gratitude and esteem but combines the two. Darcy's affection follows an initial sexual interest; Elizabeth's sexual interest develops in conjunction with other forms of emotional attachment. Austen reconciles sex, love and marriage by melding physical affection, gratitude and esteem with compatibility, equality and mutual understanding, in the merging of individuals who combine self-respect with respect for the other.

Austen offers the prospect of a marriage which seems to hold a promise of life. Heilbrun finds this prospect also in the relationship of the Crofts in *Persuasion* and in *Bleak House* but otherwise rarely in nineteenth-century literature. Such a marriage bears the marks of friendship;[23] for Austen the key to happiness in marriage is companionship. Elizabeth and Darcy discover, as do Emma Woodhouse and Knightley and Anne Elliot and Wentworth, that men and women have much more in common than they initially think and that they can be friends. In Alfred Adler's view, the acceptance of such comradeship is an 'index of a true reconciliation' of sexual roles and of an 'equilibrium between the sexes' (41). Austen presents an ideal of relations between the sexes that three-quarters of a century later, in Olive Schreiner's pronouncement, still is regarded as revolutionary:

> The one and only ideal is the perfect mental and physical life-long union of one man with one woman. That is the only thing which for highly developed intellectual natures can consolidate marriage . . . . [N]o legal marriage can make a relationship other than impure in which there isn't this union. (151–2)

The discovery of friendship opens the way to the fusion of sex and love. As Anthea Zeman points out, Elizabeth is not 'sexually shocked' by Lydia's elopement but she is by Charlotte's engagement to Collins because of 'the full stop she has put, by accepting a man she does not love, to sexual and emotional fulfillment'. Austen's point, as Zeman observes, is that a woman's integrity requires that she achieve 'the right climate for sexual happiness' (170–1). That climate is the relationship of equals in a marriage based on mutual affection and reciprocal concern.

Hardy reminds us that Austen's characters are 'always creatures of strong feeling'.[24] Elizabeth discovers the strength of erotic inclination in herself and others, and she perceives the dangers it poses by its power to sway the judgement. What is needed, however, is not the repression of sexual propensity but its control and moderation by a fusion or melding with love, with the latter's provision of mutual affection, gratitude and esteem. As Spacks notes, although Elizabeth's recognition of her feelings increases her vulnerability by increasing her desire to please, it also makes 'her more subtly conscious of the feelings of others', and she is able to recognise Darcy's own new willingness to please.[25] We witness 'the generation of feeling by feeling',[26] a phenomenon described also in *Northanger Abbey* and *Emma*. Their 'mutually successful acts of attribution' allay their fears, free them from solipsism and open the way to a genuine human relationship, in which each party's growing knowledge and awareness is matched by and nourishes the other's.

We watch the progress of Elizabeth's feelings:

> she lay awake two whole hours, endeavouring to make them out. She certainly did not hate him. No; hatred had vanished long ago . . . . The respect created by the conviction of his valuable qualities, though at first unwillingly admitted, had for some time ceased to be repugnant to her feelings; and it was now heightened into somewhat of a friendlier nature, by the testimony so highly in his favour. . . . But above all, above respect and esteem, there was a motive within her of good will which could not be overlooked. It was gratitude. – Gratitude, not merely for having once loved her, but for loving her still. . . . She respected, she esteemed, she was grateful to him, she felt a real interest in his welfare. . . . (*PP*, 265–6)

At last, on Darcy's return to Longbourn, on walking out, 'Elizabeth was secretly forming a desperate resolution; and perhaps he might be doing the same'; and after Darcy's plea that she let him know what her feelings now may be, Elizabeth

> gave him to understand, that her sentiments had undergone so material a change . . . as to make her receive with gratitude and

pleasure, his present assurances. The happiness which this reply produced, was such as he had probably never felt before; and he expressed himself on the occasion as sensibly and as warmly as a man violently in love can be supposed to do. . . . [H]e told her of feelings, which, in proving of what importance she was to him, made his affection every moment more valuable. (365–6)

In this climate of reciprocal affection and esteem the near-fatal division between the sexes disappears. The relationship between the sex act and the maintenance or achievement of identity is restored. The division within the individual psyche is healed. In her relationship with Darcy, Elizabeth stabilises her ego by the avoidance of repression and inhibition on the one hand and of indulgence on the other, she enjoys a sense of freedom, and she is confirmed in her sense of self-worth. A joking exchange that 'takes their true motives for granted'[27] marks the end of her emotional odyssey and her distinctive episode of the 'drama of woman'. In response to her father's inquiry about her intention to marry Darcy, she is impelled to an unusual seriousness by the prospect of her unexpected happiness:

'I do, I do like him,' she replied, with tears in her eyes, 'I love him. Indeed he has no improper pride. He is perfectly amiable.' (*PP*, 376)

6 *Mansfield Park:* The Revolt of the 'Feminine' Woman

No other novel of Jane Austen's has stimulated such diverse interpretations as *Mansfield Park* and no other heroine such divergent responses as Fanny Price. Reconciling these differences begins with recognising that this novel presents Austen's deepest probe of the patriarchal family itself. In the other major novels, because of the father's absence or ineffectuality, the daughters are partly insulated from the worst effects of direct patriarchal rule. But in *Mansfield Park* these effects are fully and fairly examined, and we observe the faults in the family structure at the heart of the patriarchal order.

Recently, in discussion of *Mansfield Park*, critics have tended to develop one or the other of two emphases – (1) the novel is about the threat to an existing society and its reform or vindication[1] or (2) it is about a heroine of principle[2] – and they have been led, in Joseph Wiesenfarth's apt summary, to ask the following question: 'Does or does not *Mansfield Park* show that a meaningful personal freedom and integrity are viable within a traditional pattern of morals and manners?'[3]

Wiesenfarth answers the question affirmatively. The central theme of *Mansfield Park*, he says, is 'the threat to the integrity of the self that comes from an easy life lived without principle'. The central conflict thus is within the self rather than between the self and a threatening family or society. Fanny 'refuses not to be free within the bounds of duty, and duty does not direct her to sacrifice herself either to the consequence or to the convenience of others' (107, 90). However, a number of other critics who admire the heroism of Fanny Price regard it as demanded of her in a battle with her family and social environment.[4] In this view Fanny embodies the self's desire to preserve its independence, and the family and society seek to subject her to their authority.[5]

At issue also among the admirers of Fanny is Austen's purpose in writing *Mansfield Park*. In Ryals's opinion, she wished to examine 'what it means to have formed a central core of self' in a 'modern *Zeitgeist* . . . destructive of individual integrity and wholeness of being' (347, 359). At the other extreme, Donovan suggests that Austen wished to set herself 'the most difficult artistic challenge': could she 'deprive her heroine of all the outward graces and . . . command our admiration for strength of character alone'?[6]

In all of Austen's novels, the society is patriarchal in nature. Women are regarded as inferior and dependent, and their activities are devalued. This standing is imposed upon them by education and social training. From infancy a girl is taught to revere the male; in adolescence she discovers the economic and social foundations of male superiority. She is brought up to be subordinate, praised for being 'feminine', and offered 'advantages' to acquiesce; failure to please becomes a special liability. Since she is judged not as an individual but as a member of a stereotyped group, she finds it difficult to develop a separate ego. Playing the 'feminine' role, she moves in a vicious circle: the less she exercises her freedom to under-stand, the fewer resources she discovers in herself and the less she dares to affirm herself as a subject. Her situation invites collusion with her masters, a circumstance that in turn feeds their arrogance and prompts their blindness. Marriage is her chief means of support and the chief justification of her existence. But, since patriarchal values prevail, her position in marriage in all probability remains subservient and supportive.

In *Pride and Prejudice* Austen focuses on the problem of suitable marriage. In *Mansfield Park* she emphasises the broader problem of how the patriarchal system endangers its members' personalities and destinies, in terms, specifically, of how by coercion and restriction it works to stifle the potential for selfhood of Fanny Price. This interest accounts for several features of its plot: *Mansfield Park* is the only one of Austen's novels that follows the development of the heroine's personality and character within the patriarchal environment over a period of years; it gives as much attention to the relations of parents and children as to the relations of the sexes; it shows more interest in the making of wrong marriages than of right ones; and it dares, as a proof of its honesty, to feature a heroine whose best-known trait is her passivity.

At the core of the patriarchal society is a family unit dedicated to accumulating property and transmitting it to its biological descen-dants. Mansfield Park, home of the Bertram family, is a model of the patriarchal order, exemplifying the spirit of hierarchy and the assumption of male primacy over the female. Sir Thomas is master at the Park and the principal patriarchal figure: grave, Olympian, seeing only what he wants to see. Reminiscent of General Tilney of *Northanger Abbey*, he is more broadly and positively conceived. His acts proceed, we are told, from a concern for himself and society and a wish to do right, and he first appears as the guardian of what is good and proper. However, he soon reveals defects: a narrowly conceived plan of education, a moral blindness and vulgarity, and a smug authoritarianism. In directing his childrens' lives, he is guided by an obtuse preference for worldly advantage; in facing an apparent challenge to his authority, he exhibits the corrosive effects on character of despotic rule. Sir Thomas's oldest son, Tom Bertram, in accord with the principle of primogeniture, enjoys a favoured place among his children. But Tom shows by his selfishness and self-indulgence the debilitating effect of encouraging a sense of superiority and privilege early in the minds of male children.

The females at the Park are subordinate figures whose fates are decided by the marriages they make. Lady Bertram is an extreme example of the reduction of the female to virtual non-being by the patriarchal system. Having achieved a fortunate alliance, she has no further sense of purpose in life. She is helpless without masculine support, totally selfish and self-centred, too indolent even to enjoy her daughters' social success. She thinks more of her dog than of her children and misses her husband only when his return reminds her that he has been gone.

Maria and Julia Bertram are the female offspring of patriarchalism: 'remarkably fine' in appearance and in cultivation of drawing-room graces; raised in idleness and without purpose except to marry well; selfish, vain and insensitive. Although both girls outwardly comply with the process of their dehumanisation, they strive to escape the boredom and the constricted life of their society. Marriage seems to offer a means to gain freedom from parental control as well as to achieve status and economic security, but they find that it is an exchange of one confinement for another. Trained in the direction of insincerity about her sexual interests, a girl such as Maria Bertram, in de Beauvoir's eyes, is fated for adultery: in marriage the 'sole concrete form her liberty can assume' is infidelity (176). Her final disgrace exhibits both society's double standard (*MP*, 468) and the danger to the female in a sexist society of succumbing to sexual temptation.

In *Mansfield Park* the abuses of the patriarchal system, not the transgressions or follies of individuals, are Austen's main subject. All of the characters, with the possible exception of Mrs Norris, possess the potentiality of suitable behaviour were they to live in a different setting. Even the system's champion, Sir Thomas, is no villain. His intentions are good, and at the conclusion he not only acknowledges his errors but modifies his behaviour. Faulty upbringing – the inculcation of faulty values and selfish attitudes – accounts for the conduct of both parents and children. As in *Pride and Prejudice* and *Emma* the emphasis on wealth, position and sexual stereotyping weakens the personality both of those who benefit and of those who do not. But no one in *Mansfield Park* is as independent or assertive as Elizabeth Bennet or Emma Woodhouse.

Austen stresses four closely related problems encountered in the patriarchal family: the absence of love and understanding between parents and children; the failure of female education; the cultivation of shallow goals and inadequate moral standards; and the perversion of courtship and marriage.

The first of these is a principal cause of the misbehaviour of the Bertram children. In Sir Thomas's view the members of a patriarchal family exist for the sake of its advancement. He is not outwardly affectionate, and his reserve represses the flow of his children's spirits towards him (19). Having placed them under the care of a governess, with proper masters, he believes that they could need nothing more. As a result 'their father was no object of love to them, he had never seemed the friend of their pleasures, and his absence was unhappily most welcome. They were relieved by it from all restraints' (32). Thus the moral and social education of the Bertram children is handicapped by the absence of close personal attachment to their parents.

Whether or not one accepts Wiesenfarth's statement that the education of Fanny Price is the subject of *Mansfield Park*, the failure of female education is an important issue. The training characteristic of a patriarchal society blocks the emotional development of the young, hinders development of a capacity for independent action, and fails to inculcate an adequate foundation of moral principle. It prepares young women only to carry out their limited function, which is to add lustre to a family while part of it and to add to its greatness when they leave it by marriage. Thus Sir Thomas saw his daughters 'becoming in person, manner, and accomplishments, every thing that could satisfy his anxiety' (20). But, in Denis

Donoghue's view, 'the sins of Julia and Maria have been prefigured . . . by instances of their defective education' (50);[7] and the faulty upbringing of the Crawfords is the source of their failures in principle and judgement. For all their promising talents and early acquired information the Bertram sisters (and their brother Tom and the Crawfords as well) are deficient in self-knowledge, generosity and humility. At issue is the difference between an education that emphasises 'accomplishments' and that models behaviour on social example and one that emphasises the interiorisation of values. Even though Fanny escapes her cousins' formal schooling, she does not escape the broader educating effects, the social conditioning, of being brought up as a dependent female in a patriarchal society.

Austen's third criticism is that patriarchalism encourages shallow goals and inadequate moral perception. Its values permeate the individual psyche and poison personal relationships. All the prominent adults are self-centred and guided by materialism. The society encourages self-gratification in young males, since they are protected by their favoured position; and it turns young females away from any substantial activity in favour of an interest in appearance, manners, accomplishments and admiration. The children of both sexes pursue selfish goals, engage in a constant battle for personal superiority, and view freedom as an escape from external restraint.

The fourth principal fault – the corruption of courtship and marriage – is as important an issue as the failure in education. Austen depicts the same materialistic attitude towards the making of marriages as in *Pride and Prejudice*, and she explores the marriage theme with nearly the same intensity. Since Maria Bertram regards her happiness as assured by Rushworth's large fortune, she regards it as 'her evident duty to marry' him if she can (*MP*, 38–9). Marriage is also Mary Crawford's object, provided she can marry well. Sir Thomas expects his daughters' marriages to produce alliances advantageous to the family, and Lady Bertram is stirred for almost the only time in the novel by the prospect of Fanny's marrying a man of such good estate as Henry Crawford. Mary Crawford sums up the view of marriage in her society; it is the transaction in which people expect the most from others and are themselves the least honest; one should marry as soon as it can be done to advantage (43, 46). She promises that by marrying her brother Fanny will have 'the glory of fixing one who has been shot at by so many; of having it in one's power to pay off the debts of one's sex! Oh, I am sure it is not in woman's nature to refuse such a triumph' (363). All the daughters in *Mansfield Park* are in danger of being forced to omit love from the pattern of courtship and adopt unnatural and self-defeating behaviour.

The plot of *Mansfield Park* turns on two events: an abortive revolt against the restraints of patriarchalism by its favoured offspring and a successful revolt against its constraints by Fanny Price. In the first revolt the 'corrupted' children of patriarchy seek independence in order to indulge their whims, but their rebellion moves them towards moral chaos. In the second revolt, however, Fanny Price, seeking to preserve her moral integrity and selfhood from the depersonalising demands of the patriarchal society, rehabilitates the moral order.

The cause of the first revolt is the upbringing of the Bertram children (and of the Crawfords and Mr Yates). They put personal pleasure and gratification of vanity above all else. The occasion is Sir Thomas's absence. The means is a private theatrical performance. In the opinion of Edmund and Fanny, to stage it in their father's house while he is absent and in some danger would show great want of feeling (125). They also believe that he would regard it as unfit for home representation (137) and a threat to the privacy and propriety of the house (153). Edmund at first stands firm with Fanny in upholding the authority of Sir Thomas and defending decorum. When, however, he enters into the activity, Fanny is left alone as the defender of the patriarchal order, wretched in her personal predicament. The first revolt collapses with Sir Thomas's unexpected return. It was shallowly conceived and lacked substance, the result of infantile egotistic impulses: the behaviour of the 'corrupted' children would destroy both the system and what remained of their own selfhood. However, with Sir Thomas reinstated as master, nothing changes and nothing is learned.

In the second revolt a morally mature, responsive and sensitive Fanny Price defends her freedom to choose a husband in accord with personally defined criteria in the face of a concerted and un-compromising attack by the parents and children of patriarchy. The narrative presents an inescapable discrepancy between the needs of the individual and the demands of society. The female has the additional burden of overcoming the side-effects of her identification as 'the Other'. Thus, in opposing her male masters, Fanny is plagued by feelings of anxiety and guilt. However, despite the efforts of the society at indoctrination and coercion, at the crucial moment she retains the will and courage to defend her moral autonomy, and she proves that she alone of the patriarchal children is free. Her astonishing act of defiance is inherently subversive of the patriarchal order, since she places a higher value on her personal salvation than on her social salvation. It implicitly aims a death blow at that order, since at the heart of the change it would bring is a fundamentally different concept of personal relationships. That the person who strikes this saving blow is apparently most fully the system's creature and victim provides the novel's considerable dramatic and sympathetic force.[8]

Fanny Price first appears to be the model of a passive, submissive female, formed for and created by a patriarchal society. She is gentle, affectionate, desirous of doing right and endowed with great sensibility. Her disposition and humble circumstances encourage timidity and very low self-esteem. Unlike her cousins she subordinates personal pleasure to other considerations (*MP*, 131), values fond treatment (365), and is concerned to please and do her duty. In the eyes of the representatives of the system, Fanny perfectly fits the stereotype of female and wife (264–5, 293–4). Austen gives special attention to Fanny's relationship with Sir Thomas; they appear to carry to an extreme the types of the patriarchal father and the submissive daughter. Fanny's awe and fear of Sir Thomas's opinion and her desire to please him are constantly emphasised (320–1). His advice is that of an 'absolute power' (280). She is afraid that she will not appear properly submissive.

Thus prior to her revolt Fanny's behaviour exhibits much of the false humility, the psychological paralysis and the emotional dependence rooted in low self-esteem that Daly describes as a product of the internalisation of masculine opinion by the female in an androcentric society (50–4). She appears to be a partner in what Janeway describes as the collusion of weakness and power to preserve subordination by the withdrawal of the weak from the possibilities of action (107–9). Fanny's case seems almost a perfect illustration of de Beauvoir's representation of the formation of the 'feminine' woman (261–2, 267–9, 337).

However, Fanny's personality is more complex than those around her perceive. Her taste is strong (*MP*, 337), she is responsive to the natural environment and to anything that warms her imagination with scenes of the past (85–6), and she is clever and has a quick apprehension as well as good sense (22). She is perceptive and reactive to those around her, as shown particularly by her disgust at what she believes to be Henry Crawford's want of feeling (328-9). She is not to be won by gallantry and wit or without the assistance of sentiment and feeling and seriousness on serious subjects. Since her feelings are strong, her words often spring directly from them, but she retains sufficient objectivity to judge herself.[9] There is always a kernel of stoical independence in her makeup, as Mrs Norris notes: 'she certainly has a little spirit of secrecy, and independence, and nonsense, about her' (323). Fanny has a devotion to principle, a determination to do her duty, and many of the feelings of youth and pride.

During the first revolt Fanny recognises her debt to the patriarchal society, appreciates its values, is cautious about self-assertion, and keeps her poise amid the claims of judgement and of the heart. She defends that society more satisfactorily than its more favoured members. Edmund tells his father that only Fanny has judged rightly throughout, and she is embraced by the latter as his sole faithful and upright child.

Subsequently, Sir Thomas treats Fanny with a new kindness, and her health and beauty markedly improve, as she seems to have earned a place in the patriarchal order. But the outcome is only temporary. The aborted theatricals were a dress rehearsal for the later, more reprehensible breakaway of the Bertram sisters and the Crawfords. Furthermore, Fanny's recognition and promotion follow upon her appearing to fill, as Sir Thomas's natural daughters did not, the role of a model patriarchal child. In fact, as Fanny's worth is recognised, the patriarchal order moves to appropriate her will and exploit her gifts. In the remainder of the novel her integrity and selfhood come under attack by three males whose goal is her submission. The response is Fanny's revolt.

Henry Crawford authors the first attack on Fanny's integrity and selfhood. Attracted by her new spirit and improved appearance, he decides to amuse himself by gaining her love. Since he wishes only to satisfy his masculine compulsion to dominate, her resistance stimulates his interest. But he soon finds himself snared in his own net. As his thoughts turn from flirtation to marriage, two themes emerge: the increase in his interest as he perceives how well Fanny fits the patriarchal idea of a model wife; and the inconceivability to all that she can refuse his offer. Henry ticks off her qualifications: strong affections, a dependable temper, a quick and clear understanding, manners that 'were the mirror of her own modest and elegant mind', and strong principles, gentleness and modesty. He especially praises 'that sweetness which makes so essential a part of every woman's worth in the judgment of man, that though he sometimes loves where it is not, he can never believe it absent'. Mary Crawford assures him that Fanny 'is the very one to make you happy' (294–5). Like Darcy at Hunsford, he cannot believe that he can ask Fanny in vain. Unlike Darcy, he is kept by his masculine egotism from ever quite recognising her reality.

Mary Crawford encourages Henry in his suit with the arguments of convention: Fanny's upbringing must influence her to accept, and her gentle and grateful disposition would assure her consent even if he were less pleasing (293). To these constraints upon Fanny are added her gratitude to Crawford for William's promotion and her sense of the improvement in his behaviour (328). But Fanny's objection is deeply rooted: she perceives an absolute incompatibility of personality and attitudes. She has often been oppressed by his disposition; still more does she object to his character. She has seen him behaving very improperly and unfeelingly (349). Her most serious charge: 'And, alas! how always known no principle to supply as a duty what the heart was deficient in' (329).

The attack from Sir Thomas is even more threatening and oppressive because it brings the patriarchal father and his dutiful 'daughter' into direct conflict. The encouragement Fanny has received from Sir Thomas and her own increased affection for him only add to the pressure upon her. She appears doubly ungrateful because she has received a genteel upbringing beyond her expectations. Upon her refusal of Crawford, Fanny is thrust back into her former fearful relationship with Sir Thomas, augmented by an increase in guilt.

The scenes between Sir Thomas and Fanny illustrate how the patriarchal system demands the female's submission and self-effacement. For all of his merits Sir Thomas represents the parent as tyrant. In accord with his notions of marriage and the relations of parents and children, he believes that after his sanction nothing remains but Fanny's consent. Consequently he is dumbfounded by her assertion that she cannot return Crawford's 'good opinion'. Three times he asks if she refuses him, uncomprehending. His displeasure mounts as he finds no acceptable explanation (315–17). Finally, he addresses her with the cold accents of the patriarchal father whose authority has been defied (the accents of Richardson's Mr Harlowe); his words reflect the assumptions that support the patriarchal family structure:

> It is of no use, I perceive, to talk to you. . . . I will, therefore, only
> add, as thinking it my duty to mark my opinion of your conduct
> – that you have disappointed every expectation I had formed,
> and proved yourself of a character the very reverse of what I had
> supposed. . . . I had thought you peculiarly free from wilfulness of
> temper, self-conceit, and every tendency to that independence of
> spirit, which prevails so much in modern days, even in young
> women, and which in young women is offensive and disgusting
> beyond all common offence. But you have now shewn me that
> you can be wilful and perverse, that you can and will decide for
> yourself, without any consideration or deference for those who
> have surely some right to guide you. . . . The advantage or dis-
> advantage of your family – of your parents – your brothers and
> sisters – never seems to have had a moment's share in your
> thoughts on this occasion. . . . You think only of yourself; and
> because you do not feel for Mr. Crawford exactly what a young,
> heated fancy imagines to be necessary for happiness, you resolve
> to refuse him . . . and are, in a wild fit of folly, throwing away
> from you such an opportunity of being settled in life . . . as will,
> probably, never occur to you again. (318–19)

Understanding the import of Sir Thomas's speech is crucial to
understanding the basic relationship between Fanny Price and the
society of Mansfield Park. The words are those of the dominant
patriarchal male parent. Sir Thomas expresses the system's
intolerance of any independence of spirit and identifies as wilful and
ungrateful any concern for self that opposes the parents' wishes. He
places the interest of the family above those of individual members.
He places material values and a concern for status and security in
the society above personal aspirations and emotional happiness. He
finds any deviation from its standards more reprehensible in the
female than in the male. Fanny is a subverter of the patriarchal
order, to a worse degree even than the 'corrupted' children.

Sir Thomas decides that kindness may be the best way to work
with such a gentle-tempered girl. But his retreat from a dogmatic
and demanding position is only tactical. He still intends to
manipulate her, and he hopes for a resolution in accord with his
wishes. In encouraging Crawford's departure he hopes that she will
miss Crawford and that she will regret her loss of importance (366),

and in sending Fanny to Portsmouth he hopes that abstinence from elegance and luxury will induce in her a juster estimate of the value of Crawford's offer (369).

Fanny too hopes that time will favour her. She

> trusted . . . that she had done right, that her judgment had not misled her; for the purity of her intentions she could answer; and she was willing to hope . . . that her uncle's displeasure was abating, and would abate farther as he considered the matter with more impartiality, and felt, as a good man must feel, how wretched, and how unpardonable, how hopeless and how wicked it was, to marry without affection. (324)

Fanny here identifies the source of her revolt: the defence of her right to make a marriage choice in accord with her own view of what would constitute her happiness or welfare. At issue is the question of location of authority over the self. The individual who seeks self-fulfilment is in conflict with the patriarchal order that would subordinate the individual to the group. As in all of Austen's novels, the clash occurs in most striking fashion in the female's choice of a spouse, where the pressure of the patriarchal society to conform is most severe and potentially traumatic.

The attack from Edmund Bertram is the most dangerous of the three. It occurs when Crawford's behaviour is attracting favourable response from Fanny and when Sir Thomas has substituted siege for assault. Edmund is Fanny's first and principal friend, towards whom she has a respectful, grateful, confiding, tender feeling (37). Since he casts himself in the role of a mediator and seeks to provide a rationale for surrender, his attack comes in insidious form.

At the outset Edmund is the protector and mentor of Fanny, but as the story unfolds he reveals two deficiencies in moral development: his powers of moral discrimination are not as fine as hers, and his adherence to what he believes is right is less firm. He lapses twice in behaviour: he joins in the revolt of the 'corrupted' children, and he joins in the attempt to coerce Fanny into a bad marriage. Despite his attractive qualities, his kindness to Fanny and their affinity in feeling and principles, Edmund is susceptible to the same impulse for self-indulgence and pursuit of selfish goals that guides the others.

Edmund too is a scion of paternalism. His sexism is not as aggressive or overt as Crawford's or Sir Thomas's, but it is well ingrained. For example, his use of stereotyping is implicit in his criticism of Mary Crawford: 'No reluctance, no horror, no feminine – shall I say? no modest loathings!' (455). His attitudes on marriage also are in perfect accord with those of his patriarchal society. He is entirely on Sir Thomas's side and hopes for a match (335).

At first Fanny is reluctant to talk to Edmund because she assumes that they think too differently, but when he professes his objection to marriage without love, especially where her happiness is at stake, he appears to be wholly on her side (346–7). However, in Edmund's words, 'the matter does not end here'; Crawford's is no common attachment. Edmund perseveres with the hope of creating that regard which has been lacking. His gentle admonition is as firmly patriarchal as Sir Thomas's bluster: '. . . let him succeed at last, Fanny, let him succeed at last. You have proved yourself upright and disinterested, prove yourself grateful and tender-hearted; and then you will be the perfect model of a woman, which I have always believed you born for' (347). Briefly he tries to explain away the problem of their different tempers. Finally, he summons up the traditional arguments for woman's submission. There are, first of all, his assumptions about the differences between marriage roles. Henry Crawford will be

> a most fortunate man . . . to attach himself to such a creature – to a woman, who firm as a rock in her own principles, has a gentleness of character so well adapted to recommend them. He has chosen his partner, indeed, with rare felicity. He will make you happy, Fanny, I know he will make you happy; but you will make him every thing. (351)

Then there are his assumptions about her obligations of duty and gratitude and her need to be rational (meaning practical or prudent): 'I cannot suppose that you have not the *wish* to love him – the natural wish of gratitude.' Finally, because he cannot free himself from traditional assumptions about woman's nature, he assumes that her resistance must reflect the force of her attachment to the Park (348). If she can get used to the idea of Crawford's being in love with her, a return of her affection should follow (356). Edmund has completely missed the point of Fanny's objection.

Fanny's devotion to principle and sense of duty to self is as unyielding to Edmund's attack as it was to Sir Thomas's. Her anguish is even greater: 'Oh! never, never, never; he never will succeed with me' (347). Her justification is the same: one should not marry without love; she cannot love where she does not admire (348). To his suggestion that when Crawford's love becomes familiar to her it will become agreeable and to the charge, conveyed by Crawford's sisters, that a woman who would refuse such an offer must be out of her senses, Fanny makes the fullest and most forthright defence of the independence and power of woman's feeling and of woman's right to choose for herself and the most direct attack on sex-role stereotyping to be found in Austen's novels. In context, Fanny's sense of self, her honesty and her directness are amazing:

> I *should* have thought . . . that every woman must have felt the possibility of a man's not being approved, not being loved by some one of her sex, at least, let him be ever so generally agreeable. Let him have all the perfections in the world, I think it ought not to be set down as certain, that a man must be acceptable to every woman he may happen to like himself. . . . In my situation, it would have been the extreme of vanity to be forming expectations on Mr. Crawford. . . . How was I to have an attachment at his service, as soon as it was asked for? His sisters should consider me as well as him. . . . [W]e think very differently of the nature of women, if they can imagine a woman so very soon capable of returning an affection as this seems to imply. (353)

Mansfield Park describes a confrontation between Fanny Price's inextinguishable integrity and her exploitative, dehumanising environment. Her heroism lies in constancy to an ideal of selfhood in the face of circumstances which she has no means or hope of changing. Fortuitously, all ends well. Austen does not doom her heroine to the dreadful consequences of either marriage to Henry Crawford or persistence in refusing him. The Crawfords' misbehaviour frees her from his suit and opens Edmund's eyes to Mary's unsuitability. Sir Thomas then discovers his own errors of belief and judgement. Reasonably soon after his disappointment, Edmund discovers where his true interest lies.

Critics often emphasise how *Mansfield Park* differs from Austen's other work: for example, an apparently passive and priggish heroine; a heavily didactic tone; the separation of moral principle from personal charm. But, although Austen's 'mind grew graver' in her later novels,[10] in the most essential points her interests in all of them are the same. The central concern is the relationship between the individual and society. The centre of attention is the 'drama of woman'. Although with different emphases, all of Austen's heroines experience the problem of female powerlessness, all of them encounter heavy pressure to compromise their ideals, and all of them, except Emma Woodhouse, are forced to assume masks. Austen approaches the problem from opposite directions: in the stories of Elinor Dashwood, Fanny Price and Anne Elliot she concentrates on the problems of powerlessness in the face of a complex system of repression and suppression; in the stories of Elizabeth Bennet, Emma Woodhouse and Marianne Dashwood she stresses the need, if one is to cope with the demands of a patriarchal society, for a clear understanding of one's self, of others and of one's circumstances.

Fanny Price's nearest likeness is Anne Elliot, then Elinor Dashwood. All three painfully play the 'role of compelled observer'.[11] Each loves in silence where she has little hope of success. Since each already sees clearly, there is little emphasis in their stories on developing the ability to make correct judgements. Each brings a 'necessary moral cohesion' to her world.[12] Fanny Price and Anne Elliot are Austen's 'solitary heroines', her heroines of 'no "consequence" '.[13] They must resist heavy external pressure to accept an inauthentic existence, so that their ability to withstand both temptation and threat, to hold fast to principle and selfhood, that is, their possession of a core of self, is more severely tested and more clearly demonstrated than any other Austen heroine's. Most substantially, these two, as Benjamin Whitten says of Anne, see the dangers of marriage to the wrong man, and they possess the power of their instincts which allows them 'to sense the truth about others' and which infuses them 'with the strength of character to maintain . . . [their] beliefs in the face of opposition'.[14] In *Mansfield Park* and *Persuasion* not the protagonist but her world or her lover grows and changes.

However, Fanny Price and Elizabeth Bennet also face basically similar situations, though their responses are different. Each attempts to think for herself and to do what is wisest; each views marriage as a relationship between two individuals; each resists a marriage urged on her to a man of whom she cannot approve; each is determined to act in the manner which would best constitute her happiness; and each, in the opinion of others, is 'perverse'. Similarly, although Fanny Price and Emma Woodhouse are opposites in social circumstances, personal advantages and personality, Fanny's heroic stand and Emma's 'humbling' bring them to very nearly the same personal resolution of their difficulties. In both stories, Austen's fullest treatments of the influence of patriarchal principles in the family, she is willing to hold on to the best features of the patriarchal order while changing the worst, whereas in *Persuasion* she depicts that order in apparently irreversible decline.

The firmest link uniting the novels is Austen's concern for the heroine's freedom to choose in marriage. In *Sense and Sensibility*, in *Pride and Prejudice*, and in *Emma*, as well as in *Mansfield Park*, the heroine encounters the male's assumption that he need only to ask to be accepted. But for Austen's heroines marriage is impossible without love: it involves choosing a partner on the basis of mutual affection and shared emotion, and the right to personal choice is inalienable. Such an insistence, natural enough in our age, was boldly subversive in hers.

All of the novels stress that before marriage there must be friendship and companionship and that mutual esteem is the foundation of true happiness. In *Pride and Prejudice* and *Emma*, the plots permit a complementary emphasis on the importance of sexual attraction in good marriages. In *Mansfield Park*, however, since more attention is paid to the making of bad marriages than to the making of good ones and since the main ingredients of a bad marriage are incompatibility of temperament and interests and mercenary or exploitative intent, Austen especially emphasises, as the source of equilibrium between the sexes, the slow growth of love from affection and long-standing friendship. In a society that views marriage as primarily a practical affair and personal compatibility as of secondary importance, this emphasis suggests her modernness, not her conservatism; Austen shows what, in a modern view, a marriage ought to be.

Fanny's heroism extends beyond the 'principle of self-control' that Mary Lascelles cites (238) to include, as Donovan points out, devotion to an ideal or an idea of life,[15] a loyalty displayed by Austen's other heroines but nowhere else so vigorously attacked or desperately defended. Placed in the most humble and humbling of circumstances of all of Austen's heroines and apparently imbued with the sense of otherness of the indoctrinated female, Fanny, in extreme circumstances, clings to the power to judge and to act, the power of one who cannot and will not be reduced to an object. Fanny 'in tears stands against the authority of all her world',[16] in the ultimate crisis of the female under the rule of the male. In this single, crucial instance, Fanny Price, so unlikely a candidate, embodies woman as acting and perceiving rather than opposing or submitting. Rich describes the phenomenon that Austen dramatises:

> Sometimes this [the courage of women] involves tiny acts of immense courage. . . . [O]ften it involves moments, or long periods, of thinking the unthinkable, being labeled, or feeling, crazy; always a loss of traditional securities. Every woman who takes her life into her own hands does so knowing that she must expect enormous pain, inflicted both from within and without. (215)

Fanny's resistance to the presumptuous Crawford, the tyrannical Sir Thomas and the obtuse Edmund provides Austen's moments of purest dramatic power.

In *Mansfield Park* Austen depicts, as Ryals observes, 'what it means to have formed a central core of self'; Fanny 'will be none other than her true self' (346). Like Clara Middleton in *The Egoist* she cannot be a prize awarded to a man. That 'proper pride', which is the bulwark of selfhood and which is sustained by conscience and instinct, prompts her to rebellion. She affirms, hesitantly at first but finally forthrightly, that she is entitled to an individual life. By holding to the power to choose, she gives her behaviour a dimension of liberty.

From examination of the contention between Fanny Price and the patriarchal social order of Mansfield Park, one answers the questions cited at the outset with confidence: Fanny Price is a 'heroine of principle'; the main concern of the novel is her welfare; the patriarchal society at the Park is the 'enemy'; the contention springs from the latter's attempt to dictate Fanny's marriage choice; and Fanny's ordeal and triumph provide the dramatic centre of the novel. One also perceives that Fanny is potentially a victim of the social order, never its foe; that the society is on trial; that any advantage she receives from it is accidental; that she becomes its preserver; and that the threat to the social order results from its own shortcomings. To the question identified by Wiesenfarth – is a meaningful personal freedom and integrity viable within a traditional pattern of morals and manners? – the answer would appear to be a cautious 'yes'. The true needs of the self and of the society are not incompatible. But an equilibrium is reached only after a very painful ordeal for the heroine and a difficult lesson painfully learned by the leaders of the established order. At the heart of the matter Austen is concerned about the threat to selfhood of a social system that subordinates the needs of the individual to those of the society; she depicts the most pressing and disturbing form of this danger – the victimisation of the female.

Austen's treatment of Mary Crawford confirms the point. In the eyes of many readers the charming and gifted Mary far outshines the presumably dull heroine. Yet Fanny enjoys a final 'triumph' and Mary a 'defeat'. The most common explanation is that Austen's didactic intention inhibited or deflected her personal preference and artistic judgement.

Unquestionably the presentation of Mary Crawford serves the author's intellectual and moralising purpose. But to assume that these purposes are adequately met by the trite association of charm with moral obtuseness and dullness with moral discernment discounts Austen's artistic capability and possibly her intelligence. What is important to recognise is that Fanny and Mary are both raised in a patriarchal order and thus are both potentially 'victims' of that order. The reader need not feel uncomfortable about the mixture of attractive and unattractive qualities in Mary Crawford. *Mansfield Park* is not a book divided against itself. The divergence in the fates of Fanny and Mary is a result of the differences in their relationships to the society. Their personality differences accentuate the irony of the contrast in their fortunes. Despite her apparent subjugation, Fanny's position as 'outsider' helps her to develop the capability to take a moral stand (a moral education in reverse), and it shields from corruption a natural capacity for moral judgement, whereas Mary's favourable position, along with the pressure of positive reinforcement, subverts any inborn moral capacity and encourages only pragmatic, materialistic and cynical attitudes, hallmarks of the 'privileged' female and the 'corrupted' child in the patriarchal society.[17] Mary Crawford's behaviour displays the power of environmental conditioning to determine gender role-playing.

Thus Mary Crawford is an actual victim of the patriarchal order, just as Fanny is a potential victim. She is rich, beautiful, gifted with wit and humour and musical skill, and courageous. Nevertheless, the faults of her upbringing display themselves quickly. These defects, we are repeatedly told, are the product of her exposure to a selfish and materialistic society. The point is made most forcefully by Edmund, following his breaking off from Mary:

This is what the world does. For where, Fanny, shall we find a woman whom nature had so richly endowed? – Spoilt, spoilt! –

No, her's is not a cruel nature. I do not consider her as meaning to wound my feelings. The evil lies yet deeper; in her total ignorance, unsuspiciousness of there being such feelings, in a perversion of mind which made it natural to her to treat the subject as she did. She was speaking only, as she had been used to hear others speak, as she imagined every body else would speak. Her's are not faults of temper. She would not voluntarily give unnecessary pain to any one. . . . Her's are faults of principle, Fanny, of blunted delicacy and a corrupted, vitiated mind. (*MP*, 455–6)

(He has spoken earlier of her mind being tainted [269].) In corroboration, the narrator says that Miss Crawford had 'shewn a mind led astray and bewildered, and without any suspicion of being so; darkened, yet fancying itself light' (367). For Mary the victim, as for Louisa Gradgrind of *Hard Times*, there is no happy ending. Though discontented with her life, she cannot free herself. The warping of her nature by her environment (469) has been going on too long and too persistently for her to acquire the needed self-knowledge. She is forever a victim, caught between two worlds and essentially undeserving of her fate.

Rather than being cautious and conservative or nostalgic and fearful of the future, *Mansfield Park* challenges convention and the status quo and looks forward. It examines selfhood, condemns a decaying environment that relegates women to a state of subjection, and expresses the importance and difficulty of being free and the need to preserve order by commitment to action.[18] It does not expose the dangers of individuality or counsel retreat to a life of art, ritual and imposed form.[19] Finally, it supports the belief that there is a 'feminist' element in Austen's fiction. Austen presents Fanny Price as representative of an oppressed sex. Unaware of the conflict between herself and the family structures that have provided a crippling security, she is forced by necessity to speak from the self. But in defending her integrity and her personal freedom to choose, an effort that is more moving in that she makes a stand, alone and weak, against the patriarchal family and the world, Fanny Price defends the birthright of every human being.

7 *Emma:* The Flight from Womanhood

I

Critics generally view *Emma* as a novel of education in which Emma Woodhouse, a young woman with 'the power of having rather too much her own way, and a disposition to think a little too well of herself' (*E*, 5), comes to understand her own emotional nature, the ascendancy of reason over imagination, the true nature of the world about her, the limits of her control over the world, and her moral responsibility. She is described as an egotist, and her problems are viewed as problems within her own personality – excessive pride, lack of control over her imagination and self-deception. Her greatest faults are a love of power and a desire to dominate, which she overcomes through a process of self-discovery and the acquisition of self-knowledge. The outcome is a contraction of her social freedom and an expansion of her emotional and moral life.

Within this pattern, however, one finds disagreement about Austen's view of Emma's education, whether it contributes to her well-being by teaching her to see the world clearly and to recognise its virtues or whether it proves both painful and disillusioning;[1] about George Knightley's nature and role, whether he is the novel's 'normative or exemplary figure' or also fallible;[2] and about the outcome, whether the novel ends constructively (the more popular view) or with the essential sources of discord intact.[3] The most striking disagreement is about the final relationship between Emma and Knightley. At one extreme Emma's education includes a lesson in the supremacy of the male; at the other, events display a turn away from patriarchal principles.[4] The view also appears that *Emma* is written in protest against patriarchalism; but the fuller treatments of this idea in the 1970s end in a surprisingly pessimistic judgement of the novel's final effect.[5] W. A. Craik's observation in

1965 that *Emma* is Austen's 'most misunderstood work' remains apt (125).

Austen's interest in the 'drama of woman' provides the framework for a new approach to explanation of her purposes in *Emma*. To begin with, several distinctive points about the novel acquire an enhanced value and consonance when one regards them from this perspective. The most significant one is Emma's unorthodox view that marriage for her is unnecessary. Almost equally important are the observations that Austen subjects Emma to possibly the most severe self-examination of all of her heroines and that she carries Emma 'as close to viciousness as any author could dare to take a heroine designed to be loved'.[6] Finally, Knightley is described as a 'fallible mentor', which suggests that Austen is interested less in elevating an imperfect and inferior Emma than in advancing two fallible human beings; and our attention is called to the counterposing of the apparently fortunate Emma and four socially deprived or reduced females. Set against the background of Austen's interest in the 'drama of woman', these ideas prompt a reading that answers the following questions: (1) what is the explanation of Emma's 'monstrous egoism'? (2) why does she reject marriage, and what meaning should one attach to the marriage that she finally makes? (3) why does she take so long to discover the 'true feeling of love'? (4) what are the changes in her at the end? (5) is Austen's purpose limited to describing Emma's growing-up? and (6) what is Knightley's role and what changes, if any, does he undergo?

II

Austen writes about the period in a young woman's life before she enters marriage, when she is tempted by the possibility of an alternate mode of living. The society is patriarchal. Roles are prescribed and gender types are clearly defined. Governance is assigned to the male. This unequal relationship leads to a view of woman as inferior and to male tyranny in various forms: for example, in *Emma*, Mr Woodhouse's demanding dependence, Knightley's assumption of moral and intellectual superiority, and Frank Churchill's mischievous manipulation.

De Beauvoir summarises the general situation that a young woman faces. As she matures she discovers that men control the world and that she must consent to becoming an object in

submission and adoration. She is taught that she will gain value in
men's eyes not by increasing her own worth but rather by modelling
herself upon their dreams. If she makes a stand against the world,
she soon sees that the struggle is too unequal. Slowly she buries her
childhood and enters submissively upon her adult existence. A
contradiction exists, however, between her status as a real human
being and her vocation as a female. How can she give up her ego?
She may linger in suspension between the time of childish independence and that of womanly submission. Usually, though with
some resistance, she accepts her femininity.

Finding a balance between the demands of self and the demands
of others thus may be the most serious problem that a young woman
faces. Austen describes two forms of response. Elinor Dashwood,
Fanny Price and Anne Elliot display complex systems of repression
and suppression; Elizabeth Bennet and Emma Woodhouse and,
with qualification, Catherine Morland and Marianne Dashwood,
challenge the social environment but seem obliged to learn to adjust
to it. Emma's response, however, is unique. Of Austen's heroines
only she is apparently free to marry or not to marry, and only she
deliberately resists the prospect of domestic confinement from the
outset. Her closest likeness is Elizabeth Bennet, but Emma's will to
rule is stronger and her search for self-knowledge lasts throughout
the book.

Emma is Austen's most artful, ironic and objective treatment of
the 'drama of woman'. Emma Woodhouse embarks on a 'flight
from womanhood'.[7] She resists taking her place in the adult female
world because she sees that a woman's place is one of dependence
and assumed inferiority. She spurns the 'feminine' role, as signified
by her rejecting marriage and asserting her independence of others'
control. Although in the traditional critical view her behaviour is
wilful and eccentric and any criticism of the social environment is
little more than incidental, the special nature of Emma's behaviour,
as well as the attention that Austen also gives in the novel to the
inequality of the sexes, the indignity of marriage and the plight of
single women, raises doubt that her primary purpose is to illustrate
individual idiosyncrasy or immaturity.

As de Beauvoir indicates, were Emma's career to follow the
traditional pattern, we would watch her struggle to overcome the
active forces within her in the process of accepting a passive,
dependent role. But Emma, endowed with energy, spirit, imagination and intelligence, and encouraged by uniquely favourable

circumstances, refuses to surrender her autonomy, to become 'feminine'. She rejects the idea that a woman must charm a masculine heart. In a society where one's freedom and identity depend upon the possession of power, she adopts the prerogatives of the privileged male as her own. Her attempt to turn the tables may explain Austen's labelling her a heroine whom no one would much like but herself.

Does Emma's 'flight from womanhood' produce a constructive change in her life? Emma may be her own mistress, but she is bound by a false, crippling code. Although she is free not to marry, she is not free to marry as she pleases; and although she rejects the woman's role handed to her, she is not free, apparently, to be whatever it is within her nature to be. If, finally, she acquiesces to patriarchal rule or if her self-assertion, like that of the 'corrupted' children of *Mansfield Park*, follows the lure of a false freedom, then the outcome will be tragic. But neither the tone nor the events justify such a conclusion. Emma's 'flight from womanhood' turns to pursuit and ends in achievement of a true freedom and equality.

The fact that the patriarchal society is less on view in *Emma* than in *Mansfield Park* does suggest that the heroine's main conflict is within herself rather than with her society and that the basic movement is from self-delusion to self-recognition. But Austen's focus is always dual, on one's struggle within the self and with the world – a balancing of contrary and complex forces. In *Emma* the two contests are clearly linked: the struggle within Emma is between internalised patriarchal values and her instinctive sense of selfhood, the self versus the world internalised rather than the self divided.

The psychological sphere is often the principal theatre of action for a young woman. Society's expectations become part of her internal criteria of normal feminine achievement, so that the 'being' follows the 'doing' assigned and learned, even though this pattern may ignore her individual capabilities. Lady Bertram of *Mansfield Park* is an extreme example of one who has followed this path; Isabella Knightley is a more common case. Emma Woodhouse, however, feeling herself obliged to become passive and dependent at an age when 'the will to live and to make a place in the world is running strong', tries to 'be' something else. Unlike Fanny Price and Anne Elliot, who develop their inner lives deeply and become more attached to their feelings, Emma takes the aggressive path chosen by Elizabeth Bennet of challenging the threatening social forces. She rejects her assigned sex role.

Emma may feel some confusion about gender identity. In one theory a young girl with a mother to love and to follow achieves 'personal' identification; that is to say, motivated primarily by love and admiration, she identifies with the mother and adopts her values, attitudes and personal traits. But Emma's mother 'died too long ago for her to have more than an indistinct remembrance of her caresses' (*E*, 5). Instead, Emma's development appears to follow the course of 'positional' identification, that is, an identification with the position or role of a model that represents a fantasised projection into the situation and behaviour of the model. The model attracts emulation because of his or her role or status.[8] The distinction may offer a useful insight into Emma's behaviour. Without a mother whose loving, guiding presence might have eased her passage into conventional womanhood, Emma's most influential model is a male figure, Knightley, whose position and role she comes to wish for herself.

Furthermore, unlike Austen's other heroines, Emma apparently has no sense of insecurity, social or financial: 'Emma Woodhouse, handsome, clever, and rich, with a comfortable home and happy disposition, seemed to unite some of the best blessings of existence; and had lived nearly twenty-one years in the world with very little to distress or vex her.' She experiences little restraint from Miss Taylor, her governess (*E*, 5); and in her relation with her father there is a partial inversion of roles, in that she manages the household, directs conversation, orders events in consideration of his moods and compensates by her tact and certainty for his indecisive and capricious ways.

Although Emma is not genuinely free, she appears to have a degree of liberty unusual for her sex. She is her own boss, she enjoys rank and privilege as an inheritor, and she has the prospect of continuing independence. Understandably, she attempts to define her world from a centre of self, and it is unlikely that she will do without what gives her pleasure (40). In many respects her circumstances and attitudes resemble those of an elder or only son rather than those of a daughter – 'the power of having rather too much her own way, and a disposition to think a little too well of herself' (5) – and her immediate problem is his also: boredom.

With reason, then, Emma seeks to separate herself from the conditions that produce women's dependence and subordination and from the women who can not escape them. She will not accede to the role of passive, complaisant female:

Emma did not find herself equal to give the pleased assent, which no doubt he [John Knightley] was in the habit of receiving, to emulate the 'Very true, my love,' which must have been usually administered by his travelling companion; but she had resolution enough to refrain from making any answer at all. She could not be complying, she dreaded being quarrelsome; her heroism reached only to silence. (113–14)

Emma perceives that subordinates must please but not the powerful. Miss Bates's behaviour reflects the self-abasement and the self-reduction of the female who attempts to overcome the spectre of non-being by denying the self. Emma's revulsion may explain her scorn, and her wish to be among the wielders of power rather than among its victims may contribute to her cruel treatment of Miss Bates at Box Hill.

One potential source of danger to her independence, Emma believes, is the emotion of love. Paradoxically, although she sees that to have a loving relationship is the most important thing in marriage, she fears the power of love to overcome one's self-control. It moves individuals to action and behaviour which contradict reason and cause a loss of will; it raises the threat of one's being undervalued, of being taken as a fluttery, dependent creature, a 'female', rather than as a person of intellect and dignity (63–4); and it may direct one contrary to one's best intentions (412–13). If love is dangerous for a man, with his advantages, how much worse for a vulnerable female, as the predicament of Jane Fairfax illustrates. Not having experienced love, Emma is pleased by the idea that she is safe from emotional involvement (84).

Marriage, too, may be a threat to independence. It is generally viewed as an arrangement of convenience, with economic improvement the first consideration and social improvement the second, and in courtship the male usually has the advantage. Mr Elton, for example, is 'a very handsome young man' who knows 'the value of a good income as well as anybody' and 'does not mean to throw himself away' (66). Subsequently he captures the 'charming Augusta Hawkins', who 'was in possession of an independent fortune', and we are assured that he 'had caught both substance and shadow – both fortune and affection' (181–2). Whereas Mr Elton follows his practical interest, Mr Weston 'had only himself to please in his choice; his fortune was his own'. Thus he can afford to marry a portionless woman who is 'well-judging and truly amiable' and enjoy the 'proof of its being a great deal better to chuse than to be chosen, to excite gratitude than to feel it' (17). The marriage is a stroke of extraordinary good luck (18) for Miss Taylor, as George Knightley is willing to remind her.

Initially, Emma's view of marriage corresponds to the general view (and to Knightley's). It is necessary for women who lack financial security, and it can be called happy if it provides one with a pleasant home. On such grounds she justifies her attempt to match Harriet Smith with Mr Elton (74–5). But, with none of the usual inducements herself, she does not see how marriage could change her own state for the better: she is not in love nor does she expect to be, and she lacks neither fortune, employment nor importance. In fact, if she were to marry, she 'must expect to repent it'. She could never 'expect to be so truly beloved and important; so always first and always right in any man's eyes' as she is now in her father's (84). In considering Mr Elton's unexpected proposal, she recognises that practicality is the cause, resents the position that women are in, and delights in her freedom (135). As a woman of sense, spirit and ample means, she wishes to avoid the moral, spirtual and practical losses that marriage would entail. Like Clarissa Harlowe a half century earlier and Gwendolyn Harleth a half century later, she defends the single state as an alternative.

In place of the conditions that restrict women, Emma seeks to create those that would give her control of her life. But her revolt initially is misdirected by her assimilation of patriarchal values. In order to be listened to and have her opinion approved, she replaces 'feminine' docility with 'masculine' self-assertion. In reaction to the contingency of women's lives, she sets out to be 'a manager of destinies'. Emma's treatment of Harriet Smith, who fits the stereotype of the 'feminine' woman, is patronising and condescending, as a male mentor's would be. She manipulates Harriet freely, although 'for her own good', and she manages the task of finding her a suitable husband with all the concern for security and suitability of a patriarchal father: 'This is an attachment which a woman may well feel pride in creating. This is a connection which offers nothing but good. It will give you every thing that you want – consideration, independence, a proper home – it will fix you in the centre of all your real friends . . .' (74).

Knightley attributes Emma's lack of outstanding attainment in the common female accomplishments to insufficient industry and patience. In fact, she is more attracted by the 'masculine' activities of self-assertion and command. She competes with the Knightley brothers to prove the superiority of her judgement, a 'masculine' attribute. Sulloway calls her 'condescending control and manipulation of Harriet Smith . . . a parody of what Wollstonecraft analyzes as the male "condescencsion of protectorship" ' (324). Her distorting fancy bends facts to fit her ideas and fuels her pride in her 'masculine' ability to rule wisely.

But Austen is as sensitive to what may be the drawbacks of exercising control over one's life as she is to the need for it. While events remind the reader of the likely fate of the dependent female, Emma discovers the hazards of an independent life. The 'masculine' behaviour that she copies is as restrictive as the 'feminine' behaviour that she repudiates and poses as great a threat to selfhood. It produces the same sense of isolation and of unsatisfactory relationships. Emma finds that she is in danger of moving beyond reach of what she most desires.[9] It also encourages an egotism that blinds her to the real existence of others and stimulates in her the 'masculine' treatment of women that had repelled her. Like other characters in Austen's fiction who combat male oppression by strength of will, good fortune and the mastery of 'masculine' behaviour patterns, she risks a dangerous dehumanisation.[10] The obvious comparison is with Mrs Elton. Both seek to dominate and manipulate, and they contend for rule in Highbury. At Box Hill, when Emma yields to the impulsive display of aggressive egotism, the identification between them seems nearly complete. Mrs Elton is a vulgar version of what Emma could become. But Emma can still respond sensitively to others' needs and deficiencies and feel guilt for her boorishness. She soon arrives at a just opinion of Mrs Elton's worth, although slower to see their likeness; and as she moves towards a clearer understanding of herself, the contrast between them deepens.

The risks to Emma of continuing in the initial direction of her flight are illustrated by the conduct of three other female characters in Austen's novels who have followed that course. In *Emma* Mrs Churchill is branded as heartless, unreasonable and tyrannical, the complete usurper of masculine rule, whose marriage illustrates the dangers of imbalance in the relationship of husband and wife, whichever sex is dominant. In *Pride and Prejudice* Lady Catherine de Bourgh, strong-willed and socially pampered, has passed through the metamorphosis that Emma is entering and emerged a shrew. Finally, Lady Susan, like Emma, attempts to acquire and exercise the power identified with the male, with equivocal results. The cost for all three appears to exceed the benefit.

Emma offers Austen's fullest rendering of the plight of single women: Mrs Weston (formerly Miss Taylor) makes a fortunate escape from the single life; Harriet Smith and Miss Bates are stereotypically 'feminine', examples of the highly manipulable and the pathetically dependent; and Jane Fairfax faces the alienation that in this society threatens even the gifted and accomplished. In Emma's behaviour towards the last two one sees how very close she comes to sealing herself off from fellow-feeling.

Austen describes the situation of Miss Bates bluntly:

> Miss Bates stood in the very worst predicament in the world for having much of the public favour; and she had no intellectual superiority to make atonement to herself, or frighten those who might hate her, into outward respect. She had never boasted either beauty or cleverness. Her youth had passed without distinction, and her middle of life was devoted to the care of a failing mother, and the endeavour to make a small income go as far as possible. (*E*, 21)

Miss Bates is a model of the reduction of women and the antithesis of Emma, who scorns her compliance as well as her gabbling. Her existence almost invites Emma's insult at Box Hill, when the latter joins the male egotist Frank Churchill in self-indulgent jesting at the expense of the vulnerable old maid. However, Emma's self-anger and mortification when she perceives how cruelly she has treated Miss Bates signal her turning back from her flight from womanhood. She begins to realise how recklessly she has followed the dictates of a false and alien self: 'Never had she felt so agitated, mortified, grieved, at any circumstance in her life. She was most forcibly struck. The truth of his representation there was no denying. She felt it at her heart. How could she have been so brutal, so cruel to Miss Bates!' (376).

The history of Jane Fairfax forcefully illustrates the grounds for Emma's flight from womanhood. Jane Fairfax is a young woman of great beauty, elegance and superior accomplishment, almost without flaw or fault and Emma's superior in many respects – except that she is poor and powerless. For this single reason, Jane is forced into dependence and disguise. Her career is the opposite of Emma's; she is marked by circumstances to be a victim of the system.

Despite her beauty, goodness and talent, she is constantly patronised by the mediocre. At twenty-one she appears destined to disappear into the limbo world of the governess, which she bitterly likens to slavery (165). Finally, she is mistreated by the young male, Frank Churchill, who imposes on her a humiliating and potentially compromising secret engagement and, at the same time, teases her in her helplessness as if she were his possession, not his wife-to-be. Jane's only serious fault is a lack of openness. But, as she explains, she always had a part to play, and she had to protect herself from Emma's condescension (459). Knightley finally excuses this mistake in judgement because she ran a greater risk than Churchill did if their engagement were disclosed, and Emma does so because she discovers the power of strong feeling to cloud one's judgement.

   In trying to distance herself from the common plight of single women, Emma attempts to join the ranks of their oppressors. In addition to jealousy of the esteem in which Jane is held and envy of the attention her accomplishments receive, Emma needs to believe that she is superior to Jane for the sake of her own sense of security. If she is sure of the distance between them, she should be safe from the dangers that threaten even women like Jane. Emma's imagination comes to her aid. She places Jane at the centre of an intrigue of which she is the victim and thus attributes to her an emotional susceptibility to which Emma believes herself immune. Reassured about her own invulnerability Emma can look 'at Jane Fairfax with twofold complacency; the sense of pleasure and the sense of rendering justice, and [she] was determining that she would dislike her no longer' (167).

   Later, when her vision is no longer clouded by her egotism, Emma recognises the tragedy of Jane Fairfax's situation. When the circumstances of Jane's secret engagement are fully disclosed, Emma feelingly defends her 'deviation from the strict rule of right': 'If a woman can ever be excused for thinking only of herself, it is in a situation like Jane Fairfax's. – Of such, one may almost say, that "the world is not their's, nor the world's law" ' (400). Emma learns enough about love to understand the cause of Jane's error: 'It must have been from attachment only, that she could be led to form the engagement. Her affection must have overpowered her judgment' (419). Since she long ago had dismissed Frank Churchill as a possible suitor, her anger at his paying attention to one young woman while engaged to another is a protest against the harm that such self-indulgent conduct can do.

Austen calls Emma an 'imaginist'. Imagination is both 'a power that penetrates the inner meaning of reality' and 'a power that creates substitutes for reality'.[11] In her flight from womanhood Emma tries to shape the world to her desires, both to create a protective role for the self and to gain a sense of freedom from the world of female experience. But imagination can not transform reality, her attempt inhibits her discovery of her true nature, and the danger arises that 'by limiting reality to its own ideas the imagination . . . [will lose] its control not only of others but of itself and . . . [be] controlled by what possesses it'.[12] Emma risks separation from a creative relationship with her fellow human beings. Fortunately, she does not become so lost in her activity as 'imaginist' that she cannot make the choice finally between detachment and participation.

In sum, Emma's flight from womanhood is self-defeating in a variety of ways: (1) it falsifies her perception of reality; (2) her identification with the behaviour of the oppressor forces her to live vicariously and restricts the growth of meaningful personal relationships; and (3) her adoption of the masculine role limits her ability to recognise and pursue her deepest personal needs and interests. Emma's behaviour becomes aggressive and dogmatic, selfish and self-absorbed. She acts unfeelingly and insolently and sets a bad example for others. She misinterprets what she sees and makes judgements from incomplete knowledge. She imagines that the games she invents are real and slides into self-deception. Through the arrogance of believing herself in the secret of the feelings of others and proposing to arrange their destinies, she performs actual mischief. Her vulnerability continues, rather than decreases, because she becomes susceptible to flattery, blinds herself to the needs and liabilities of her sex, seems unaware of the existence of others, and becomes involved, for unflattering reasons, where she had intended to supervise. Although Emma seeks to escape the female's confined existence, she does not escape the stamp of the female stereotype in the eyes of others, such as Philip Elton and Frank Churchill. She fails to recognise the world's independence from her control and her dependence on the world. She is ignorant of the true nature of love and of her own emotional and sexual needs. She finds her vaunted isolation frustrating, and she feels the weight of loneliness and melancholy. Unable to acquire the control over her life that she expected, she discovers her own incompleteness.

How truly false Emma's illusion of freedom and power is and how fully her false self exposes her to, rather than protects her from, the control of another is seen in her duping by Frank Churchill. The latter is one of Austen's clever young men who 'live by their wits and their charm . . . [and] whose end in life is pleasure'.[13] His favourable position in the patriarchal order enables him to manipulate others, particularly women, with little fear of the consequences. Because of his economic dependence, like Willoughby and Wickham he does so to advance his own interests; he is not so seriously in need but that, like Henry Crawford, he also does so to gratify his vanity.

Emma wants the same power to control others that males seem to possess. She would use it more for the pleasure of the act, for the satisfaction of feeling her power, whereas Churchill, needing less reassurance, would use it more for the pleasure of secret management. But Emma, in her massive egotism, mistakenly views him as only another one of her subjects (*E*, 206). Churchill, in turn, encourages Emma to create her own image of him. Each, of course, views the other as an object to manoeuvre. Their flirtation is a sham. Emma, to gratify her vanity, is using Churchill to make herself the centre of attention; and he, with unnecessary complication, is screening his serious relationship with Jane Fairfax. The difference is that Emma plays a part from a need to affirm her identity. She pursues her course blindly and, in a sense, innocently. But Churchill enjoys plotting and is practised at the game. At Box Hill he creates a mock court and places Emma at the centre as its ruler. But he controls the 'mock ruler' as he controls Emma herself, and she little understands the extent of his control. When she learns of his deception, she experiences the most dreadful humiliation of all of Austen's heroines. She admits that she has been 'completely duped' (399), taken in by a cleverness superior to her own.

Two lessons emerge for Emma from this painful experience: the first advances Austen's familiar theme of the importance of openness in human affairs. Roles, disguises, intrigues, games are signs of false relationships. They are the instruments by which the powerful manipulate the weak and which the weak adopt to survive. They are encouraged by the structure of the patriarchal society, which provides the privileged male, such as Churchill, with freedom from accountability and which forces on the vulnerable female, such as Jane Fairfax, the need to dissemble and, in broader terms, to accept an incomplete life. Knightley proclaims the true hollowness of Churchill's performance:

Very bad – though it might have been worse. – Playing a most dangerous game. Too much indebted to the event for his acquittal. – No judge of his own manners by you. – Always deceived in fact by his own wishes, and regardless of little besides his own convenience. – Fancying you to have fathomed his secret. Natural enough! – his own mind full of intrigue, that he should suspect it in others. – Mystery; Finesse – how they pervert the understanding! My Emma, does not every thing serve to prove more and more the beauty of truth and sincerity in all our dealings with each other? (445–6)

Emma's second lesson is that adopting a false self has increased her vulnerability and deepened her ignorance of her true wishes. Elizabeth Bennet's words could well be Emma's: 'Had I been in love, I could not have been more wretchedly blind. But vanity, not love, has been my folly. . . . I have courted prepossession and ignorance, and driven reason away. . . . Till this moment, I never knew myself' (*PP*, 208). Emma has tried to exercise power as men do. But in her competition with Churchill she discovers that he retains an advantage by reason of custom and circumstances; she still is judged by the stereotype that she thought she had escaped; and she has continued to be an object of manipulation when she hoped to enjoy that power herself. From her attempt to be a manipulator she learns the principle that Fanny Price defends against the manipulator – that the essence of selfhood is freedom to decide one's own destiny. Although Emma later good-humouredly acknowledges the resemblance between her earlier behaviour and Churchill's – 'I think there is a little likeness between us' (*E*, 478) – in her response to the discovery of his duplicity and her duping she finally embraces her womanhood; in just anger as well as injured pride, she demands that the oppressor change his ways:

What right had he to come among us with affection and faith engaged, and with manners so *very* disengaged? What right had he to endeavour to please, as he certainly did – to distinguish any one young woman with persevering attention, as he certainly did – while he really belonged to another? – How could he tell what mischief he might be doing? – How could he tell that he might not be making me in love with him? – very wrong, very wrong indeed. (396–7)

III

In resisting the pressure to conform to a 'feminine' stereotype, Emma embraces the 'masculine' stereotype. Then the false self that she has created encounters the social realities of the patriarchal order. But Emma is not defeated by this collision, as some critics believe. She moves to a centre that balances feminine and masculine personal qualities in a unified whole.

Emma Woodhouse's situation is similar to Emma Bovary's in that they confront the possibility of finding no course of action suited to their consciousness of themselves as individuals or of finding no single human being who can comprehend what is happening to them.[14] But in *Emma* the potential for tragedy is muted. Emma Woodhouse has the money which is the key to escaping subjection; her keen intelligence can not be permanently diverted from the truth; she has the courage and the desire to accept actuality and genuinely wants to change; she is not fixed by nature or nurture in a single pattern but can grow in response to new influences; and, finally, she finds the single human being who can understand and appreciate her uniqueness. The issue is decided by the triumph of Emma's core gender identity over the fantasy of being a male and by the learning experience – psychological, emotional and cognitive – that both she and Knightley undergo.

Indisputably, *Emma* is a novel about education, in the course of which Emma Woodhouse acquires self-knowledge. At that point agreement almost ends. To resolve the major issues – the value for Emma of her education, Knightley's nature and role, the outcome of events and the final relationship between Emma and Knightley – one must recognise that *Emma* also is a novel about the need for openness and equality between individuals, as shown in the relationship between men and women. Austen insists that the happiness of the individual requires both self-knowledge, represented by the discovery and integration within the self of the range of possibilities of human behaviour, and concord between the sexes, represented by the integration of two selves, male and female, through the dissolution of artificial social and psychological barriers. The two subjects are complementary and interdependent: achievement of openness and equality requires self-knowledge, but without hope of the former a full and true self-knowledge is difficult to attain. To these two subjects one should add a third of only slightly less prominence: *Emma* is a novel about the responsibility of those who possess power to protect, rather than to oppress, those without it. Finally, one must recognise that the movement towards self-knowledge and mutuality involves Knightley as well as Emma. The self-knowledge gained by either will produce only frustration and despair unless matched by that gained by the other. Emma and Knightley both seek openness and equality, but they do not initially recognise this intention or pursue it wisely.

Emma obviously lacks self-knowledge. Robert Liddel describes her as simply a 'very wrong-headed heroine'.[15] But there is more to Emma, even in her most arrogant and deluded moments, than this view acknowledges. Although at first she is unduly proud of her judgement (*E*, 24), she is often right about matters, and she displays a considerable potential for self-examination (67, 231). She wishes to be the centre of attention, is jealous of competitors, and is most gracious when she feels superior (167–8); but she is not intentionally or generally unkind, and she is sensitive to others when her vanity is not involved (363). Although she is 'not unwilling' to receive more credit for her attainments than she deserves, she knows she could be better (44, 227), a sign of basic good sense, like her lack of pride about her beauty (39) and her ability to see the complexity of a point that Knightley would resolve by an either/or. Emma possesses initiative, the ability to organise, an active conscience, imagination, wit and intelligence – a mind, in Marilyn Butler's apt phrase, 'potentially cool and tough' (253). She strays from the judicious because of a fear of being taken as a 'female', internalised patri-archal values and her ignorance of the nature of love. But Emma's education is a process of correction, not of restructuring. She must fail in some serious way in order to learn to distinguish between her strengths and limitations and her sensible and foolish wishes and to be forced to look into herself for the cause of her humiliation.

Emma can and does learn. To begin with, she is not as irrational or arbitrary as she sometimes appears to be or as, in her remorse, she accuses herself of being. Even during her most assertive period she experiences moments when her conscience will not acquit her (*E*, 166, 180), and at times she questions her conduct, although she may overlook her doubts (67, 155, 166, 187). There is truth in her opinions often and signs of common sense, as well as signs of vanity (264, 194). She comes to recognise the perceptivity of the Knightley brothers, despite her rivalry with them (135), and she comes to admit her errors: that she was grossly mistaken about Harriet and Elton (134, 141), that her behaviour could have encouraged Elton to look in her direction, that she was foolish to be so active in match-making (136–7), that she wronged Jane Fairfax (203, 291), and that she played the fool in her relations with Frank Churchill (425).

As Douglas Bush observes, Emma undergoes 'the fullest and severest self-examination pursued by any Austen heroine except Anne Elliot, whose case is quite different' (157). She discovers how similar her interest in managing people was to that of Churchill, whom she vigorously condemns (*E*, 399, 478). She learns with what 'insufferable vanity' she believed in her superiority to others and what mischief she did (412–13). She learns that she is feared rather than loved by others whose good opinion she expected (376–7, 391). She learns how limited is her capacity to shape the world to her wishes and how elusive and precarious is the autonomy she prizes. By the end of the story Emma substitutes humility for pride and self-reproach for self-assertion (375–6, 407–8, 411–12, 415, 425, 477). She retains her basic independence and strength of judgement, but she acquires a sense of consideration and a control of feeling (408). She is no longer impelled to measure her worth by contending with Knightley or another male for superiority in judgement (478, 480). She hopes that 'every future winter of her life . . . would yet find her more rational, more acquainted with herself, and leave her less to regret when it were gone' (423).

Emma also discovers the power of loneliness and melancholy, and she comes to understand her own heart (403). With the sudden triumph of her instinctive nature over false values, she learns the true character of her feeling for Knightley (407) – that her happiness depends on being first in interest and affection with him (412). She learns that men and women have much more in common than she had thought. She moves from pursuit of a spurious and damaging autonomy to embrace of a 'mature dependence', the ability to distinguish clearly between ego and object and hence to be able to value the latter for its own sake, that is, to give as well as to receive.[16] Emma becomes both a different and a better woman.

Her most important lesson is that she learns to accept her woman-hood, as shown by her reference to her intimacy with Harriet Smith as 'the worst of all her womanly follies' (*E*, 463), her description of her involvement with Frank Churchill as 'an old story, probably – a common case – and no more than has happened to hundreds of my sex before' (427), and her denunciation of Churchill's exploiting the system's partiality to his own sex (396–9). However, her dismay at the defeat of her dream of freedom is dispelled by her discovery that she can be valued for her intelligence and dignity and that a male exists with whom she can live in a relationship of reciprocal affection and respect.

This last discovery marks the climax of the theme of openness and equality. In Austen's view individual happiness requires the union of two selves as well as the use of one's full human potential. Such a union, based on 'truth and sincerity' in personal relationships (446), depends upon equality between the sexes, mutual respect and candour. After achieving their own concord, Knightley exclaims to Emma that they have 'every right that equal worth can give, to be happy together' (465). Mrs Weston places the final seal of approval on the match: 'It was all right, all open, all equal. No sacrifice on any side worth the name. It was a union of the highest promise of felicity in itself, and without one real, rational difficulty to oppose or delay it' (468).

Knightley endorses the ideal of openness and equality well before he can be a partner in such a relationship. His praise of the match between Miss Taylor and Mr Weston shows that he admires a balance of qualities between the sexes and suggests what he wants in a wife: 'A straight-forward, open-hearted man, like Weston, and a rational unaffected woman, like Miss Taylor, may be safely left to manage their own concerns' (13). Later, in conversation with Emma he praises an 'open temper':

> Jane Fairfax is a very charming young woman – but not even Jane Fairfax is perfect. She has a fault. She has not the open temper which a man would wish for in a wife.

> Jane Fairfax has feeling . . . I do not accuse her of want of feeling. Her sensibilities, I suspect, are strong – and her temper excellent in its power of forbearance, patience, self-controul; but it wants openness. She is reserved, more reserved, I think, than she used to be – And I love an open temper. (288–9)

Even before his agreement with Emma, Knightley shows his enthusiasm for a union of equals: 'He [Churchill] is a most fortunate man. . . . At three and twenty to have drawn such a prize! . . . Assured of the love of such a woman – the disinterested love . . . every thing in his favour, – equality of situation . . . equality in every point but one [income] . . .' (428). He castigates Churchill for the selfishness and love of intrigue which corrupt the understanding and are the antitheses of the 'beauty of truth and sincerity' that one hopes for in an intimate relationship (446).

Emma seeks openness and equality with equal vigour and with greater immediate cause: as a sign of her worth in her own and in others' eyes (117). As much as any thing, Emma wants to be able to speak freely and to be thought interesting. She desires 'equal footing and perfect unreserve'. She looks for the qualities in a friend that eventually she and Knightley discover in each other – intelligence, forbearance, mutuality of interests and candour (6). Elton's proposal is insulting because it is so crassly impersonal. At last, with Harriet, as bested rival, safe in London and with her own marriage plans settled, Emma 'could talk, and she could listen with true happiness' (451). She believed that the 'disguise, equivocation, mystery, so hateful to her to practise, might soon be over. She could now look forward to giving him that full and perfect confidence which her disposition was most ready to welcome as a duty' (475). Truth and sincerity are the guarantors of openness and equality in personal relationships. Emma and Knightley become lovers, finally, because they can be friends. Nowhere else is Austen so insistent that her heroine's marriage is one of equals. 'The perfect happiness of the union', the novel's final phrase, describes a personal integration as well as a wedding.

However, before this union can occur, both Knightley and Emma must overcome the ingrained patriarchal attitudes which prompt Emma to emulate the privileged male and which lead Knightley, like Darcy, to assume a superiority because of his sex. Emma must mature, which means that she must free herself from fear of a woman's life; but, equally important, Knightley must accept her maturing, which means that he must learn to treat her not as a child or stereotypically but as an equal. Both must learn to accept the world with its faults: Emma, by discovering the self-defeating effects of her elaborate defence, and Knightley, by learning to tolerate fallibility in others through a discovery of his own failings.

Both are in the dark about themselves at the beginning. Both are inhibited by egotism from fully exercising rational judgement. They prescribe for others in accord with the corrupt power relationships of patriarchy. But Emma shows a greater capacity for self-questioning than Knightley; in fact, his inability to question his own judgement spurs her to oppose him. Knightley speaks confidently out of the sufficiency of his ego, and Emma speaks compulsively in defence of hers (66–7). Both adopt the role of mentor, Emma with Harriet

Smith, Knightley with Emma; but they are fallible mentors, and eventually each acknowledges selfish motive in assuming the role, and probable error. Like Elizabeth Bennet and Fitzwilliam Darcy, each in the end gratefully thanks the other for what each has learned. Both tend to be assertive and dogmatic. In their first confrontation, on Emma's role in the Taylor – Weston match (11–13), Knightley is starchy, authoritarian, pedantic, abstract and unyielding. Emma perceives his reductive intent. In fact, she is closer to the truth than he is. The exchange suggests at the outset that their limitations and distinctions may be comparable.

That Emma and Knightley are lovers unconsciously and will become lovers avowedly the reader quickly perceives. But first both have a discovery to make about their emotions. They are in danger of being insensitive to others and to their own emotional needs, Emma through her quest for immunity and Knightley through his self-rectitude. Each is saved by a propitious surrender to feeling, almost against principle and better judgement, to which each, however, in joy at the discovery made of the self and the other, happily acquiesces. As John Hagan describes the sudden turn, 'It is passion which spins the plot at this point, not reason' (561). Rather than love's birth and growth, the reader watches the discovery of love already in place and the removal of obstacles to its fulfilment.

In view of the aspiration of both Emma and Knightley to assert sovereignty over the other, the meetings between them often have the form of a contest, even a duel. Joseph Duffy believes that the stakes are mutual conquest,[17] and Sulloway believes that the result is Emma's 'enslavement and her muted sufferings in an irrational, humorless society' (326); but Austen assesses the problem of sexual relationship less grimly. In her novels some men – Darcy, Wentworth, Knightley – 'begin to liberate themselves toward wholeness'.[18] Although both Emma and Knightley exercise control over the lives around them, they discover that they can have the human companionship they desire only if they are willing to recognise the human reality of others.

In addition to the obstacle of Emma's flight from womanhood, the lovers must overcome Knightley's reluctance to acknowledge her substantiality as a person. Knightley seems at first a forbidding authority figure (*E*, 60–4). His views of women and marriage appear conventional: marriages are made primarily to attain security, and 'happily married' means well provided for; Harriet Smith 'is a pretty little creature' and 'in good hands she will turn out a valuable woman' (58); he is not averse to arranging a sensible match (61). His attitude towards Emma initially is that of a patriarchal male parent: Emma is a child-woman to him. He is thirty-seven and she is twenty. He will not recognise that the passing years have reduced the gap between their understandings. He regards her judgement as under the power of fancy and whim rather than guided by reason (98–9). He has no fault to find with her person and acquits her of personal vanity, but he says that she is spoiled, and he bestows grave looks on her when he is displeased (69). When Emma is divided between tears and smiles over Miss Weston's departure and marriage, Knightley gives her a heavy-handed moral lesson (11). When she claims credit for arranging the match, he scolds her for vanity (12–13). He rebukes her for relishing a 'delightful inferiority' in Harriet, but he 'relishes . . . [her] delightful inferiority to himself'.[19]

But like Emma's, Knightley's personality is more complex than often is acknowledged. He has a sense of humour (*E*, 59–60) and can enjoy Emma's teasing (144). He finds her physically very attractive. He acknowledges 'a sincere interest' in her, there 'is an anxiety, a curiosity in what one feels for Emma', and he wonders 'what will become of her' (38–40). He explains his admiration and concern as that of 'a partial old friend', but he has been in love with her at least from the time of the expectation of Frank Churchill's arrival (432).

Despite his apparent reserve, Knightley's personal feelings, particularly those unrecognised by him, affect him strongly.[20] He is most severe to Emma when she challenges the superiority of his understanding. His odd wish that he 'should like to see Emma in love, and in some doubt of a return; it would do her good' (*E*, 41) appears to stem from frustration as well as constructive intent. Most important, from near the end of the first book, Knightley is jealous of Frank Churchill. The effect on his judgement is obvious, although he will not recognise it; and it puzzles Emma:

> To take a dislike to a young man, only because he appeared to be of a different disposition from himself, was unworthy the real liberality of mind which she was always used to acknowledge in him; for with all the high opinion of himself, which she had often laid to his charge, she had never before for a moment supposed it could make him unjust to the merit of another. (150–1)

Austen's irony is obvious. Knightley must discover the irrational foundations of love and his own susceptibility to emotional impulse. His jealousy awakens him to the real nature of his regard for Emma and instigates his quest for self-knowledge. Far from being the novel's 'normative and exemplary figure', an unerring mentor, Austen's representative of the 'patriarchal ideal', or a Pygmalion who creates his wife in his own image, Knightley is, like Emma, a fallible human being moving towards an understanding of his human limitations and his human possibilities.

As much as Knightley praises an 'open temper' and practises such 'openness' in criticising Emma (which 'was not particularly agreeable' to her), he has not learned to welcome an 'open temper' in another (11). Hence their relationship at the outset is uneven and uneasy (10). Knightley can not accept Emma as an individual or an equal or treat her intelligence and her judgement as worthy of his respect. Although Emma does not want to quarrel with him, she wants recognition (65, 98–9, 135). She is discontented in a relationship in which she always seems to be in the wrong (98–9); she refuses to deny her own intelligence (113–14). Her resistance moves her at times to foolish extremes, such as persisting in an action when she suspects it is wrong (48) or contradicting Knightley just to show her independence (58–60, 146–7). Facing his assumption of superiority, she frequently seems reduced to defending her self-esteem (67).

On the whole Emma is more sensitive than Knightley about their relations. She can restrain herself when she does not agree, rather than break the peace or appear to be quarrelsome (58, 97, 112, 206, 276). When they do argue, she is eager to make up. Accused of a fault, she looks for a means of reconciliation that will leave her self-respect intact (98–9). She is willing to allay his anxiety if she can do so without being insincere (171). On some occasions she acknowledges that he is right and she is wrong (135, 291, 375–6).

Of the two Emma is more open to self-examination: 'She did not always feel so absolutely satisfied with herself, so entirely convinced that her opinions were right and her adversary's wrong, as Mr. Knightley. He walked off in more complete self-approbation than he left for her' (67). She displays considerable common sense at times about her own feelings (264–5). She is capable of seeing the merit of something even when it contradicts her wishes (50–1). When she truly blunders, as at Box Hill, her remorse is quick and full, and she feels justly rebuked and grateful for Knightley's counsel (374–6).

At times Emma's insight appears the keener. On several occasions she offers a valid criticism of Knightley. For example, she questions his apparent assumption that a man has only to propose to be accepted, and his indignation at Harriet Smith's refusal of Robert Martin contradicts his disavowal of the criticism (59–60). In the most important instance, a discussion of Frank Churchill, she describes at length how poor a judge Knightley is of the difficulties of dependence (145–6). One senses from the undercurrent of feeling that Emma is expressing her sensitivity to the differences in their own circumstances and perhaps in the circumstances of men and women in general: 'you have not an idea of what is requisite in situations directly opposite to your own'. (Knightley later admits that because of his favourable situation he tends to be unbending.) Emma rebukes him sharply: he is 'very fond of bending little minds; but where little minds belong to rich people in authority' he would have little success. She reminds him that where there are 'habits of early obedience and long observance to break through . . . it might not be so easy to burst forth at once into perfect independence. . . .' She cries out: 'Oh! the difference of situation and habit! I wish you would try to understand what an amiable young man may be likely to feel in directly opposing those, whom as child and boy he has been looking up to all his life' (147–8). Again, Emma seems to be stirred by the correspondence to her own relations with Knightley (and more broadly, to the relations of men and women). She appears to be trying to persuade him of the difficulty and complexity of being dependent and of the difficulty of life for those who are not in circumstances as favourable as his. Again, Emma's insight is the keener.

Still, Knightley has always provided Emma the standard by which she judges other men, and slowly her admiration turns to love. At first her regard seems impersonal. His 'downright, decided, commanding sort of manner – though it suits *him* very well' – would be insufferable if copied by a younger man (34). However, on the four occasions when, consciously or unconsciously, she compares him with Frank Churchill, each time he becomes more distinctly the model of male excellence.

On the first occasion, she is disappointed when Churchill fails to exhibit the qualities she admires, which, not surprisingly, are those she attributes to Knightley: rationality, moderation and an unselfish warmth of heart (205). Emma's own expressions of regard for Knightley, meanwhile, are becoming more personal and more discriminating:

I know no man more likely than Mr. Knightley to do the sort of thing – to do any thing really good-natured, useful, considerate, or benevolent. He is not a gallant man, but he is a very humane one . . . and for an act of un-ostentatious kindness, there is nobody whom I would fix on more than on Mr. Knightley. (223)

In a second comparison of the two men, she stops just short of naming Knightley as the man she could be attracted to (320). Then, at Mr Weston's ball, she consciously admires Knightley's handsomeness and virility, and for the first time she regards him as a potential lover:

She was more disturbed by Mr. Knightley's not dancing, than by any thing else. . . . [H]e ought to be dancing, – not classing himself with the husbands, and fathers, and whist-players . . . so young as he looked! – He could not have appeared to greater advantage perhaps any where, than where he had placed himself. His tall, firm, upright figure, among the bulky forms and stooping shoulders of the elderly men, was such as Emma felt must draw every body's eyes; and, excepting her own partner, there was not one among the whole row of young men who could be compared with him. . . . [W]ith what natural grace, he must have danced, would he but take the trouble. – Whenever she caught his eye, she forced him to smile. . . . (325–6)

Their emotions move nearer and nearer to the surface. Following his rebuke of her behaviour at Box Hill, she wants him to forgive her. When he hears of her visit of amends, his look acquires a 'glow of regard', and he takes her hand (though she may have offered it). Emma recalls the scene with 'great satisfaction' (385–6).

A third time she measures Churchill by the standard Knightley provides, this time with indignant disapproval of the former: 'So unlike what a man should be! – None of that upright integrity, that strict adherence to truth and principle, that disdain of trick and little-ness, which a man should display in every transaction of his life' (397). At last the truth becomes clear: 'How long had Mr. Knightley been so dear to her? . . . She saw that there never had been a time when she did not consider Mr. Knightley as infinitely the superior, or when his regard for her had not been infinitely the most dear. She saw, that in persuading herself, in fancying, in acting to the contrary, she had been entirely under a delusion, totally ignorant of her own heart . . .' (412). After reconciling with Churchill, for the last time, now overtly, she compares the two men: 'she had never been more sensible of Mr. Knightley's high superiority of character. The happiness of this most happy day, received its completion, in the animated contemplation of his worth which this comparison produced' (480).

The growth in the fervour and openness of Emma's love corresponds to Knightley's changing attitude towards her, as marked by the abandonment of his paternalism. Just as Captain Wentworth looks with reviving interest at Anne Elliot after he observes how attractive she is to William Elliot, Knightley becomes aware that his love for Emma is sexual rather than familial as a result of his jealousy of Frank Churchill. Shaken from his flattering mentor's role and facing the possibility of losing Emma altogether, he begins to look upon her as an independent and worthy fellow being. The change has taken hold by the time of the cancellation of the first attempt to hold Mr Weston's ball (262).

On the occasion of the ball itself, after verifying that Emma had wanted Elton to marry Harriet, Knightley resists giving a lecture. Instead, he offers peace in the contest of egos. He acknowledges that Emma has a serious spirit and a reliable one. She admits her error and credits him with the discernment she lacked. He graciously returns the compliment. Emma's immense pleasure at this recognition of her adulthood leads to their first lovers' steps:

'I shall not scold you. I leave you to your own reflections.'

'Can you trust me with such flatterers? – Does my vain spirit ever tell me I am wrong?'

'Not your vain spirit, but your serious spirit. – If one leads you wrong, I am sure the other tells you of it.'

'I do own myself to have been completely mistaken in Mr. Elton. . . .'

'And, in return for your acknowledging so much, I will do you the justice to say, that you would have chosen for him better than he has chosen for himself. . . .'

Emma was extremely gratified. . . .

'Whom are you going to dance with?' asked Mr. Knightley.

She hesitated a moment, and then replied, 'With you, if you will ask me.'

'Will you?' said he, offering his hand.

'Indeed I will. You have shown me that you can dance, and

you know we are not really so much brother and sister as to make it at all improper.'

'Brother and sister! no, indeed.' (330–1)

Afterwards, 'this little explanation with Mr. Knightley gave Emma considerable pleasure' (332). Her self-respect has been confirmed by the man she admires. She has gained recognition in his eyes as a sensible, independent person, no longer a child or a 'feminine' woman.

Henceforth Knightley treats Emma as an independent adult rather than as his pupil or charge. Concerned over signs of an attachment between Churchill and Jane Fairfax, he decides that 'he must – yes, he certainly must, as a friend – an anxious friend – give Emma some hint' as a matter of duty:

> A variety of evils crossed his mind. Interference – fruitless interference. . . . Yet he would speak. He owed it to her, to risk any thing that might be involved in an unwelcome interference, rather than her welfare; to encounter any thing, rather than the remembrance of neglect in such a cause. (349–50)

Similarly, in rebuking Emma for Box Hill, Knightley shows a sensitivity that bespeaks a new relationship. He professes that in acting as a mentor again he is exercising a privilege 'rather endured than allowed'. Emma's reaction, however, is one 'only of anger against herself, mortification, and deep concern' (374–6). Finally, in declaring his love for her, Knightley plainly acknowledges his former inconsiderate treatment: '. . . you know what I am. – You hear nothing but truth from me. – I have blamed you, and lectured you, and you have borne it as no other woman in England would have borne it. . . . God knows, I have been a very indifferent lover' (430). Knightley's actions during this last scene spring from impulse and tender consideration. 'He had come, in his anxiety to see how she bore Frank Churchill's engagement. . . . The rest had been the work of the moment, the immediate effect of what he heard, on his feelings. . . . [H]e had only, in the momentary conquest of eagerness over judgment, aspired to be told that she did not forbid his attempt to attach her' (432). Knightley is saved by a surrender to feeling that he once would have regarded as weakness. Emma's response is a wish to prevent him pain, whatever it might cost her.

The changes in each are commensurate. Knightley has discovered that Emma is the 'sweetest and best of all creatures, faultless in spite of all her faults' (433). In the discovery that he depends on another fallible creature for his happiness, he abandons his assumption of sexual superiority; his desire is no longer to rule but to serve. In an extraordinary act of consideration he offers to reside at Hartfield for the duration of Mr Woodhouse's life. Emma was 'sensible of all the affection it evinced. . . . [H]e must be sacrificing a great deal of independence of hours and habits . . .' (449). As the result of achieving mature dependence, they surrender their defences. Their marriage is a love match, an act of freely exercised choice, based on personal inclination. As in a similar exchange between Elizabeth Bennet and Fitzwilliam Darcy, they describe the end of selfish contention and the triumph of mutual esteem.

> 'Nature gave you understanding: – Miss Taylor gave you principles. You must have done well. My interference was quite as likely to do harm as good. It was very natural for you to say, what right has he to lecture me? – and I am afraid very natural for you to feel that it was done in a disagreeable manner. I do not believe I did you any good. The good was all to myself, by making you an object of the tenderest affection to me. I could not think about you so much without doating on you, faults and all; and by dint of fancying so many errors, have been in love with you ever since you were thirteen at least.'
>
> 'I am sure you were of use to me,' cried Emma. 'I was very often influenced rightly by you – oftener than I would own at the time. I am very sure you did me good.' (462)

Emma and Knightley experience a liberating move towards wholeness. Blessed equally with energy and vitality, they have ignored, repressed or turned away from properties of their human nature which the society has stigmatised as 'feminine', especially the emotional properties associated with tenderness, giving and sacrifice. However, they finally overcome the psychological barrier of personality stereotypes and acknowledge the range of 'masculine' and 'feminine' impulses that each possesses. By uniting their formerly divided selves, they establish the basis for mutuality and reciprocity in their marriage relationship.

The marriage of Emma and Knightley is based on the spirit of equality and mutual respect that will permit 'truth and sincerity' to rule. It is a marriage that holds the fullest promise of life, one in which the female is openly admired and shares decisions and in which there is mutual trust and a healthy sense of companionship. It is a marriage in which each recognises the human reality of the other, accepts the other's individuality and independence, and feels right and secure enough in their relationship to want to give rather than to receive. Mutual good will governs their actions, as in the decision to reside at Hartfield. Abandoning her flight from womanhood, Emma finds in Knightley a companion for herself and a partner in the duties and cares she will eventually face (450).

8 *Persuasion:* A Mature Dependence

In *Persuasion*, her last treatment of the 'drama of woman', Jane Austen affirms her life-long support of women's freedom. With unusual intensity of feeling and concentration of purpose and with a remarkable unity of form and idea, she guides Anne Elliot to happiness and self-fulfilment in marriage, despite the obstacles of patriarchalism. Recognition of this purpose clarifies the novel's thematic bond with her earlier works and resolves many of the problems of structure and content.

Persuasion has troubled critics because of an unfinished text and apparent shifts in approach, tone and thematic emphasis. By contrast with Austen's earlier heroines, Anne Elliot, at twenty-seven, seems to have lost her chance for marriage with love. Although she can balance emotion, reason and imagination and has a sufficient knowledge of the world to make confidently the judgements that trouble Austen's younger heroines, for her the period of crucial decisions has passed. Thus the novel is described as autumnal in tone, requiem-like, until the final magical deliverance, when Anne is conveyed from the 'world' of country families and landed gentry, which has become for her a decaying, trivial 'world', into a new society of natural aristocrats.

Critics differ about the focus of moral interest in *Persuasion*, the moral development of character, the centre of action, and the use of fantasy. Agreeing that Austen gives unusually strong emphasis in the novel to locating responsibility for decisions within the individual, they differ about whether she upholds eighteenth-century values or sympathises with new values.[1] Does moral development of character occur at all,[2] only in Frederick Wentworth,[3] or in both heroine and hero?[4] Do both principals contribute to their eventual reconciliation or does all the active doing belong to Wentworth?[5] Concern about plausibility leads to suggestions that the novel is like a fairy tale or that the dénouement is a product of fantasy.[6]

In describing Anne Elliot's struggle to preserve her sense of selfhood, discover a purpose for her life, and establish a loving, sharing relationship in marriage, Austen employs a number of familiar themes:

(1) The worst cases of vanity, egotism and self-obsession still are males, and these faults derive primarily from their privileged status. In the character of Sir Walter Elliot Austen reduces the male egotist to comic ineffectuality; in the character of William Elliot she creates his menacing opposite, the consummate hypocrite. Wentworth's masculine pride causes an eight-year separation from Anne Elliot.

(2) Austen again indicts sexual stereotyping and the assignment of sex roles. All three Elliot sisters endure a trivial existence. Mrs Smith is the 'final embodiment of a fate that haunts all her [Austen's] novels. . . . the entirely unsupported woman'.[7] Anne Elliot's resourceful and decisive actions at Lyme and elsewhere expose the falsity of sexual stereotyping.

(3) Austen condemns marriages based on patriarchal principles and made for personal advantage. Lady Russell, Elizabeth Elliot and William Elliot, who support them, are discomfited. Her mother's history warns Anne of the unfavourable prospects of a marriage based on other than mutual respect, equality and love (*P*, 4).

(4) As elsewhere, Austen deplores concealment and celebrates openness in human behaviour. For Anne Elliot and Mrs Smith concealment is a defence against inequitable social circumstances; for William Elliot it offers a means of exploiting others that reflects the male's relative immunity from consequences (like his counterparts Frank Churchill and Henry Crawford). Anne and Wentworth move from concealment to openness, putting aside the poses encouraged by pride or social need and presenting their true selves to each other.

(5) In Anne Elliot Austen again depicts a courageous young woman whose vision of personal integrity guides her at the risk of her emotional and physical security. She is a 'solitary heroine', like Fanny Price, not a 'role-breaker', like Emma Woodhouse. Her stoic heroism and disciplined moral character invest Anne with a dignity unmatched by her younger 'sisters'.

(6) Austen stresses again the duality of human personality, as opposed to the bipolarity at the heart of sexual stereotyping.

On the former she bases her view of the ideal love relationship.
(7) The concept of duality allows for development of a wide range of attributes within each individual. Anne Elliot and Wentworth display characteristics assigned to the sexes separately; they learn that for their personal and mutual happiness they must achieve an equilibrium among these internal properties and they must balance the needs of each as equal individuals.

In *Persuasion* Austen also adds to or modifies what she has said before. The result, in Bush's description, is 'the deepest or highest plane of drama that Jane Austen ever reached' (181).

(1) The theme of imagination is less prominent than in earlier novels, but there is a stronger emphasis on feeling. Although Anne Elliot hides her emotions almost completely, the reader, by his access to her thoughts, experiences the physical and psychological ordeal that she undergoes. Wentworth is the most headstrong of Austen's heroes – and the most attractive. *Persuasion* is concerned with the quality of emotion as well as with the intensity. Rightness of feeling is the principal measure of Anne's superiority to others, and its presence in Wentworth, in contrast with William Elliot, marks him as worthy of her love.
(2) Although Austen's heroines eventually speak out against prejudicial social distinctions, they often do so obliquely. Anne Elliot's discussion with Captain Harville of firmness in feeling is the fullest and most direct comment in the novels on the conditions of life for a woman. The substantive issues of sexual discrimination seem closer to the surface in this work than ever before.
(3) Austen particularly celebrates women's strength in *Persuasion*. Outwardly less spirited than her younger counterparts, Anne possesses an unmatched depth and firmness of commitment to an ideal of personal and sexual fulfilment.
(4) Anne Elliot is Austen's most isolated heroine. Although in the climax of *Mansfield Park* the solitude of Fanny Price matches that of Anne, the latter exists as an adult in a state of near non-being from the outset.
(5) Anne Elliot also is Austen's most mature heroine, almost without flaw. Her feelings at twenty-seven are the riper and deeper emotions that come with suffering. Experience, the power of her instincts and her moral probity confirm her judgement and

support her acts. She has built a core of self as a source of self-awareness and self-assurance. Consequently, she escapes the narcissism of her father and sister, refuses to repeat her mother's mistakes, avoids self-pity, and can be confident that she and Wentworth will understand each other before long. Anne Elliot possesses 'true' autonomy – 'self-possession' or 'mastery of self' – as opposed to the 'false' autonomy that Emma Woodhouse at first pursues – a 'self-sufficiency' which relieves one from dealing with others openly and mutually.

In *Persuasion* Austen finally 'blows up' the patriarchal family. Throughout the novels she has favoured formation of a family type based on free choice in marriage and lasting mutual affection rather than on parental selection and expediency; but the new family, while turning away from kin and rejecting male hegemony, remained in close contact with the old. In *Northanger Abbey*, despite the warning of General Tilney's tyranny, the marriage of Catherine and Henry held out the possibility of accommodation between the female and the patriarchal order. In *Mansfield Park* that order apparently was temporarily rehabilitated through the 're-education' of the father. But in *Persuasion* Austen depicts the patriarchal family as spiritually bankrupt and futile. In its place she offers the conjugal family; in place of primogeniture, the self-made man; and in place of marriage for family advantage, individual choice on the basis of personal relationship. Anne Elliot leaves her paternal abode forever.

The discredited patriarchal family in *Persuasion* symbolises a discredited patriarchal society. Its principal representatives are Sir Walter and William Elliot. With the former Austen satirises the relationship between the vanity of the male and his social advantages: Sir Walter's house is the 'palace of egotism'. Surrounded by mirrors, he does away with the world and is the prisoner of himself. Feeling has atrophied (*P*, 26), social discourse has become stultifying and insipid (226), and parental duties have been abandoned. On those who still accept his authority or his claims to deference his egotism exerts a destructive influence. He is an easy victim of the unscrupulous.

Just as Sir Walter illustrates the patriarchal male becoming a fool, William Elliot illustrates him becoming a monster. The latter combines self-love and social privilege with ambition and calculation to form Austen's most deliberate and dangerous hypocrite. Unlike her other 'villains' – Willoughby, Wickham, Churchill and

Crawford – William Elliot does not act out of need or a love of mischief, but his financial and social advantages unite with a cold, dark egoism to compose a force for evil (199).

Although at first Anne finds William Elliot attractive and sensible, she soon comes to regard him as a 'disingenuous, artificial, worldly man, who has never had any better principle to guide him than selfishness' (208). The idea of marriage to him briefly excites her by the prospect of being the mistress of Kellynch, as she feels a tug of the vanity that has conquered the rest of her family, but her impression of his moral character tells her that 'we should not suit' (159). Well before she learns fully of his villainy from Mrs Smith, she has sensed that she cannot trust him, that he lacks openness.

But Austen plays down the threat these characters pose: Sir Walter is a comic figure, and William Elliot is brushed aside when need be. She is more interested in a third danger, less obvious but more critical for her heroine: the harm to men and women of sexual stereotyping. Anne's sense of life will not be complete without bonding with a like-minded person, but such bonding is impossible as long as either one's understanding of one's own nature or that of others is clouded by prejudice, false preconceptions and sexual politics. Apparently in order to concentrate on this problem Austen avoids putting Anne through an initial experience of courtship, relieves her of the need to acquire self-knowledge, and reduces the reader's concern for her vulnerability by making her already the recipient of nearly the worst that the society can inflict.

Although both sexes must make the same journey to knowledge of the self and of others, in *Persuasion* Anne has already gone as far as she can alone. She must hope for, and await, Wentworth's catching up. But the passage for the young male is difficult because his advantages foster self-satisfaction and indifference to the problem. He is taught to regard attributes identified with women as signs of weakness and those identified with men as signs of strength, a conditioning that deprives him of an opportunity to express his feelings and to be gentle and that inhibits mutuality in his heterosexual relations. Spurred by his sense of superiority, he is ready to resort to prejudicial generalisations to explain or justify his or others' behaviour. Wentworth is not a fool or a hypocrite, but he is trapped by circumstances, sexual bias and masculine egotism. Before he can discover his own full nature or what a woman is, he must, like the female, exorcise the internalised patriarchal presence. Before he can achieve communion with the other sex, he must unite his divided self. The greatest danger to Anne Elliot from the patriarchal order is that Wentworth can not see himself and others clearly.

The women of *Persuasion*, especially, show how that order can damage one's personality and control one's behaviour. Elizabeth Elliot, as the eldest daughter, handsome and without Anne's resources of mind and spirit, has absorbed her father's pride of family, love of form and consciousness of rank; but at twenty-nine she has begun to feel the emptiness of her life (7). She has been swindled by the masculine universe; her anger at William Elliot, whom she had liked for himself 'and still more for being her father's heir', cannot be forgotten. Such were

the cares to alloy, the agitations to vary, the sameness and the elegance, the prosperity and the nothingness, of her scene of life – such the feelings to give interest to a long, uneventful residence in one country circle, to fill the vacancies which there were no habits of utility abroad, no talents or accomplishments for home, to occupy. (8–9)

The narrator contrasts the sources of happiness for Elizabeth and Anne: 'the origin of one all selfish vanity, of the other all generous attachment' (185).

Mrs Clay is the last of Austen's predatory females. Like the Elliot sisters, she has been forced into a subordinate status; like Lady Susan she tries to exploit the oppressive system's weaknesses: where vanity rules, a 'clever young woman, who understood the art of pleasing', may seize advantage (15). Walter Elliot is the deeper hypocrite (her 'selfishness was not so complicate nor so revolting as his' [215]); she deceives in order to survive, he adds to power he already has.

Lady Russell is a woman of good sense and good intentions, and she loves Anne Elliot like a daughter. Her view of marriage, however, is shaped by patriarchal values. Well provided for, like Emma Woodhouse she sees no need to marry but attempts to guide the marital destiny of another. On three occasions she counsels Anne by patriarchal standards, such as the wealth in property of the prospective husband. Although acting always with integrity and solicitude, Lady Russell represents a threat to Anne's possibilities of happiness, the menace of one who 'loves' her but whose advice would hold her in social bondage. On the first occasion, she persuaded Anne that her engagement to Wentworth was 'a wrong thing' (27). By the time of Charles Musgrove's offer, however, Anne has come to recognise her previous mistake and leaves 'nothing for advice to do' (29). On the third occasion, Lady Russell predicts a personal relationship with Mr Elliot adequate for a marriage of such great social advantage, and she dangles the bait before Anne of her mother's place as Lady Elliot of Kellynch Hall (159); but Anne again escapes the trap (211).

Anne Elliot, of course, is the worst injured of the women in *Persuasion*. She apparently has lost her chance for personal happiness in marriage, and she will not wed for any other reason. Rejecting the sterile interests of her father and sister, she is nobody to them (5). She is 'on the shelf', a spinster of twenty-seven who can only try to make herself useful in others' families. She dwells in spiritual solitude, her self-esteem in danger because of her near reduction to non-being. At the opening of the story her condition is one of physical decline and emotional depression.

Like Elinor Dashwood and Fanny Price, Anne Elliot is in love and knows it; she is not, as Elizabeth Bennet and Emma Woodhouse are, in the process of discovering her true feelings about a man. But unlike Fanny Price, Anne enjoys hope of a return of her love well before the end of the story; and, unlike Elinor Dashwood, who is sure of Edward Ferrars's regard, Anne is not helpless to improve the chances of eventual union. *Persuasion* concentrates on a single problem: the obstacles to intimacy caused by sexual stereotyping.

Anne broke her engagement with Wentworth eight years earlier, at nineteen, because she was persuaded by Lady Russell that it 'was a wrong thing – indiscreet, improper, hardly capable of success, and not deserving it' (27). She believed that she was 'being prudent, and self-denying principally for *his* advantage' (28). Wentworth, however, misinterpreted her behaviour. His ego was seriously wounded by her apparent doubt of his worth as a man. Judging her by the stereotype of 'feminine' behaviour, he discovered in her only signs of 'feminine' weakness which his 'masculine' temper could not endure. Without attempting to understand Anne's reasons for breaking the engagement, he blamed her for timidity in the face of family pressures where he looked for strength of mind and feeling (61). 'Feeling himself ill-used' (28), he went away and did not communicate again.

Since Anne does seem to fit the feminine stereotype, Wentworth's misjudgement has support from appearance as well as from assumption. Whereas he, at their first meeting, is described as 'a remarkably fine young man, with a great deal of intelligence, spirit and brilliancy', Anne is described as 'an extremely pretty girl, with gentleness, modesty, taste, and feeling' (26). Lady Russell thinks of her as being 'peculiarly fitted by her warm affections and domestic habits' for marriage (29), and in her domestic relations she is constantly engaged in the 'feminine' tasks of ministration and reconciliation (39, 46).

This 'femininity' partly is imposed by Anne's environment and partly reflects the development of potentialities within her nature. In the first instance, in circumstances the very opposite of Emma's, Anne has received repeated lessons 'in the art of knowing our own nothingness' (42). Confronted by indifference to her well-being, she must repress her feelings and try to handle conflicts by absorbing them rather than by aggressive assertion. Compelled to be an observer of life, she is glad to be of some use, any use, rather than be 'rejected as no good at all' (33). Thus the 'feminine' role is nearly inescapable for her. (When hopes have passed one by, 'in a generous woman resignation takes the form of forbearance'.[8]) But the 'feminine' role encourages passivity and dependence rather than the active behaviour associated with the 'masculine' role. It may cause one's manners to be false to one's feelings, and it may induce psychological paralysis from a sense of hopelessness, guilt and anxiety.

At the same time that the patriarchal system discourages development of the instrumental side of women's nature, it stimulates development of the expressive side. Women are encouraged to become nurturant, responsive and kind in their relationships. It presses them to develop traits of patience, endurance and fortitude as well as sensitivity to the emotional atmosphere of personal relationships. Anne finds such traits invaluable when a chance for personal happiness reappears; moreover, they represent a mode of response that Wentworth must learn to appreciate if that chance for them both is to become a reality.

Austen brings Anne Elliot closer to the experience of total alienation than any other heroine except Fanny Price, and her treatment of the subject is fuller and more intense in *Persuasion* than in *Mansfield Park*. Anne and Fanny are Austen's heroines of no consequence; they are exploited but not valued. They fall into no self-deception and pass through no awakening as do Catherine Morland, Elizabeth Bennet and Emma Woodhouse. Instead, they are subjected to a severe assault from without on a core of self that they struggle to retain intact. They are cast, however, in the role of the victim as subject and not as object. Each possesses a firm sense of her own and other people's reality and identity, and one observes them acting and perceiving, not only acted upon and perceived. Although each is tempted to accept the false security of subjugation, she has the courage to make an assertion of selfhood, an act which brings her into conflict with the instruments of social control.

One commentator observes that *Persuasion* is Austen's 'darkest treatment' of the 'perils of the free spirit in its search for social identity'.[9] So precarious does life seem, so unreasonable are the consequences of apparently reasonable choice, that the conclusion prompts another observer to think that the novel is possibly a fairy tale after all.[10] And perhaps it would be, except that *Persuasion* rings with the truth of the 'drama of woman' and of Austen's vision of human possibilities. Although the active doing is largely Wentworth's – he is the one who learns and grows – Anne's mind and feelings, as Tave points out, are 'ever at the center';[11] and the reader's concern for her fate is the key to his imaginative, emotional and moral engagement. Events may swirl about Anne apparently beyond her control, but the issue, metaphorically, is her life or death; and no one can escape the excitement of learning with her what these events may hold. Despite her initial enervation no Austen heroine possesses a more deeply felt, vital and diverse emotional life.

Anne Elliot's conversation with Captain Harville about constancy in men and women, which prompts Wentworth to reopen his heart to her, is the pivotal event in the story and conveys its central issue. In summary,

Anne initially states that *no* woman could soon forget a man she truly loved and, with her own experience undoubtedly in mind, that a woman does not forget a man as soon as a man forgets a woman. Such a distinction, however, is perhaps women's fate rather than their merit, because they 'live at home, quiet, confined' where their feelings prey upon them, whereas men have always a profession or business to occupy them and weaken their impressions. When Harville points out that Benwick had no such distraction, Anne asks whether it must not then be man's nature which explains the brevity of his grief. Harville insists on the opposite: on the basis of the resemblance between bodily and mental frames he asserts 'that as our bodies are the strongest, so are our feelings'. Anne takes up the analogy: women's feelings must then be the most tender. Although a man is more robust than a woman, he is not longer-lived. In view of the labours, hardships and risks to which he is subjected, 'it would be too hard indeed . . . if woman's feelings were to be added'. When Harville argues that history and literature prove women's fickleness, Anne rejects such accounts as creations of men – 'I will not allow books to prove any thing.' But she doubts that either point can be proven, since she and Harville begin with a bias towards their own sex and build every circumstance in its favour. Then Harville describes the sufferings of a sailor when he leaves his family and 'the glow of his soul' when he returns. Anne eagerly exclaims that such 'true attachment and constancy' are not 'known only by woman' and that men are 'capable of every thing great and good' in their married lives. The only privilege she would claim for her sex, the result of unenviable differences in circumstances, 'is that of loving longest, when existence or when hope is gone' (*P*, 232–5).

The conversation reveals Anne's hard-won knowledge, confidence and objectivity. She is aware of her condition and the condition of women in her society. With confidence in her own identity, she can press her argument thoughtfully and vigorously despite masculine opposition. She is free in her mind and feelings to speak with understanding and without rancour about circumstances painful to her as an individual and as a woman. She believes in mutuality and reciprocity of thought and feeling as the proper bases of relationships between the sexes.

Anne speaks within Wentworth's hearing. By insisting that women feel as deeply as men do and can continue to love when hope is lost and that men are as capable of true attachment and constancy as women, she counters the false image of the differences between men and women that has kept Wentworth from her. Since she obviously draws upon her own history and feelings, he is persuaded that she still loves him as strongly as he loves her. His eyes now fully open to the strength and depth of Anne's character, he perceives that the female stereotype is inadequate to describe her powers and that, having developed her own values and followed them, she is her own woman. Anne previously has contemplated her relations with Wentworth with a sense of optimism: 'Surely, if there be constant attachment on each side, our hearts must understand each other ere long. We are not boy and girl, to be captiously irritable, misled by every moment's inadvertence, and wantonly playing with our own happiness' (221). Wentworth, at last, acts on the opportunity for reconciliation that he now believes to exist.

Far from the purely feminine figure that Wentworth thought her, Anne unites 'feminine' feeling with 'masculine' action. She is delicate, an 'elegant little woman', but she also has fortitude and the capability of decisive performance (53, 58, 109–11, 122). As circumstances permit or require, she displays both the instrumental and the expressive modes. The different reactions of Anne and Wentworth to Louisa Musgrove's fall at the Cobb in Lyme dramatise that the range of possible behaviour in men and women includes the traits of both stereotypes, that is, that human nature is dualistic rather than bipolar. Anne shows the clear head and promptness of decision that one expects from the male. Wentworth collapses against the sea wall in shock and calls out for help as if all his strength had gone. Anne shows 'masculine' energy and presence of mind; Wentworth shows 'feminine' emotion and weakness. The episode refutes the myth that only men can be strong and resourceful in emergencies and that emotionalism is a feminine trait. Wentworth discovers Anne's true strength of character, and he encounters a variety of feelings within himself whose existence he had not suspected.

From this point on Anne takes the lead in determining the course of events. Her self-esteem improves, and her mood changes from depression and resignation to hopeful excitement as she realises that she is attractive to another man and still loved by Wentworth. Once she perceives that the latter is again free to love her, her passivity fades, and she begins, tactfully but unmistakably, to encourage his reviving interest. Anne does not intend to lose him again by default.[12]

Anne Elliot has always been the sort of woman that Wentworth desires, one who combines a 'strong mind, with sweetness of manner'. She joins a deeply tender nature with the strength of character to maintain her beliefs in the face of opposition. She adds a wisdom and self-assurance acquired through suffering from her own and others' mistakes. She is free from the prejudices of her society. She proves herself capable of judging and managing particular situations. The most self-aware, knowledgeable and mature of Austen's heroines, she surpasses the conventional limits of woman's nature.

In *Persuasion*, unlike in her previous novels, Austen treats the fate of her hero and heroine as a subject that can be decided apart from their milieu. Captain Wentworth is a self-made man with independent means; Anne Elliot has achieved mastery of self. One problem, primarily, keeps them apart: Wentworth's resort to sexual stereotyping to explain Anne's rejection of him. Like Darcy and Knightley, he must learn to judge men and women as individuals and to base his personal relationships on the recognition of individual worth and mutual respect; unlike them, he undergoes his learning experience alone. Both his fate and Anne's depend on his success.

Wentworth has made his fortune rather than inherited it. He has exhibited the 'masculine' attributes of energy, enterprise and fearlessness; and he has 'been lucky in his profession'. He 'was brilliant, he was headstrong' (*P*, 27); and he is proud of his abilities and his accomplishments. When Anne rejects his proposal, his pride is deeply hurt. He believes that she 'questioned his estimate of himself, doubted his worth as a man, and did not love him enough to resist the persuasion to give him up'.[13] 'Totally unconvinced and unbending' (*P*, 28) in his opinions, he leaves the country abruptly.

Wentworth's attitude reveals that patriarchy's greatest threat to Anne Elliot's happiness is the warping of his judgement by the inculcation of sexual stereotypes. In the grip of his ego he feels his own particularity and readily generalises about the opposite sex. His conversation with his sister Mrs Croft about women aboard naval vessels (68–9) shows how little he esteems women's substance. In reacting to the broken engagement, he never considers Anne's particular circumstances.

The model for the 'superior' male sex encourages renouncing and overcoming rather than taking in and creating. Convinced of the rightness of his own judgement, Wentworth reduces the problem of moral choice for Anne to one of will. Like Knightley, with male self-assurance he believes that after one decides what is right all one needs in order to act on one's beliefs and bear down opposition is firmness of character.[14] Failing to recognise that Anne has sacrificed her inclination to her sense of the right, of human fallibility and of duty, he sees her as lacking courage, decision and firmness, that is, as 'feminine'.

Wentworth is a victim of his bias, as well as Anne. He has been deeply hurt; he cannot forgive her; he wishes to forget her. He 'remains trapped within feelings that regard himself', a 'version of self-centeredness, which often becomes self-righteousness in the first half of the novel'.[15] This reaction leads him to a foolish error with almost tragic results.

On his return to Somersetshire, Wentworth's object is to marry (*P*, 61). Anne Elliot was still in his thoughts when he 'seriously described the woman he should wish to meet with. "A strong mind, with sweetness of manner" . . .' (62). Believing still in Anne's susceptibility, he stresses the first quality, so that when he meets Henrietta Musgrove, who seems to possess Anne's presumed complaisance, and Louisa Musgrove, who seems to possess the strong mind that Anne apparently lacks, he praises Louisa and urges her to instil her own spirit into Henrietta: 'It is the worst evil of too yielding and indecisive a character, that no influence over it can be depended on. – You are never sure of a good impression being durable. Every body may sway it; let those who would be happy be firm . . .' (88). At Lyme, Louisa's 'firmness', which is only wilfulness, and Wentworth's 'complaisance' lead to her near-fatal fall. Subsequently, Wentworth realises that through his own 'weakness', his own lack of decisiveness and of high standards, he is implicitly committed to a woman that he can not love or admire.

How is one persuaded that Wentworth will prove worthy of Anne Elliot? Austen limits his errors to mistakes in judgement prompted by male vanity. Otherwise he is regarded by the narrator and by Anne as extremely attractive in every respect. By contrast with Sir Walter Elliot, he is a self-made man, modest, energetic, independent and self-confident. By contrast with William Elliot, he is open. To balance his 'somewhat self-satisfied behavior with the young women, we are presented with a carefully prepared scene between him and Mrs. Musgrove, designed to show . . . his compassion'.[16] After the episode on the Cobb, Wentworth changes rapidly, the only character besides Anne to exhibit moral development. When we discover that his *only* fault is his male pride, we become confident, as Anne declares herself to be, that a way will be found to overcome that problem, that he will acquire a clear understanding of his own mind and heart.

Wentworth's breakthrough begins at the Cobb. Only then, as he tells Anne later, did he begin to comprehend himself (*P*, 241). From that episode he learns to appreciate her true strength of character and to see the foolishness of his own ideas. At Lyme

he had learnt to distinguish between the steadiness of principle and the obstinacy of self-will, between the darings of heedlessness and the resolution of a collected mind. There, he had seen every thing to exalt in his estimation the woman he had lost, and there begun to deplore the pride, the folly, the madness of resentment, which had kept him from trying to regain her when thrown in his way.

From that period his penance had become severe. (242)

Wentworth sought 'a strong mind, with sweetness of temper'. He discovers how excellent a description this is of Anne, that she has always been the sort of woman he desires. Immediately following that episode he begins to re-establish intimacy with her. When he resumes his old habit of command, he shows a 'deference for her judgment' that for Anne is a source of pleasure and a proof of friendship, a step forward as significant as the comparable step towards mutual respect had been for Emma and Knightley (117).

Wentworth's breakthrough represents self-recognition rather than self-transformation, but the effect is one of rebirth just the same. He acknowledges the errors of his egotism. Of Louisa Musgrove's accident he says, 'It had been my doing – solely mine. She would not have been obstinate if I had not been weak' (183). He admits the error for which Emma Woodhouse severely criticises Frank Churchill: appearing to engage the affections of a young woman for whom one does not really care or of two young women at the same time. Finally, he recognises that only his pride has kept him and Anne apart:

'Tell me if, when I returned to England in the year eight [1808] . . . if I had then written to you, would you have answered my letter? would you, in short, have renewed the engagement then?'

'Would I!' was all her answer; but the accent was decisive enough.

'Good God!' he cried, 'you would! It is not that I did not think of it, or desire it, as what could alone crown all my other success. But I was proud, too proud to ask again. I did not understand you. I shut my eyes, and would not understand you, or do you justice. This is a recollection which ought to make me forgive every one sooner than myself. Six years of separation and suffering might have been spared.' (247)

Thus Wentworth removes the wall between himself and Anne by breaking down the wall within his own psyche. He does not have to develop 'feminine' emotion and sensitivity; he has strong feelings and is sensitive to others, as his attentions to the bereaved Captain Benwick and to Mrs Musgrove attest. He discovers 'feminine' feelings within him that may guide, even overpower, 'masculine' judgement at crucial moments and in important areas of behaviour (109–11). He discovers 'weaknesses' within himself that he would formerly have ascribng   where Anne has been strong. He discovers his error in understanding the causes of his own behaviour and therefore the likelihood of his error in explaining hers (241). Recognising his own weakness and poor judgement, he realises that restraint and devotion to principle are needed to control impulse and enthusiasm (242). But he discovers that 'natural' feelings may guide one wisely. Had he followed his 'natural' impulse to write to Anne upon his return to England, rather than his 'artificial' pride, he would have prevented much suffering by both.

After he discovers how seriously he has misjudged Anne's actions and misled himself, Wentworth fears that Anne lacks his new knowledge. He doubts that she can judge him except as his past actions would falsely guide her. But Anne has freed herself from such obstacles to right judgement long ago, and she has been watching his slow progress. At the propitious moment she finds the way to convey her belief that men and women have an equal capacity for love and fidelity; and each recognises that power in the other. Wentworth discovers that Anne does not judge him by the conventional standard but by what he now believes himself to be. He feels an upsurge of joy: 'You do us justice indeed. You do believe that there is true attachment and constancy among men' (237). And with their reconciliation Anne finds the future open to her again.

In Bakan's opinion, 'overemphasis on the development of the ego will obscure, indeed repress, the communion feature of the psyche' (56). After suspending his ego's restriction of what it will entertain and what it will not, Wentworth comes to see his mixed or dual nature clearly. Both he and Anne show 'feminine' emotion and 'masculine' decision. They discover themselves to be and come to accept each other as being both assertive and yielding, independent and dependent, strong and gentle. In learning about their own needs, they learn to recognise the reality of other people's needs. They achieve 'mature dependence', the capacity to differentiate between ego and object and 'therewith a capacity for valuing the object for its own sake and for giving as well as receiving'.[17] Their final relationship is reciprocal, harmonious, equilibrious; it provides a model for the overcoming of other separations (*P*, 240–1).

Austen's primary interest in her novels is the quest for freedom and happiness. Her concern is most intense in *Persuasion*, where she explores the deeper emotions, broader experience and riper judgement of maturity and the suspense of a last, or a second, chance. She foregoes describing the maturing experience itself, so important in her previous novels except *Mansfield Park*, and she plays down the direct influence of active social forces in favour of concentrating on the movement of feeling between hero and heroine when their own actions will decide their fates. Never before had Austen expressed strong feeling so effectively, so closely linked human activity with emotional meaning as well as with rationality, so strongly emphasised rightness of feeling – that is, so fully stressed the dual nature of human personality.

The process of self and mutual discovery that Austen describes, with its promise of equality and joyous union between the sexes, can be likened to a movement towards a concept of androgynous being. At the heart of the matter lies a dualistic view of human nature which conceives of the 'masculine' and the 'feminine' as separate aspects of personality that may coexist but may also vary more or less independently in every individual.[18] According to Dijkstra,

> The ideal of the androgyne, as it developed in the late eighteenth century and throughout the nineteenth, expresses one of the most ancient concepts of Western civilization, that of the original, harmonious, sexually integrated constitution of the person before being divided into the artificial, externalized opposites of male and female. (63)

In particular, in the nineteenth century

> adherence to variously developed concepts of the androgynous nature of the soul of man became the affirmation of a balanced personal identity beyond the artificial contrasts created by industrialized bourgeois society to make its system of dominance and submission, struggle and the externalization of selfhood, a self-perpetuating one. With the rise of capitalism the function of sex was becoming more and more a matter of economics. . . . Woman was forced to gather into herself all humanist qualities,

all sweetness and light, all softness and compassion; she became the passive component in a dualism which allowed the male to arrogate to himself all active, aggressive . . . qualities of personality. (63–4)

Austen's ideal of personality appears to follow the model of the androgynous personality: a balance of 'masculine' and 'feminine' characteristics, without either group dominating or subsuming the other. The healthy person would, as Marilyn Farwell observes, have traits identified with both genders:

> Intuition would be as valid a way to knowledge as rationality; but for the androgynous mind . . . intuition would qualify the rational just as the rational would qualify intuition. . . . [T]he androgynous mind would be free from the confining sex stereotypes which society now imposes but would not therefore be asexual or unisexual.[19]

A principal advantage of such a personality, in the form that Austen envisions, is a greater sense of selfhood and individuality: such a person is freer than others to develop his or her values and goals, has access to a wider range of experience, is better acquainted with both the emotional and the rational meaning of human activity, is more aware of the variability, vulnerability and contradictions of human relations, and is thus freer to engage with other human beings along the full range of human responses. Ann Ferguson's model for the ideal androgynous person appears to describe the model for human becoming that Austen dramatises:

> . . . [H]uman beings have a need (or a potential) for free, creative, productive activity which allows them to control their lives in a situation of cooperation with others. Both men and women need to be equally active and independent; with an equal sense of control over their lives; equal opportunity for creative, productive activity; and a sense of meaningful involvement in the community.[20]

Austen's major pairs of lovers – Elizabeth Bennet and Fitzwilliam Darcy, Emma Woodhouse and George Knightley, Anne Elliot and Frederick Wentworth – possess or acquire these qualities as a condition of their readiness for self-fulfilment, reciprocal love and mutual happiness.

In Austen's view, without a radical change in the conventional concept of male and female roles and personality an ideal love relationship is impossible. The cooperation characteristic of such a relationship requires close and direct emotional engagement, a sense of the other party as a person in his or her own right, and a strong continuing sense of mutual dependence, respect and love. Such a relationship between two mature people is one of love between equals. The potential for attaining such a love relationship exists within individual human nature – in its variety and plasticity – but it is a potential at odds with the dominant structure of social relationships. In *Persuasion* again, and most determinedly, Austen dramatises the possibility that individuals may attain that ideal relationship despite such obstruction. Moreover, since in *Persuasion* the offending society is less stable, less vigorous than heretofore (witness the decay of the patriarchal family), the hope for broader social change is implicitly greater.

Notes and References

Chapter 1: Introduction

1. Within the last twenty years see, for example, W. Allen, 'Jane Austen', in W. Heath (ed.), *Discussions of Jane Austen* (Boston, Mass.: Heath, 1961) pp. 51–7; P. Beer, *Reader, I Married Him* (London: Macmillan, 1974); F. W. Bradbrook, *Jane Austen and Her Predecessors* (Cambridge University Press, 1967); J. Brown, *Jane Austen's Novels* (Cambridge, Mass.: Harvard University Press, 1979); L. Brown, *Bits of Ivory* (Baton Rouge, La.: Louisiana State University Press, 1973); D. Bush, *Jane Austen* (New York: Macmillan, 1975); M. Butler, *Jane Austen and the War of Ideas* (Oxford University Press, 1975); D. Cecil, *A Portrait of Jane Austen* (London: Constable, 1978); P. DeRose, *Jane Austen and Samuel Johnson* (Washington, DC: University Press of America, 1980); D. Donoghue, 'A View of "Mansfield Park" ', in B. C. Southam (ed.), *Critical Essays on Jane Austen* (London: Routledge & Kegan Paul, 1968) pp. 39–59; R. Donovan, 'The Mind of Jane Austen', in J. Weinsheimer (ed.), *Jane Austen Today* (Athens, Ga.: University of Georgia Press, 1975) pp. 109–27; A. Duckworth, *The Improvement of the Estate* (Baltimore, Md.: Johns Hopkins Press, 1971); J. M. Duffy, Jr, 'Moral Integrity and Moral Anarchy in *Mansfield Park*', *ELH*, 23 (1956) 71–91, and 'The Politics of Love: Marriage and the Good Society in *Pride and Prejudice*', *University of Windsor Review*, 11 (1976) 5–26; J. Kennard, *Victims of Convention* (Hamden, Conn.: Archon Books, 1978) ch. 1; M. Krieger, *The Classic Vision* (Baltimore, Md.: Johns Hopkins Press, 1971) pp. 221–43; A. W. Litz, *Jane Austen* (New York: Oxford University Press, 1965); T. Lovell, 'Jane Austen and the Gentry', in D. Laurenson (ed.), *The Sociology of Literature* (University of Keele, 1978) pp. 15–37; D. Mansell, *The Novels of Jane Austen* (London: Macmillan, 1973); H. Mews, *Frail Vessels* (London: Athlone Press, 1969) ch. 4; K. Moler, *Jane Austen's Art of Allusion* (Lincoln, Neb.: University of Nebraska Press, 1968) 'Introduction'; D. Monaghan, *Jane Austen: Structure and Social Vision* (London: Macmillan, 1980); J. Nardin, *Those Elegant Decorums* (Albany, NY: State University of New York Press, 1973); J. Odmark, *An Understanding of Jane Austen's Novels* (Oxford: Basil Blackwell, 1981); G. Ryle, 'Jane Austen and the Moralists', in Southam, *Critical Essays*, pp. 106–22; Southam, '*Sanditon*: the Seventh Novel', in J. McMaster (ed.), *Jane Austen's Achievement* (New York: Barnes & Noble, 1976) pp. 1–26; H. Steeves, *Before Jane Austen* (New York: Holt, Rinehart & Winston, 1965) ch. xix; J. Stewart, 'Tradition and Miss Austen', in Southam, *Critical Essays*, pp. 123–35; D. Stone, 'Victorian Feminism and the Nineteenth-Century Novel', *Women's Studies*, 1 (1972) 69–72; S. Tave, *Some Words of*

Jane Austen (University of Chicago Press, 1973); I. Watt, 'Serious Reflections on *The Rise of the Novel*', *Novel*, 1 (1968) 205–18; J. Wiesenfarth, *The Errand of Form* (New York: Fordham University Press, 1967); A. Wilson, 'Evil in the English Novel', *Kenyon Review*, 29 (1967) 167–94.

2. D. W. Harding, 'Regulated Hatred: An Aspect of the Work of Jane Austen', in Heath, op. cit., pp. 41–50; M. Mudrick, *Jane Austen: Irony as Defense and Discovery* (Princeton University Press, 1952).

3. For example, see F. O'Connor, 'Jane Austen: The Flight from Fancy', in Heath, op. cit., p. 68; D. Van Ghent, *The English Novel* (New York: Harper, 1961) p. 100; M. Schorer, 'The Humiliation of Emma Woodhouse', in I. Watt (ed.), *Jane Austen: A Collection of Essays* (Englewood Cliffs, NJ: Prentice-Hall, 1963) p. 105; Mansell, op. cit., pp. 112–15; L. Lerner, *The Truthtellers* (New York: Shocken Books, 1967) p. 164; Y. Gooneratne, *Jane Austen* (Cambridge University Press, 1970) p. 18; N. Auerbach, 'O Brave New World: Evolution and Revolution in *Persuasion*', *ELH*, 39 (1972) 126; S. Siefert, *The Dilemma of the Talented Heroine* (Montreal: Eden Press, 1978) p. 66; and J. Newton, *Women, Power, and Subversion* (Athens, Ga.: University of Georgia Press, 1981) 'Introduction' and ch. 2. See also R. Polhemus, *Comic Faith* (University of Chicago Press, 1980) pp. 27–30; and J. Sherry, '*Pride and Prejudice*: The Limits of Society', *SEL 1500–1900*, 19 (1979) 609–22.

4. H. W. Garrod, 'Jane Austen: A Depreciation', in Heath, op. cit., p. 34.

5. Anthony Burgess, 'The Book is Not for Reading,' *New York Times Book Review*, 4 Dec. 1966, p. 1.

6. Frank Bradbrook, *Jane Austen: Emma* (London: Edward Arnold, 1961) p. 13.

7. Extract from G. H. Lewes, 'The Lady Novelists', in Southam (ed.), *Jane Austen: The Critical Heritage* (London: Routledge & Kegan Paul, 1968) p. 141.

8. Beer, op. cit., p. 25. See also J. Brown, op. cit., pp. 156–64, 170; Butler, op. cit., pp. 1–3; Cecil, op. cit., p. 68; H. Corsa, 'A Fair but Frozen Maid: A Study of Jane Austen's *Emma*', *Literature and Psychology*, 19 (1969) 101–21; and E. Figes, *Patriarchal Attitudes* (New York: Stein & Day, 1970) p. 159; Kennard, op. cit., pp. 13, 23; Mews, op. cit., pp. 42, 47, 60; Monaghan, 'Jane Austen and the Position of Women', in D. Monaghan (ed.), *Jane Austen in a Social Context* (London: Macmillan, 1981) pp. 105–21; S. Myers, 'Womanhood in Jane Austen's Novels', *Novel*, 3 (1970) 225–32; E. Steeves, 'Pre-Feminism in Some Eighteenth-Century Novels', *Texas Quarterly*, 16 (1973) 52; H. Steeves, op. cit., pp. 376–8; Stone, op. cit., pp. 70–2; J. Todd, *Women's Friendship in Literature* (New York: Columbia University Press, 1980) pp. 268–71; and A. Zeman, *Presumptuous Girls* (London: Weidenfeld & Nicolson, 1977) pp. 27–9.

9. M. Wilson, *Jane Austen and Some Contemporaries* (London: Cresset Press, 1938) pp. 34–42.

10. L. Trilling, 'Mansfield Park', in *The Opposing Self* (New York: Viking, 1959) pp. 209–10; D. Daiches, 'Jane Austen, Karl Marx, and the Aristocratic Dance', *American Scholar*, 17 (1948) 289–90; and P. Thomson, *The Victorian Heroine* (London: Oxford University Press, 1956) pp. 58–9.

11. Mary Ellmann, *Thinking About Women* (New York: Harcourt, Brace and World, 1968) pp. 42, 211–12.

12. Robert Donovan, '*Mansfield Park* and Jane Austen's Moral Universe', in *The Shaping Vision* (Ithaca, NY: Cornell University Press, 1966) pp. 153–4.

13. For example, see Auerbach, 'O Brave New World', p. 126, and the chapter

on *Pride and Prejudice* in *Communities of Women* (Cambridge, Mass.: Harvard University Press, 1978); A. Chandler, ' "A Pair of Fine Eyes": Jane Austen's Treatment of Sex', *Studies in the Novel*, 7 (1975) 98; C. Heilbrun, *Toward a Recognition of Androgyny* (New York: Knopf, 1973) pp. 74–8; M. Hummel, 'Emblematic Charades and the Observant Woman in *Mansfield Park*', *TSLL*, 15 (1973) 253; D. C. Measham, 'Sentiment and Sentimental Psychology in Jane Austen', *Renaissance and Modern Studies*, 16 (1972) 79; and G. Wagner, *Five for Freedom: A Study of Feminism in Fiction* (Rutherford, NJ: Fairleigh Dickinson University Press, 1973) p. 41.

14. Lloyd Brown, 'Jane Austen and the Feminist Tradition', *NCF*, 28 (1973) 321–38.

15. Alison Sulloway, 'Emma Woodhouse and *A Vindication of the Rights of Women*', *Wordsworth Circle*, 7 (1976) 320–32.

16. Ellen Moers, *Literary Women* (New York: Doubleday, 1976) pp. 70–1.

17. Marian Fowler, 'The Feminist Bias of *Pride and Prejudice*', *Dalhousie Review*, 57 (1977) 47–64.

18. Susan MacDonald, 'Passivity and the Female Role in *Pride and Prejudice*', *Women and Literature*, 6 (1978) 36, 44.

19. Warren Roberts, *Jane Austen and the French Revolution* (New York: St Martin's Press, 1979) pp. 155–202. Relevant discussion also appears in Siefert, op. cit., and in L. Robinson, 'Why Marry Mr. Collins?' in *Sex, Class, and Culture* (Bloomington, Ind.: Indiana University Press, 1978) pp. 178–99.

20. P. Spacks, *The Female Imagination* (New York: Knopf, 1975).

21. P. Spacks, *Imagining a Self: Autobiography and Novel in Eighteenth-Century England* (Cambridge, Mass.: Harvard University Press, 1976).

22. Sandra Gilbert and Susan Gubar, *The Madwoman in the Attic: The Woman Writer and the Nineteenth-Century Literary Imagination* (New Haven, Conn.: Yale University Press, 1979).

23. Susan Gubar, 'Sane Jane and the Critics: "Professions and Falsehood" ', *Novel*, 8 (1975) 250–1.

24. Similarly, in Lovell's view, 'Paradoxically, Jane Austen endorsed the narrow view of women in the conservative ideology of her novels while simultaneously denying it in the act of writing them', but Lovell does not detect anxiety, guilt or outrage as a cause or effect (op. cit., p. 35); Wagner concludes that women, in a male world, are 'forced into some self-protective dissimulation and that cunning which is the analogy of art' (op. cit., p. 45); and Newton finds in *Pride and Prejudice* evidence of the 'subversion, indirection, and disguise [which] are natural tactics of the resisting weak' (op. cit., 9), although Elizabeth Bennet's rebellion finally 'works in the interests of tradition' (79) which require that she 'dwindle by degrees into a wife' (84).

25. Monaghan, in a review of 'recent feminist interpretations' of Austen ('Jane Austen and the Feminist Critics', *Room of One's Own*, 4 [1979] 34–9), found that 'feminist critics' tend: (1) to reshape the facts known of her life to present an image of 'the woman as artist as victim'; (2) to interpret from her failure to live up to the 'ideals of modern feminism' that 'she tamely accepted female subservience'; and (3) to fail to understand that the conception of marriage in Austen's society undercuts both the position that she 'accepted female subordination' and the position, as offered by L. Brown, that she was a feminist in the liberationist sense of the word. The Austen that Monaghan approves of appears in Spacks's treatment in *The Female Imagination*

– 'a complex woman who is at once fully convinced of the innate equality of women and of her society's tendency to underrate and dehumanize them and yet is confident that women can fulfill themselves within this society' – and it is this Austen, essentially, that the present study describes. In 'Jane Austen and the Social Critics: Recent Trends', *English Studies in Canada*, 2 (1976) 280–7, Monaghan describes the role of women as 'one of the least satisfactorily examined aspects of Jane Austen's work'.

26. P. Spacks, 'Muted Discord: Generational Conflict in Jane Austen', in Monaghan, *Jane Austen in a Social Context*, p. 177.

27. Lee Edwards, 'The Labors of Psyche: Toward a Theory of Female Heroism', *Critical Inquiry*, 6 (1979) 45, 49.

28. S. Goldberg, *The Inevitability of Patriarchy* (New York: William Morrow, 1973) p. 30.

29. A Rich, *Of Woman Born* (New York: Norton, 1976) p. 57.

30. Goldberg, op. cit., p. 78.

31. K. Sacks, 'Engels Revisited: Women, the Organization of Production, and Private Property', in M. Rosaldo and L. Lamphere (eds), *Woman, Culture, and Society* (Stanford University Press, 1974) pp. 208, 220.

32. S. Ortner, 'Is Female to Male as Nature is to Culture?' in Rosaldo and Lamphere, ibid., pp. 72–80.

33. L. Stone, *The Family, Sex and Marriage in England 1500–1800* (New York: Harper and Row, 1977) p. 660.

34. See also H. Payne, rev. art., 'The Eighteenth-Century Family: An Elusive Object', *Eighteenth-Century Life*, 5 (1978) 48–61; G. Schochet, *Patriarchalism in Political Thought* (New York: Basic Books, 1975); E. Shorter, *The Making of the Modern Family* (New York: Basic Books, 1975); and R. Trumbach, *The Rise of the Egalitarian Family* (New York: Academic Press, 1978). M. Burgan discusses Austen's 'implicit critique of the patriarchal hierarchy as a proper foundation for social organization' in 'Mr. Bennet and the Failures of Fatherhood in Jane Austen's Novels', *JEGP*, 74 (1975) 536–52.

35. J. Spence and R. Helmreich, *Masculinity & Femininity* (Austin, Texas: University of Texas Press, 1978) pp. 3–4, 17–18, 118.

36. In recent years the traditional view has been vigorously disputed. One objection is that research on the subject favours a 'nurture' theory rather than a 'nature' theory (Figes, op. cit., p. 9). Another is that a behaviour may reflect 'a very general cultural theme. Since women must work within a social system that obscures their goals and interests, they are apt to develop ways of seeing, feeling, and acting that seem to be "intuitive" and unsystematic.' Furthermore, 'cultural stereotypes order the observer's own perceptions' (Rosaldo, 'Woman, Culture, and Society: A Theoretical Overview', in Rosaldo and Lamphere, op. cit., p. 30). A third objection emphasises the problem of discriminating between biological woman and cultural woman (C. Thompson, 'Cultural Pressures in the Psychology of Women', in J. Miller [ed.], *Psychoanalysis and Women* [New York: Brunner/Mazel, 1973] p. 61). J. Chafetz says that 'given present evidence, no precise line between organism and environment, gender and role, can be drawn' (*Masculine/Feminine or Human?* [Itasca, Ill.: F. E. Peacock, 1974] p. 4). Similarly, E. Janeway insists 'that a large part (at least) of . . . [the] psychological differences between the sexes . . . are the result of learned behavior, of social training and

acculturation' (*Man's World, Woman's Place* [New York: William Morrow, 1971] p. 91).

37. See L. Agress, *The Feminine Irony* (Rutherford, NJ: Fairleigh Dickinson University Press, 1978) pp. 35–6; L. Appignanesi, *Femininity and the Creative Imagination* (London: Vision Press, 1973) pp. 6–10; J. Bardwick, *Psychology of Women* (New York: Harper & Row, 1971) p. 100; M. Daly, *Beyond God the Father* (Boston, Mass.: Beacon, 1973) p. 15; Ellmann, op. cit., p. 87; V. Gornick and B. Moran (eds), *Woman in Sexist Society* (New York: Basic Books, 1971) p. xiii; Figes, op. cit., pp. 149–50; K. Millett, *Sexual Politics* (New York: Doubleday, 1970) p. 26; Spence and Helmreich, op. cit., pp. 14, 17–19; and Thompson, op. cit., p. 57.

38. See Agress, op. cit., pp. 57–67; N. Chodorow, 'Family Structure and Feminine Personality', in Rosaldo and Lamphere, op. cit., pp. 43–66; Figes, op. cit., pp. 24–6, 160; and Gornick and Moran, op. cit., p. xii.

39. See Chafetz, op. cit., p. 109; Figes, op. cit., pp. 21–2; Spence and Helmreich, op. cit., pp. 5–6.

40. See Daly, op. cit., pp. 23–4; Janeway, op. cit., pp. 98, 100; Rosaldo, in Rosaldo and Lamphere, op. cit., pp. 28–9; and Thompson, op. cit., p. 61.

41. Chafetz, op. cit., p. 165.

42. Chafetz, op. cit., pp. 166–7; Daly, op. cit., p. 172.

43. R. Sampson, *The Psychology of Power* (New York: Pantheon Books, 1966) p. 233.

44. See J. Calder, *Women and Marriage in Victorian Fiction* (New York: Oxford University Press, 1976) p. 182; Millett, op. cit., pp. 39, 43; and I. Tayler and G. Luria, 'Gender and Genre: Women in British Romantic Literature', in M. Springer (ed.), *What Manner of Woman* (New York University Press, 1977) pp. 98–9.

45. See also Daly, op. cit., p. 143; Figes, op. cit., p. 159; and Thompson, op. cit., pp. 58–9.

46. See R. Seidenberg, 'For the Future – Equity?' in Miller, op. cit., p. 345.

47. Rich, op. cit., p. 57.

48. Thompson, op. cit., p. 57.

49. F. Dell, *Love in the Machine Age* (New York: Octagon Books, 1973) pp. 28–9.

50. See Figes, op. cit., pp. 76, 87, 176.

51. Chafetz, op. cit., p. 222; also see Thompson, op. cit., p. 61.

52. K. Horney, 'The Flight from Womanhood', in Miller, op. cit., p. 5.

53. See Mews, op. cit., chs 1–2; M. Benkovitz, 'Some Observations on Women's Concept of Self in the 18th Century', pp. 37–54, and R. Halsband, 'Women and Literature in 18th Century England', pp. 55–72, in P. Fritz and R. Morton (eds), *Woman in the 18th Century and Other Essays* (Toronto: Hakkert, 1976); S. Rowbotham, *Hidden from History* (London: Pluto Press, 1973) chs 3, 4; B. Schnorrenberg, with J. Hunter, 'The Eighteenth-Century Englishwoman', in B. Kanner (ed.), *The Women of England* (Hamden, Conn.: Archon Books, 1979) pp. 183–228; E. Steeves, op. cit., p. 222; and F. Vigman, *Beauty's Triumph* (Boston, Mass.: Christopher Publishing House, 1966) p. 30.

54. Schnorrenberg, op. cit., p. 202; see Roberts, op. cit., p. 155. For discussion of Wollstonecraft, see A. Kleinbaum, 'Women in the Age of Light', in R. Bridenthal and C. Koonz (eds), *Becoming Visible: Women in European History*

(Boston, Mass.: Houghton Mifflin, 1977) p. 231; B. G. MacCarthy, *The Later Women Novelists 1744–1818* (Dublin: Cork University Press, 1947) pp. 189–96; M. Quinlan, *Victorian Prelude* (New York: Columbia University Press, 1941) pp. 139–43; Sheila Rowbotham, *Women, Resistance and Revolution* (New York: Pantheon Books, 1972) pp. 40–5; E. Steeves, op. cit., p. 231; Sulloway, op. cit., p. 320; and Vigman, op. cit., pp. 30–5.

55. E. Steeves, op. cit., pp. 55–6.

56. See Moers, op. cit., p. 125, and Spacks, *Imagining a Self*, ch. 3. Elaine Showalter, in *A Literature of Their Own* (Princeton University Press, 1977), omits eighteenth-century women novelists from her study of the literary subculture of female writers because, in her opinion, they 'refused to deal with a professional role, or had a negative orientation toward it' (18) and did 'not see their writing as an aspect of their female experience, or as an expression of it' (19).

57. J. Richetti, 'The Portrayal of Women in Restoration and Eighteenth-Century English Literature', in Springer, op. cit., p. 67.

58. Lloyd Brown, 'Jane Austen', pp. 321–2; see also M. LeGates, 'The Cult of Womanhood in Eighteenth-Century Thought', *Eighteenth-century Studies*, 10 (1976) 21–39.

59. See discussions by MacCarthy, op. cit., p. 86; Tayler and Luria, op. cit., p. 106; and Zeman, op. cit., pp. 4, 10.

60. K. Rogers, 'Inhibitions on Eighteenth-Century Women Novelists: Elizabeth Inchbald and Charlotte Smith', *Eighteenth-Century Studies*, 11 (1977) 63.

61. Rogers, 'Richardson's Empathy with Women', in A. Diamond and L. Edwards (eds), *The Authority of Experience* (Amherst, Mass.: University of Massachusetts Press, 1977) pp. 128–9.

62. Rogers, 'Inhibitions', p. 64.

63. See discussions in Agress, op. cit., ch. 2, also pp. 114–21; Quinlan, op. cit., p. 143; Spacks, *Imagining a Self*, pp. 58–60; and E. Steeves, op. cit., pp. 50–1.

64. Spacks, *Imagining a Self*, p. 63.

Chapter 2: Jane Austen and the 'Drama of Woman'

1. Gooneratne, *Jane Austen*, p. 26. See Q. D. Leavis, 'A Critical Theory of Jane Austen's Writings', *Scrutiny*, 12 (1944) 104–19.

2. The fullest discussion of Austen's treatment of the sexual is by A. Chandler ' "A Pair of Fine Eyes": Jane Austen's Treatment of Sex', *Studies in the Novel*, 7 (1975) 88–103. See also Bowen, 'Jane Austen', in D. Verschoyle (ed.), *The English Novelists* (New York: Harcourt, Brace, 1936) p. 105; J. Brown, *Jane Austen's Novels*, pp. 12–15; J. Fergus, 'Sex and Social Life in Jane Austen's Novels', in Monaghan, *Jane Austen in a Social Context*, pp. 66–85; G. Gould, 'The Gate Scene at Sotherton in *Mansfield Park*', *Literature and Psychology*, 20 (1970) 75–8; J. Hagstrum, *Sex and Sensibility* (University of Chicago Press, 1980) pp. 268–74; Mansell, *Novels of Jane Austen*, p. 98; J. McMaster, *Jane Austen on Love* (University of Victoria, 1978); N. Sherry, *Jane Austen* (London: Evans Brothers, 1966) pp. 100–1.

3. G. Luria, rev. of *Charlotte Brontë: The Self Conceived*, by H. Moglen, and *Jane*

Austen and the War of Ideas, by M. Butler, in *Signs*, 4 (1978) 379.

4.   Spacks, *Female Imagination*, p. 14.
5.   See Daiches, 'General Editor's Introduction', in Calder, *Women and Marriage in Victorian Fiction*, p. 9; Spacks, *Female Imagination*, pp. 319–22; and G. Stewart, *A New Mythos: The Novel of the Artist as Heroine 1877–1977* (St Albans, Vt.: Eden Press, 1977) pp. 15, 40.
6.   Rowbotham, *Women, Resistance and Revolution*, p. 44.
7.   For discussion of Fanny Burney and of Austen's ties with other late eighteenth-century women novelists, see Bradbrook, *Austen and Her Predecessors*, ch. 6; L. Brown, 'Jane Austen', pp. 321–38; E. Copeland, 'Money in the Novels of Fanny Burney', *Studies in the Novel*, 8 (1976) 24–37; R. Cutting, 'Defiant Women: The Growth of Feminism in Fanny Burney's Novels', *SEL 1500–1900*, 17 (1977) 519–30; P. Glassman, 'Acts of Enclosure', *Hudson Review*, 30 (1977) 142–4; G. Kelly, *The English Jacobin Novel 1780–1805* (Clarendon: Oxford University Press, 1976); MacCarthy, *Later Women Novelists 1744–1818*, passim; Mews, *Frail Vessels*, ch. 3; Moers, *Literary Women*, passim: Moler, *Art of Allusion*, passim, and *'Pride and Prejudice*: Jane Austen's "Patrician Hero" '*, SEL 1500–1900*, 7 (1967) 491–508; Rogers, 'Inhibitions', pp. 63–78; Spacks, *Imagining a Self* and *Female Imagination*; S. Staves, *'Evelina*; or, Female Difficulties', *MP*, 73 (1976) 368–81; E. Steeves, 'Pre-Feminism', pp. 48–57; H. Steeves, *Before Jane Austen*, chs XIII, XVIII and XIX; Tayler and Luria, 'Gender and Genre', pp. 98–121; and Zeman, *Presumptuous Girls*, pp. 3–29.
8.   Cutting, op. cit., p. 528.
9.   H. Steeves, op. cit., pp. 222–4; also see Cutting, ibid., pp. 519–30.
10. L. Brown, 'Jane Austen', p. 332.
11. Moler argues that the 'Austen novel consistently tends to define its vision of life in relation to literature' (*Art of Allusion*, p. 1).
12. E. Steeves, op. cit., p. 54.
13. W. Magee, 'The Happy Marriage: The Influence of Charlotte Smith on Jane Austen', *Studies in the Novel*, 7 (1975) 120.
14. See also K. Ellis, 'Charlotte Smith's Subversive Gothic', *Feminist Studies*, 3 (1976) 51; and H. Steeves, op. cit., p. 317.
15. Rogers, 'Inhibitions', p. 69; Bradbrook, *Austen and Her Predecessors*, pp. 110–12.
16. Spacks, *Imagining A Self*, p. 71.
17. For example, P. Beer says that Austen 'appears neither to have . . . [read *A Vindication*] nor to have thought at all along the same lines' (*Reader, I Married Him*, p. 25); H. Steeves concludes that she may have been influenced by Wollstonecraft's early writing because of a similarity of views but not by the later writings because of their aggressive and radical character (op. cit., pp. 379–81); and L. Brown and Sulloway argue for a significant connection between the two on the basis of textual parallels (L. Brown, 'Jane Austen', pp. 327–8; Sulloway, 'Emma Woodhouse', p. 320).
18. Rowbotham, *Women, Resistance and Revolution*, p. 42.
19. See the discussion by L. Brown, 'Jane Austen', pp. 324–7.
20. See discussions by Auerbach, 'O Brave New World', pp. 124–7; L. Brown, 'Jane Austen', pp. 328–32; E. Flexner, *Mary Wollstonecraft: A Biography* (New York: Coward, McCann and Geoghegan, 1972) pp. 155–61; and Sulloway,

op. cit., pp. 320–2.

21. Spacks, *Imagining a Self*, p. 89.
22. E. Steeves, op. cit., p. 48.
23. J. Mitchell, *Woman's Estate* (New York: Pantheon Books, 1971) pp. 65–6.
24. S. de Beauvoir, *The Second Sex*, trans. and ed. H. M. Parshley (New York: Bantam Books, 1970) p. 103.
25. A. Wright, *Jane Austen's Novels* (New York: Oxford University Press, 1953) p. 10.
26. One may answer Calder's question – 'Was there any other novelist in the century whose most important theme concerned the "mutual likeness" of men and women?' (*Woman and Marriage* p. 188) – by citing Austen. Polhemus, in *Comic Faith*, posits that *Emma* expresses a 'comic faith' because Austen, despite the inadequacy and constraints of Emma's patriarchal society (p. 27), 'clearly is celebrating the potential and relative freedom of . . . [her] life and giving her audience and herself an image of hope' (p. 42).
27. M. Murray (ed.), *A House of Good Proportion* (New York: Simon & Schuster, 1973) p. 20.
28. B. Hardy, *A Reading of Jane Austen* (London: Peter Owen, 1975) p. 191.
29. 'Letter 141', *Jane Austen's Letters to Her Sister Cassandra and Others*, ed. R. W. Chapman, 2nd edn (London: Oxford University Press, 1952) p. 483.
30. See discussion in B. Brophy, 'Jane Austen and the Stuarts', in Southam, *Critical Essays*, p. 27; Calder, op. cit., p. 25; Copeland, op. cit., p. 25; Duckworth, *Improvement*, pp. 29–30; Hummel, 'Emblematic Charades', p. 251; Moers, *Literary Women*, pp. 67–76; J. Rockwell, *Facts in Fiction* (London: Routledge & Kegan Paul, 1974) p. 85; Schorer, 'Pride Unprejudiced', *Kenyon Review*, 18 (1956) 72–91; Van Ghent, *The English Novel*, pp. 100–2.
31. Janeway, *Man's World, Woman's Place*, p. 116.
32. See Auerbach, 'O Brave New World', pp. 124–5.
33. de Beauvoir, op. cit., p. 271.
34. Daly labels this idea the theory of the 'two kingdoms' (*Beyond God the Father* p. 127).
35. Quoted in R. Miles, *The Fiction of Sex* (London: Vision Press, 1974) p. 29.
36. Tave, *Some Words*, p. 209.
37. L. Brown, *Bits of Ivory*, p. 45.
38. D. Bakan, *The Duality of Human Existence* (Chicago, Ill.: Rand McNally, 1966) p. 100.
39. See discussion by R. Heilman, '*E pluribus unum*: parts and whole in *Pride and Prejudice*', in J. Halperin (ed.), *Jane Austen: Bicentenary Essays* (Cambridge University Press, 1975) pp. 131–9.
40. D. Devlin, *Jane Austen and Education* (New York: Barnes & Noble, 1975) p. 75.
41. R. D. Laing, *The Divided Self* (London: Tavistock Publications, 1960) p. 43.
42. Clyde Ryals, 'Being and Doing in *Mansfield Park*', *Archiv*, 206 (1970) 346.
43. R. D. Laing, *Self and Others* (New York: Pantheon Books, 1969) p. 133.
44. J. Halperin concludes that 'the specific formula governing many Victorian novels . . . the ordeal leading from egoism to self-discovery, actually begins with Jane Austen', *Egoism and Self-Discovery in the Victorian Novel* (New York: Burt Franklin, 1974) p. 3.
45. Spacks, *Female Imagination*, p. 114.
46. Laing, *Self and Others*, p. 70. See B. Paris's instructive study of the 'self-actualizing' character, who attempts to be 'fully human', in *A Psychological*

Approach to Fiction (Bloomington, Ind.: Indiana University Press, 1974).

47. Bakan, op. cit., pp. 14–15, 56.
48. See the discussion of the use of the term 'androgyny' by Spence and Helmreich, *Masculinity & Femininity*, p. 109, ft. 1; and by Rich, *Of Woman Born*, pp. 76–7, ft.
49. B. Dijkstra, 'The Androgyne in Nineteenth-Century Art and Literature', *Comparative Literature*, 26 (1974) 68.
50. Heilbrun discusses 'the absolute androgyny of Jane Austen's genius' (*Toward a Recognition of Androgyny*, pp. 76–7). Todd says that Austen discovered the possibility of an androgynous ideal in a woman which could be developed through female friendships, in 'Female Friendship in Jane Austen's Novels', *Journal of the Rutgers University Library*, 39 (1977) 29–43.
51. Daly, op. cit., p. 42.
52. See N. Sherry, op. cit., pp. 92–4. In 'The Business of Marrying and Mothering', in McMaster, (ed.), *Jane Austen's Achievement*, pp. 27–43, L. Brown offers a vigorous counter-argument to this view. My basic point of disagreement is with Brown's assumption that Austen held an 'essentially bleak vision of the individual and society' (p. 38), so that he sees 'connubial felicity and the social and individual improvement which it enshrines at the end of the novels' functioning only 'as an ironic counterpoint to the dominant social realities' (p. 40).
53. O. Schreiner, *The Letters of Olive Schreiner 1876–1920*, ed. S. C. Cronwright-Schreiner (Boston: Little, Brown, 1924) pp. 151–2.
54. Murray, op. cit., p. 20.

Chapter 3: Jane Austen's Fiction Before 1810

 1. Litz, *Jane Austen*, p. 37.
 2. For discussion of their composition see Leavis, 'A Critical Theory of Jane Austen's Writings (II): "Lady Susan" into "Mansfield Park" ', *Scrutiny*, 10 (1941) 116; Litz, op. cit., p. 40; and Southam, *Jane Austen's Literary Manuscripts* (London: Oxford University Press, 1964) ch. 3.
 3. J. Rees, *Jane Austen, Woman and Writer* (New York: St Martin's Press, 1976) p. 42; H. Steeves, *Before Jane Austen*, p. 353.
 4. Mudrick, *Jane Austen*, pp. 138–9; R. Farrar, cited by Litz, op. cit., p. 39.
 5. Bush, *Jane Austen*, p. 54; J. Levine, '*Lady Susan*: Jane Austen's Character of the Merry Widow', *SEL 1500–1900*, 1 (1961) 24; Litz, op. cit., p. 41.
 6. Butler, *Jane Austen and the War of Ideas*, p. 180.
 7. Bush, op. cit., p. 54; G. Gorer, 'Poor Honey: Some Notes on Jane Austen and Her Mother', *London Magazine*, 4 (1957) 35; Butler, op. cit., p. 122.
 8. Mudrick, *Jane Austen*, p. 138; L. Kronenberger, 'Jane Austen: *Lady Susan* and *Pride and Prejudice*', in *The Polished Surface* (New York: Knopf, 1969) p. 137.
 9. Rees, op. cit., p. 43; Cecil, *Portrait of Jane Austen*, p. 84; W. A. Craik, *Jane Austen: The Six Novels* (London: Methuen, 1966) p. 5; Litz, op. cit., p. 44.
10. H. Steeves, op. cit., p. 352; Devlin, *Austen and Education*, p. 36; Leavis, 'A Critical Theory of Jane Austen's Writings (II): "Lady Susan" into "Mansfield Park" (ii)', *Scrutiny*, 10 (1942) 284.

11. Mudrick, *Jane Austen*, p. 127.
12. Lloyd Brown, *Bits of Ivory*, p. 153.
13. Rosaldo, 'Woman, Culture and Society', p. 21.
14. Litz, op. cit., p. 136.
15. See A. Adler, 'Sex', in Miller *Psychoanalysis and Women*, p. 35; Chafetz, *Masculine/Feminine*, p. 75; L. Ovesey, 'Masculine Aspirations in Women', *Psychiatry*, 19 (1956) 341–2; J. Sherman, *On the Psychology of Women* (Springfield, Ill.: Charles C. Thomas, 1971) pp. 48–9; and Thompson, 'Cultural Pressures in the Psychology of Women,' pp. 61–2.
16. Spacks, *Female Imagination*, p. 322.
17. See Calder, *Women and Marriage*, pp. 25, 44–8.
18. See discussion by Southam, *Austen's Literary Manuscripts*, chs 2–3.
19. Mansell, *Novels of Jane Austen*, p. 12.
20. See Southam, *Austen's Literary Manuscripts*, p. 62.
21. Litz accounts for this last point by the fact that 'The Watsons' is 'conceived in the barren middle-period of Jane Austen's career', whereas the 'scaffolding of characters and situations' in *Pride and Prejudice* harks back to the 1790s (op. cit., p. 87).

Chapter 4: *Sense and Sensibility:* The Risk of Being Female

1. For discussion of possible sources, see Bradbrook, *Austen and Her Predecessors*, pp. 42–9; and Butler, *Jane Austen and the War of Ideas*, p. 101.
2. Compare, for example, Butler, op. cit., pp. 182–3, 192, 194; H. Babb, *Jane Austen's Novels* (Columbus, Ohio: Ohio State University Press, 1962) p. 53; and Mansell, *Novels of Jane Austen*, p. 61.
3. See, for example, L. Brown, 'Marrying and Mothering', pp. 33–6; Bush, *Jane Austen*, p. 83; Duckworth, ' "Spillikins, paper, ships, riddles, conundrums, and cards": games in Jane Austen's life and fiction', in Halperin, *Jane Austen: Bicentenary Essays*, p. 285; L. P. Hartley, 'Jane Austen and the Abyss', *Essays by Divers Hands*, 35 (1969) 97–100; Lerner, *Truthtellers*, pp. 160–6; S. Morgan, *In the Meantime: Character and Perception in Jane Austen's Fiction* (University of Chicago Press, 1980) pp. 111–12; Nardin, *Decorums*, p. 24; and Rees, *Jane Austen, Woman and Writer*, p. 131.
4. A. Duckworth, 'Prospects and Retrospects', in Weinsheimer, *Jane Austen Today*, p. 14.
5. The first quotation is from Mudrick, *Jane Austen*, p. 91, and the second is from Mudrick, 'Jane Austen's drawing-room', in Halperin, op. cit., p. 251.
6. Henriettta Ten Harmsel, *Jane Austen: A Study in Fictional Conventions* (The Hague: Mouton, 1964) p. 47; see Hartley, op. cit., p. 97; Nardin, *Decorums*, pp. 30–5; and Rees, op. cit., p. 131.
7. Ten Harmsel, op. cit., p. 47, Bush, op. cit., p. 83, and Rees, op. cit., p. 131; Butler, op. cit., pp. 190–2, and Lerner, op. cit., p. 161; R. Garis, 'Learning Experience and Change', in Southam, *Critical Essays*, p. 66; and Litz, as cited in Duckworth, 'Prospects and Retrospects', p. 14.
8. The problem is described in several ways: a ruthless analysis of propriety (Lerner, op. cit., p. 164); the 'tensions between the instability of the individual

and the required stabilities of society' (T. Tanner, as cited by Duckworth, 'Prospects and Retrospects', p. 16); the difficulty of preserving one's 'integrity of judgment and feeling' in the face of the demands of a 'voracious social milieu' (Nardin, *Decorums*, p. 24); and the 'precarious situation of the single woman' (L. Brown, 'Marrying and Mothering', p. 33).

9. Duckworth, ' "Spillikins" ', p. 285.

10. Chrisopher Gillie, '*Sense and Sensibility*: an Assessment', *Essays in Criticism*, 9 (1959) 5.

11. Gillie, ibid., p. 8.

12. Chandler, 'A Pair of Fine Eyes', p. 90.

13. Mansell, op. cit., p. 52.

14. Spacks, *Imagining a Self*, p. 85.

15. 'On *Sense and Sensibility*', in Watt, *Jane Austen: A Collection of Essays*, p. 50.

16. MacCarthy, *The Later Women Novelists 1744–1818*, p. 107.

17. Tave, *Some Words*, p. 84.

18. A. McKillop, 'The Context of *Sense and Sensibility*', *Rice Institute Pamphlets*, 44 (1957) 77.

19. Duckworth, *Improvement*, p. 108. See Zeman's discussion of the importance of the rules of courtship, *Presumptuous Girls*, pp. 22–5; see also Fergus, 'Sex and Social Life', pp. 67–71, and J. Gornall, 'Marriage and Property in Jane Austen's Novels', *History Today*, 17 (1967) 811.

20. Tave, *Some Words*, pp. 76–7.

21. Watt, 'On *Sense and Sensibility*', p. 49.

22. H. Hartmann, *Ego Psychology and the Problem of Adaptation* (New York: International Universities Press, 1958) p. 87. Auerbach, in 'Jane Austen and Romantic Imprisonment', in Monaghan, *Jane Austen in a Social Context,* pp. 20, 24, describes the 'sense' that Elinor endorses as 'less general wisdom than . . . [an] acute perception of "the fangs of the tyger" ', a 'seismographic awareness of . . . the reality of others' power'.

23. See recent discussions by J. Brown, *Jane Austen's Novels*, pp. 59–61; A. Banfield, 'The Influence of Place', in Monaghan, *Jane Austen in a Social Context*, pp. 44–7; and, especially, Morgan, op. cit., pp. 8, 113–31.

Chapter 5: *Pride and Prejudice:* No Improper Pride

1. The dance in Austen's novels provides an emblem of the rules and rituals of social behaviour. In *Pride and Prejudice* it also signifies the sexual component in courtship and marriage rituals. Discussion of Austen's use of dance as a metaphor appears in L. Elsbree, 'Jane Austen and the Dance of Fidelity and Complaisance', *NCF*, 15 (1960) 113–36; Daiches, 'Jane Austen, Karl Marx, and the Aristocratic Dance', pp. 289–96; and Gooneratne, *Jane Austen*, pp. 8–11. As Beer observes, sometimes the frankness of reference to dancing and elegant walking as 'essential female allurements' is startling (*Reader, I Married Him*, p. 67). Love and dancing, skill in dancing as a sexual metaphor, and the ball as a metaphor of the marriage market are obviously related; in an observation such as Darcy's that a ball 'is a subject which always makes a lady energetic' (*PP*, 21) they may fuse.

2. Daiches, op. cit., p. 290.
3. See Fowler, 'Feminist Bias of *Pride and Prejudice*', pp. 54–63; and Ten Harmsel, *Jane Austen: A Study in Fictional Conventions*, ch. IV.
4. de Beauvoir, *Second Sex*, p. xxviii.
5. Hardy, *A Reading*, p. 51.
6. Zeman, *Presumptuous Girls*, p. 154.
7. For example: in *Mansfield Park* the gate scene at Sotherton and the foreshadowing in the rehearsals of *Lovers' Vows* of the main characters' eventual sexual roles; and in *Pride and Prejudice* the accounting for the initiation of Darcy's interest in Elizabeth Bennet. See Gould, 'The Gate Scene'.
8. Nardin, *Decorums*, p. 8.
9. See Garis, 'Learning Experience and Change', p. 66, and Zeman, op. cit., p. 154.
10. Hardy, in Hardy and Daiches, 'Jane Austen', in *The English Novel* (London: Sussex Publications, 1976) p. 22.
11. Litz identifies this opposition as the conflict 'between social restraint and the individual will, between tradition and self-expression' (*Jane Austen*, p. 105), and Moler summarises the view of it as a variant of the eighteenth-century 'art – nature' contrast (*Art of Allusion*, p. 75); but the contrast seems to have sharper focus than either of these descriptions provides.
12. Daly, *Beyond God the Father*, p. 127.
13. Babb, *Jane Austen's Novels*, p. 113.
14. Babb, ibid., p. 142. Monaghan (*Jane Austen: Structure and Social Vision*, pp. 66–8) notes that both Elizabeth and Darcy rely on stereotypes but considers that the solution to their problem is the recognition that 'the middle class, the gentry and the nobility are all committed to the ideal of concern for others'.
15. Tave, *Some Words*, p. 155.
16. See Halperin's discussion, *Egoism and Self-Discovery*, p. 7.
17. Babb, op. cit., p. 124.
18. See R. D. Laing, *The Politics of Experience* (New York: Pantheon Books, 1967) chs 1–2.
19. Heilman, '*E pluribus unum*', p. 136.
20. Gooneratne, op. cit.; p. 84.
21. Tave, *Some Words*, p. 139.
22. Theodore Reik, *Psychology of Sex Relations* (New York: Rinehart, 1945) p. 4.
23. Heilbrun, 'Marriage Perceived: English Literature 1873–1941', in Springer, *What Manner of Woman* p. 168.
24. Hardy, *A Reading*, p. 39.
25. Spacks, *Female Imagination*, pp. 120–1.
26. Hardy, *A Reading*, p. 49.
27. Babb, op. cit., p. 141.

Chapter 6: *Mansfield Park:* The Revolt of the 'Feminine' Woman

1. See Bush, *Jane Austen*, p. 109; Craik, *Jane Austen: The Six Novels*, p. 92; Butler, *Jane Austen and the War of Ideas*, pp. 228–9, 247; Duffy, 'Moral Integrity and Moral Anarchy', pp. 73–9; Duckworth, *Improvement*, p. 31; A. Fleishman,

'*Mansfield Park* in Its Time', *NCF*, 22 (1967) 1–16; M. Kinkead-Weekes, 'This Old Maid: Jane Austen Replies to Charlotte Brontë and D. H. Lawrence', *NCF*, 30 (1975) 399–419; Litz, *Jane Austen*, p. 118; D. Lodge, *Language of Fiction* (London: Routledge & Kegan Paul, 1966) p. 97; Lovell, 'Jane Austen and the Gentry', pp. 15, 22–4; Todd, *Women's Friendship*, pp. 247, 271; W. Walling, 'The Glorious Anxiety of Motion: Jane Austen's *Persuasion*', *Wordsworth Circle*, 7 (1976) 333–41.

2. See J. W. Donohue, Jr, 'Ordination and the Divided House at Mansfield Park', *ELH*, 32 (1965) 171, 178; Donovan, *Shaping Vision*, p. 150; M. Lascelles, 'Jane Austen and the novel', in Halperin, *Jane Austen*, p. 238; Mansell, *Novels of Jane Austen*, pp. 127–9; Ryals, 'Being and Doing', pp. 346, 359; Trilling, '*Mansfield Park*', pp. 221–30; Wiesenfarth, *Errand*, ch. 4.

3. Wiesenfarth, *Errand*, p. 86. Of interest also are the arguments of Nardin (*Decorums*, pp. 83, 85, 89) and of C. Chabot ('Jane Austen's Novels: The Vicissitudes of Desire', *American Imago*, 32 [1975] 288–308) that *Mansfield Park* is about the importance of rules and an authority beyond the self in combating the destructive power of feeling or autonomy; and of Moler (*Art of Allusion*, p. 146) that *Mansfield Park* stresses the growth into self-knowledge of its several principal characters. Several critics find flaws of construction or of conception in *Mansfield Park* (e.g., Lerner, *Truthtellers*, pp. 159–60, and R. Brissenden, '*Mansfield Park*: freedom and the family', in Halperin, Jane Austen p. 168). At the extreme R. Farrar describes *Mansfield Park* as 'vitiated throughout by a radical dishonesty', ruined by a 'dualism of motive' ('Jane Austen', *Quarterly Review*, 227 [1917] 20), and Kingsley Amis describes Fanny Price and Edmund Bertram as 'both morally detestable' ('What Became of Jane Austen?', *The Spectator*, 4 Oct 1957, repr. in Watt *Jane Austen: A Collection of Essays*, p. 142).

4. See P. DeRose, 'Hardship, Recollection, and Discipline: Three Lessons in *Mansfield Park*', *Studies in the Novel*, 9 (1977) 261–78; Donohue, op. cit., pp. 171–8; Donovan, *Shaping Vision*, pp. 153, 171; Trilling, '*Mansfield Park*', pp. 225–30; and E. Zimmerman, 'Jane Austen and *Mansfield Park*: A Discrimination of Ironies', *Studies in the Novel*, 1 (1969) 347–56.

5. See J. Burroway, 'The Irony of the Insufferable Prig: *Mansfield Park*', *Critical Quarterly*, 9 (1967) 135–8. Tave describes Fanny as redeeming her society by defending personal integrity in making a marriage choice ('Jane Austen and one of her contemporaries', in Halperin, *Jane Austen*, p. 73; Devlin says that by not submitting Fanny threatens the society and proves that she alone is free ('*Mansfield Park*', *Ariel*, 2 [1971] 35).

6. Donovan, *Shaping Vision*, p. 150.

7. See also Moler, *Art of Allusion*, pp. 111–45.

8. Luria describes Fanny Price as 'one of the most subtle portraits of female rebellion extant' (rev. of *The Female Imagination*, by Spacks, *Signs*, 1 [1976] 982); Tayler and Luria describe Fanny as the 'epitome of the young woman in touch with true moral values and able to enforce them' and as 'the most radical and rebellious of all the Austen women' ('Gender and Genre', p. 112); Hummel describes *Mansfield Park* as Austen's 'most unequivocal condemnation of her own environment's propensity to relegate its women to a state of total subjection' ('Emblematic Charades', p. 253) and finds in her

final good fortune a continuing implication of victimisation (pp. 264–5).

9. Babb, *Jane Austen's Novels*, pp. 146, 155.
10. Allen, 'Jane Austen', p. 54.
11. C. S. Lewis, 'A Note on Jane Austen', in Watt, op. cit., p. 32.
12. Tave, 'Jane Austen', p. 73.
13. Lewis, op. cit., p. 29.
14. Benjamin Whitten, *Jane Austen's Comedy of Feeling* (Ankara: Hacettepe University Publications, 1974) p. 114.
15. Donovan, *Shaping Vision*, p. 153.
16. Tave, 'Jane Austen', p. 73.
17. Morgan describes Mary Crawford as a creature and a victim of forms, categories and preconceptions. The quality of her feeling for Edmund Bertram is 'oftenest described as a desire to possess or control him'. Her idea of successful love is control (*In the Meantime*, pp. 142–8).
18. In order: Ryals, op. cit., pp. 345–60; Hummel, op. cit., pp. 251–65; Devlin, '*Mansfield Park*', pp. 30–44; and Burroway, op. cit., p. 128.
19. See Duffy, 'Moral Integrity', pp. 71–91; Duckworth, *Improvement*, ch. 1; Harding, 'Regulated Hatred', pp. 44, 47; and Todd, *Women's Friendship*, pp. 247, 257, 268.

Chapter 7: *Emma:* The Flight from Womanhood

1. For the first view, see Craik, *Jane Austen: The Six Novels*, p. 125; Devlin, *Austen and Education*, p. 28; Gooneratne, *Jane Austen*, pp. 153–4; R. Hughes, 'The Education of Emma Woodhouse', *NCF*, 16 (1961) 70; and Mansell, *Novels of Jane Austen*, ch. 6 and p. 189. For the contrasting view, see Gubar, 'Sane Jane and the Critics', pp. 255–6; D. Minter, 'Aesthetic Vision and the World of *Emma*', *NCF*, 21 (1966) 59; Spacks, *Female Imagination*, p. 321; and Sulloway, 'Emma Woodhouse', p. 323.
2. For the view that Knightley is an exemplary figure, see Bradbrook, *Jane Austen: Emma*, pp. 12, 50; A. O. J. Cockshut, *Man and Woman* (London: Collins, 1977) pp. 63–4; Kennard, *Victims of Convention*, p. 38; Moers, *Literary Women*, p. 49; Litz, *Jane Austen*, pp. 134–5; and Wiesenfarth, '*Emma*: Point counter point', in Halperin, *Jane Austen*, p. 216. For the contrasting view, see J. Burros, *Jane Austen's 'Emma'* (Sydney University Press, 1968) p. 12; Cecil, *Portrait of Jane Austen*, p. 180; J. Hagan, 'The Closure of *Emma*', *SEL 1500–1900*, 15 (1975) 545–7, 554–61; and Sulloway, op. cit., p. 331.
3. For the view that the novel ends constructively, see Bradbrook, *Jane Austen: Emma*, p. 50; M. Bradbury, 'Persuasions: Moral Comedy in *Emma* and *Persuasion*', in *Possibilities: Essays on the State of the Novel* (London: Oxford University Press, 1973) pp. 65–6; L. Brown, 'Jane Austen', p. 338; Chabot, 'Jane Austen's Novels', p. 295; Duckworth, *Improvement*, p. 177; Garis, 'Learning Experience and Change', p. 74; Halperin, *Egoism and Self-Discovery*, pp. 12–13, 28; F. Hart, 'The Spaces of Privacy: Jane Austen', *NCF*, 30 (1975) 329–31; Litz, op. cit., pp. 133–6; Mansell, op. cit., pp. 147–51; Moler,

Art of Allusion, pp. 7–10; Spacks, *Female Imagination*, p. 321; H. Steeves, *Before Jane Austen*, pp. 357–8; Watt, 'Serious Reflections', p. 218; and R. Yeazell, 'Fictional Heroines and Feminist Critics', *Novel*, 8 (1974) 34. For a more pessimistic view, see J. Bayley, 'The "Irresponsibility" of Jane Austen', in Southam, *Critical Essays*, pp. 7–8; Gubar, op. cit., pp. 255–6; Kennard, op. cit., pp. 39–40; Schorer, 'Humiliation', p. 110; Sulloway, op. cit., pp. 326–32; and A. Wilson, 'The Neighbourhood of Tombuctoo: Conflicts in Jane Austen's Novels', in Southam, *Critical Essays*, p. 199.

4. For the first view, see Bradbrook, *Jane Austen: Emma*, pp. 13–14; Corsa, 'A Fair but Frozen Maid', p. 104; C. Edge, '*Emma*: A Technique of Characterization', in H. M. Harper, Jr, and Edge (eds), *The Classic British Novel* (Athens, Ga.: University of Georgia Press, 1972) pp. 53–60; Mansell, op. cit., pp. 151, 178; and Paris, ' "Creations inside a Creation"': The Case of Emma Woodhouse', *Psychocultural Review*, 2 (1978) 119–38. For the opposite view, see L. Brown, 'Jane Austen', p. 338; Duffy, 'Emma: The Awakening from Innocence', *ELH*, 21 (1954) 53; Minter, op. cit., pp. 51, 59; and Wiesenfarth, '*Emma*', p. 217.

5. See Bayley, op. cit., p. 17; Gilbert and Gubar, *The Madwoman in the Attic*, pp. 157–63; Gubar, op. cit., pp. 254–6; A. Kettle, 'Emma', in Watt, *Jane Austen: A Collection of Essays*, pp. 117–18; and Sulloway, op. cit., pp. 320–32.

6. W. Booth, 'Point of View and the Control of Distance in *Emma*', *NCF*, 16 (1961) 112.

7. Karen Horney uses the phrase to describe a female's attempt to take refuge in a male role in order to escape the implications for her life of the view of women's nature and role in a male-dominated society ('Flight from Womanhood', p. 11).

8. See Bardwick, *Psychology of Women*, pp. 137–8, and Rosaldo, in Rosaldo and Lamphere, *Woman, Culture and Society*, pp. 28–9.

9. So startling is the resulting perversion of purpose and personality that it has led to the observation that Emma 'shows many of the symptoms of psychological disorder which are characteristic of the neurotic personality' (Bradbrook, *Jane Austen: Emma*, p. 16) and that she shows 'all the paradigmatic symptoms of a damaged human being' (Sulloway, op. cit., p. 328).

10. Morgan (*In the Meantime*, pp. 26–42) appropriately describes Emma's behaviour as based on a belief that 'tenderness means surrender of self', but she sees the problem as one of a limited personal understanding of the importance of the inner life of others. Siefert (*Dilemma of the Talented Heroine*, pp. 128–30) ascribes Emma's desire for power to a mistaken identification of the freedom to manipulate with an ontological freedom of being and ascribes her imaginative creation of fictions to a 'defense against the mediocrity which characterises her society and which she fears will overwhelm her'.

11. Spacks, *Female Imagination*, p. 6.

12. Tave, *Some Words*, p. 218.

13. Duffy, 'Emma', pp. 48–9.

14. Murray, *House of Good Proportion*, p. 23.

15. Robert Liddel, *Novels of Jane Austen* (London: Longmans, 1963) p. 109.

16. H. Guntrip, *Personality Structure and Human Interaction* (New York: International Universities Press, 1969) p. 291.

17. Joseph Duffy, 'Emma', p. 43.

18. Daly, *Beyond God the Father*, p. 42.

19. Sulloway, op. cit., p. 325.

20. Cockshut observes that 'Knightley really suffers the pull of personal motives much more fiercely than Emma does' (op. cit., p. 64).

Chapter 8: *Persuasion:* A Mature Dependence

1. E.g., for the former see Mews, *Frail Vessels*, pp. 65–8, and Walling, 'Glorious Anxiety of Motion', p. 337; and for the latter see Litz, *Jane Austen*, p. 154.

2. See A. Gomme, 'On Not Being Persuaded', *Essays in Criticism*, 16 (1966) 182.

3. See Babb, *Jane Austen's Novels*, pp. 203–4; R. S. Crane, 'Jane Austen: "Persuasion" ', *The Idea of the Humanities* vol. II, (University of Chicago Press, 1967) p. 294; Duckworth, *Improvement*, p. 195; and Garis, 'Learning Experience and Change', p. 60.

4. D. Rackin, 'Jane Austen's Anatomy of Persuasion', in G. Goodin (ed.), *The English Novel in the Nineteenth Century* (Urbana, Ill.: University of Illinois Press, 1974) pp. 53, 64; and Whitten, *Jane Austen's Comedy of Feeling*, p. 9.

5. E.g., for the first view, see Whitten, op. cit., pp. 10, 34; for the second see Gomme, op. cit., p. 182, or Tave, *Some Words*, p. 280.

6. See Duffy, 'Structure and Idea in Jane Austen's "Persuasion" ', *NCF*, 8 (1954) 273; and P. Zietlow, 'Luck and Fortuitous Circumstance in *Persuasion*: Two Interpretations', *ELH*, 32 (1965) 194–5.

7. Duckworth, *Improvement*, p. 3.

8. de Beauvoir, *Second Sex*, p. 567.

9. Litz, op. cit., p. 155.

10. Duffy, 'Structure', p. 289.

11. Tave, *Some Words*, p. 256.

12. Whitten, op. cit., p. 98 and ch. 4.

13. Ibid., p. 31.

14. See Nardin, 'Christianity and the Structure of *Persuasion*', *Renascence*, 30 (1977) 48.

15. Babb, op. cit., p. 222.

16. Whitten, op. cit., p. 55.

17. Guntrip, *Personality Structure and Human Interaction*, p. 291.

18. Spence and Helmreich, *Masculinity & Femininity*, pp. 16–18. See discussion in ch. 2; see also Showalter, 'Literary Criticism', *Signs*, 1 (1975) 456–7.

19. Marilyn Farwell, 'Virginia Woolf and Androgyny', *Comparative Literature*, 16 (1975) 435.

20. Ann Ferguson, 'Androgyny As an Ideal for Human Development', in M. Vetterling-Braggin, *et al.* (eds), *Feminism and Philosophy* (Totowa, NJ: Rowman and Littlefield, 1977) p. 63.

Bibliography

Adler, Alfred, 'Sex', in *Psychoanalysis and Women*, ed. Jean Baker Miller (New York: Brunner/Mazel, 1973) pp. 33–42.

Agress, Lynne, *The Feminine Irony* (Rutherford, NJ: Fairleigh Dickinson University Press, 1978).

Allen, Walter, 'Jane Austen', in *Discussions of Jane Austen*, ed. William Heath (Boston: Heath, 1961) pp. 51–7.

Amis, Kingsley, 'What Became of Jane Austen?', *The Spectator*, 4 Oct 1957, in *Jane Austen: A Collection of Essays*, ed. Ian Watt (Englewood Cliffs, NJ: Prentice-Hall, 1961) pp. 141–4.

Appignanesi, Lisa, *Femininity and the Creative Imagination* (London: Vision Press, 1973).

Auerbach, Nina, *Communities of Women* (Cambridge, Mass.: Harvard University Press, 1978).

———, 'Jane Austen and Romantic Imprisonment', in *Jane Austen in a Social Context*, ed. David Monaghan (London: Macmillan, 1981) pp. 9–27.

———, 'O Brave New World: Evolution and Revolution in *Persuasion*', *ELH*, 39 (1972) 112–28.

Babb, Howard, *Jane Austen's Novels: The Fabric of Dialogue* (Columbus: Ohio State University Press, 1962).

Bakan, David, *The Duality of Human Existence: An Essay on Psychology and Religion* (Chicago, Ill.: Rand McNally, 1966).

Banfield, Ann, 'The Influence of Place: Jane Austen and the Novel of Social Consciousness', in Jane Austen in a Social Context, ed. David Monaghan (London: Macmillan, 1981) pp. 28–48.

Bardwick, Judith, *Psychology of Women* (New York: Harper & Row, 1971).

Basch, Françoise, *Relative Creatures: Victorian Women in Society and the Novel, 1837–67*, trans. Anthony Rudolf (London: Allen Lane, 1974).

Bayley, John, 'The "Irresponsibility" of Jane Austen', in *Critical Essays on Jane Austen*, ed. B. C. Southam (London: Routledge & Kegan Paul, 1968) pp. 1–20.

Beer, Patricia, *Reader, I Married Him* (London: Macmillan, 1974).

Benkovitz, Miriam, 'Some Observations on Women's Concept of Self in the 18th Century', in *Woman in the 18th Century and Other Essays,* ed. Paul Fritz and Richard Morton (Toronto: Hakkert, 1976) pp. 37–54.

Booth, Wayne, 'Point of View and the Control of Distance in *Emma*', *NCF*, 16 (1961) 95–116.

Bowen, Elizabeth, 'Jane Austen', in *The English Novelists*, ed. Derek Verschoyle (New York: Harcourt, Brace, 1936) pp. 101–13.

Bradbrook, Frank, *Jane Austen and Her Predecessors* (Cambridge University Press, 1967).

———, *Jane Austen: Emma* (London: Edward Arnold, 1961).

Bradbury, Malcolm, 'Persuasions: Moral Comedy in *Emma* and *Persuasion*', in *Possibilities: Essays on the State of the Novel* (London: Oxford University Press, 1973) pp. 55–78.

Brissenden, R.F., '*Mansfield Park*: freedom and the family', in *Jane Austen: Bicentenary Essays*, ed. John Halperin (Cambridge University Press, 1975) pp. 156–71.

Brophy, Brigid, 'Jane Austen and the Stuarts', in *Critical Essays on Jane Austen*, ed. B. C. Southam (London: Routledge & Kegan Paul, 1968) pp. 21–38.

Brown, Julia, *Jane Austen's Novels: Social Change and Literary Form* (Cambridge, Mass.: Harvard University Press, 1979).

Brown, Lloyd, *Bits of Ivory: Narrative Techniques in Jane Austen's Fiction* (Baton Rouge, La.: Louisiana State University Press, 1973).

———, 'The Business of Marrying and Mothering', in *Jane Austen's Achievement*, ed. Juliet McMaster (New York: Barnes & Noble, 1976) pp. 27–43.

———, 'Jane Austen and the Feminist Tradition', *NCF*, 28 (1973) 321–38.

Burgan, Mary, 'Mr. Bennet and the Failures of Fatherhood in Jane Austen's Novels', *JEGP*, 74 (1975) 536–52.

Burgess, Anthony, 'The Book is Not for Reading', *New York Times Book Review*, 4 Dec 1966, p. 1.

Burroway, Janet, 'The Irony of the Insufferable Prig: *Mansfield Park*', *Critical Quarterly*, 9 (1967) 127–38.

Burros, J. F., *Jane Austen's 'Emma'* (Sydney University Press, 1968).

Bush, Douglas, *Jane Austen* (New York: Macmillan, 1975).

Butler, Marilyn, *Jane Austen and the War of Ideas* (Oxford University Press, 1975).

Calder, Jenni, *Women and Marriage in Victorian Fiction*, intro. David Daiches (New York: Oxford University Press, 1976).

Cecil, David, *A Portrait of Jane Austen* (London: Constable, 1978).

Chabot, C. Larry, 'Jane Austen's Novels: The Vicissitudes of Desire', *American Imago*, 32 (1975) 288–308.

Chafetz, Janet, *Masculine/Feminine or Human?* (Itasca, Ill.: F. E. Peacock, 1974).

Chandler, Alice, ' "A Pair of Fine Eyes": Jane Austen's Treatment of Sex', *Studies in the Novel*, 7 (1975) 88–103.

Chodorow, Nancy, 'Family Structure and Feminine Personality', in *Woman, Culture, and Society*, ed. Michelle Rosaldo and Louise Lamphere (Stanford University Press, 1974) pp. 43–66.

Cockshut, A. O. J., *Man and Woman: A Study of Love and the Novel 1740–1940* (London: Collins, 1977).

Copeland, Edward, 'Money in the Novels of Fanny Burney', *Studies in the Novel*, 8 (1976) 24–37.

Corsa, Helen, 'A Fair But Frozen Maid: A Study of Jane Austen's *Emma*', *Literature and Psychology*, 19 (1969) 101–21.

Craik, W. A., *Jane Austen: The Six Novels* (1965; London: Methuen, 1966).

Crane, R. S., 'Jane Austen: "Persuasion" ', *The Idea of the Humanities and Other Essays Critical and Historical*, vol. II (University of Chicago Press, 1967) pp. 283–302.

Cutting, Rose Marie, 'Defiant Women: The Growth of Feminism in Fanny Burney's Novels', *SEL 1500–1900*, 17 (1977) 519–30.

Daiches, David, 'Jane Austen, Karl Marx, and the Aristocratic Dance', *American*

Scholar, 17 (1948) 289–96.

Daly, Mary, *Beyond God the Father: Toward a Philosophy of Women's Liberation* (Boston: Beacon, 1973).

de Beauvoir, Simone, *The Second Sex*, trans. and ed. H. M. Parshley (New York: Bantam Books, 1970).

Dell, Floyd, *Love in the Machine Age* (New York: Octagon Books, 1973).

DeRose, Peter, 'Hardship, Recollection, and Disciplines: Three Lessons in *Mansfield Park*', *Studies in the Novel*, 9 (1977) 261–78.

———, *Jane Austen and Samuel Johnson* (Washington, D.C.: University Press of America, 1980).

Devlin, David, *Jane Austen and Education* (New York: Barnes & Noble, 1975).

———, '*Mansfield Park*', *Ariel*, 2 (1971) 30–44.

Dijkstra, Bram, 'The Androgyne in Nineteenth-Century Art and Literature', *Comparative Literature*, 26 (1974) 62–73.

Donoghue, Denis, 'A View of "Mansfield Park" ', in *Critical Essays on Jane Austen*, ed. B. C. Southam (London: Routledge & Kegan Paul, 1968) pp. 39–59.

Donohue, Joseph W., Jr, 'Ordination and the Divided House at Mansfield Park', *ELH*, 32 (1965) 169–78.

Donovan, Robert, '*Mansfield Park* and Jane Austen's Moral Universe', in *The Shaping Vision: Imagination in the English Novel from Defoe to Dickens* (Ithaca, NY: Cornell University Press, 1966) pp. 140–72.

———, 'The Mind of Jane Austen', in *Jane Austen Today*, ed. Joel Weinsheimer (Athens, Ga.: University of Georgia Press, 1975) pp. 109–27.

Duckworth, Alistair, *The Improvement of the Estate* (Baltimore, Md.: Johns Hopkins Press, 1971).

———, 'Prospects and Retrospects', in *Jane Austen Today*, ed. Joel Weinsheimer (Athens, Ga.: University of Georgia Press, 1975) pp. 1–32.

———, ' "Spillikins, paper, ships, riddles, conundrums, and cards": games in Jane Austen's life and fiction', in *Jane Austen: Bicentenary Essays*, ed. John Halperin (Cambridge University Press, 1975) pp. 279–97.

Duffy, Joseph M., Jr, 'Emma: The Awakening from Innocence', *ELH*, 21 (1954) 39–53.

———, 'Moral Integrity and Moral Anarchy in *Mansfield Park*', *ELH*, 23 (1956) 71–91.

———, 'The Politics of Love: Marriage and the Good Society in *Pride and Prejudice*', *University of Windsor Review*, 11 (1976) 5–26.

———, 'Structure and Idea in Jane Austen's "Persuasion" ' *NCF*, 8 (1954) 272–89.

Edge, Charles, '*Emma*: A Technique of Characterization', in *The Classic British Novel*, ed. Howard M. Harper, Jr, and Charles Edge (Athens, Ga.: University of Georgia Press, 1972) pp. 51–64.

Edwards, Lee, 'The Labors of Psyche: Toward a Theory of Female Heroism', *Critical Inquiry*, 6 (1979) 33–50.

Ellis, Katherine, 'Charlotte Smith's Subversive Gothic', *Feminist Studies*, 3 (1976) 51–5.

Ellmann, Mary, *Thinking About Women* (New York: Harcourt, Brace and World, 1968).

Elsbree, Langdon, 'Jane Austen and the Dance of Fidelity and Complaisance', *NCF*, 15 (1960) 113–36.

Farrar, Reginald, 'Jane Austen', *Quarterly Review*, 227 (1917) 11–12, 16–18.

Farwell, Marilyn, 'Virginia Woolf and Androgyny', *Contemporary Literature*, 16 (1975) 433–51.

Fergus, Jan, 'Sex and Social Life in Jane Austen's Novels', in *Jane Austen in a Social Context*, ed. David Monaghan (London: Macmillan, 1981) pp. 66–85.

Ferguson, Ann, 'Androgyny As an Ideal for Human Development', in *Feminism and Philosophy*, ed. Mary Vetterling-Braggin *et al* (Totowa, NJ: Rowman and Littlefield, 1977) pp. 45–69.

Figes, Eva, *Patriarchal Attitudes* (New York: Stein and Day, 1970).

Fleishman, Avrom, '*Mansfield Park* in Its Time', *NCF*, 22 (1967) 1–18.

Flexner, Eleanor, *Mary Wollstonecraft: A Biography* (New York: Coward, McCann and Geoghegan, 1972).

Fowler, Marian, 'The Feminist Bias of *Pride and Prejudice*', *Dalhousie Review*, 57 (1977) 47–64.

Garis, Robert, 'Learning Experience and Change', in *Critical Essays on Jane Austen*, ed. B. C. Southam (London: Routledge & Kegan Paul, 1968) pp. 60–82.

Garrod, H. W., 'Jane Austen: A Depreciation', in *Discussions of Jane Austen*, ed. William Heath (Boston: Heath, 1961) pp. 32–40.

Gilbert, Sandra M. and Susan Gubar, *The Madwoman in the Attic: The Woman Writer and the Nineteenth-Century Literary Imagination* (New Haven: Yale University Press, 1979).

Gillie, Christopher, '*Sense and Sensibility*: An Assessment', *Essays in Criticism*, 9 (1959) 1–9.

Glassman, Peter, 'Acts of Enclosure', *Hudson Review*, 30 (1977) 138–46.

Goldberg, Steven, *The Inevitability of Patriarchy* (New York: William Morrow, 1973).

Gomme, Andor, 'On Not Being Persuaded', *Essays in Criticism*, 16 (1966) 170–84.

Gooneratne, Yasmine, *Jane Austen* (Cambridge University Press, 1970).

Gorer, Geoffrey, 'Poor Honey: Some Notes on Jane Austen and Her Mother', *London Magazine*, 4 (1957) 35–48.

Gornall, J. F. G., 'Marriage and Property in Jane Austen's Novels', *History Today*, 17 (1967) 805–11.

Gornick, Vivian and Barbara Moran (eds), *Women in Sexist Society: Studies in Power and Powerlessness* (New York: Basic Books, 1971).

Gould, Gerald, 'The Gate Scene at Sotherton in *Mansfield Park*', *Literature and Psychology*, 20 (1970) 75–8.

Gubar, Susan, 'Sane Jane and the Critics: "Professions and Falsehoods" ', *Novel*, 8 (1975) 246–59.

Guntrip, Henry, *Personality Structure and Human Interaction* (New York: International Universities Press, 1969).

Hagan, John, 'The Closure of *Emma*', *SEL 1500–1900*, 15 (1975) 545–61.

Hagstrum, Jean, *Sex and Sensibility* (University of Chicago Press, 1980).

Halperin, John, *Egoism and Self-Discovery in the Victorian Novel* (New York: Burt Franklin, 1974).

Halsband, Robert, 'Women and Literature in 18th Century England', in *Woman in the 18th Century and Other Essays*, ed. Paul Fritz and Richard Morton (Toronto: Hakkert, 1976) pp. 55–72.

Harding, D. W., 'Regulated Hatred: An Aspect of the Work of Jane Austen', in *Discussions of Jane Austen*, ed. William Heath (Boston: Heath, 1961) pp. 41–50.

Hardy, Barbara, *A Reading of Jane Austen* (London: Peter Owen, 1975).

Hardy, Barbara and David Daiches, 'Jane Austen', in *The English Novel* (London: Sussex Publications, 1976) pp. 15–30.

Hart, Francis, 'The Spaces of Privacy: Jane Austen', *NCF*, 39 (1975) 305–33.

Hartley, L. P., 'Jane Austen and the Abyss', *Essays by Divers Hands*, 35 (1969) 85–100.

Hartmann, Heinz, *Ego Psychology and the Problem of Adaptation* (New York: International Universities Press, 1958).

Heilbrun, Carolyn, 'Marriage Perceived: English Literature 1873–1941', in *What Manner of Woman*, ed. Marlene Springer (New York University Press, 1977) pp. 160–83.

———, *Toward a Recognition of Androgyny* (New York: Knopf, 1973).

Heilman, Robert, *'E pluribus unum:* Parts and whole in *Pride and Prejudice*', in *Jane Austen: Bicentenary Essays*, ed. John Halperin (Cambridge University Press, 1975) pp. 123–43.

Horney, Karen, 'The Flight from Womanhood', in *Psychoanalysis and Women*, ed. Jean Baker Miller (New York: Brunner/Mazel, 1973) pp. 3–16.

Hughes, R. E., 'The Education of Emma Woodhouse', *NCF*, 16 (1961) 69–74.

Hummel, Madeline, 'Emblematic Charades and the Observant Woman in *Mansfield Park*', *TSLL*, 15 (1973) 251–66.

Janeway, Elizabeth, *Man's World, Woman's Place* (New York: William Morrow, 1971).

Kelly, Gary, *The English Jacobin Novel 1780–1805* (Clarendon: Oxford University Press, 1976).

Kennard, Jean, *Victims of Convention* (Hamden, Conn.: Archon Books, 1978).

Kettle, Arnold, 'Emma', in *Jane Austen: A Collection of Essays*, ed. Ian Watt (Englewood Cliffs, NJ: Prentice-Hall, 1961) pp. 112–23.

Kinkead-Weekes, Mark, 'This Old Maid: Jane Austen Replies to Charlotte Brontë and D. H. Lawrence', *NCF*, 30 (1975) 399–419.

Kleinbaum, Abby, 'Women in the Age of Light', in *Becoming Visible: Women in European History*, ed. Renate Bridenthal and Claudia Koonz (Boston, Mass.: Houghton Mifflin, 1977) pp. 217–35.

Krieger, Murray, *The Classic Vision: The Retreat from Extremity in Modern Literature* (Baltimore, Md.: Johns Hopkins Press, 1971).

Kronenberger, Louis, 'Jane Austen: *Lady Susan* and *Pride and Prejudice*', in *The Polished Surface: Essays in the Literature of Worldliness* (New York: Knopf, 1969) pp. 127–50.

Laing, R. D., *The Divided Self* (London: Tavistock Publications, 1960).

———, *The Politics of Experience* (New York: Pantheon Books, 1967).

———, *Self and Others*, 2nd edn (New York: Pantheon Books, 1969).

Lascelles, Mary, 'Jane Austen and the novel', in *Jane Austen: Bicentenary Essays*, ed. John Halperin (Cambridge University Press, 1975) pp. 235–46.

Leavis, Q. D., 'A Critical Theory of Jane Austen's Writings', *Scrutiny*, 10 (June 1941) 61–87; 10 (Oct 1941) 114–42; 10 (Jan 1942) 272–94; 12 (Spring 1944) 104–19.

LeGates, Marlene, 'The Cult of Womanhood in Eighteenth-Century Thought', *Eighteenth-Century Studies*, 10 (1976) 21–39.

Lerner, Laurence, *The Truthtellers: Jane Austen, George Eliot, D. H. Lawrence* (New York: Shocken, 1967).

Levine, Jay Arnold, *'Lady Susan*: Jane Austen's Character of the Merry Widow',

SEL 1500–1900, 1 (1961) 23–34.

Lewes, G. H., 'The Lady Novelists', in *Jane Austen: The Critical Heritage*, ed. B. C. Southam (London: Routledge & Kegan Paul, 1968) pp. 140–1.

Lewis, C. S., 'A Note on Jane Austen', in *Jane Austen: A Collection of Critical Essays*, ed. Ian Watt (Englewood Cliffs, NJ: Prentice-Hall, 1961) pp. 25–34.

Liddel, Robert, *Novels of Jane Austen* (London: Longmans, 1963).

Litz, A. Walton, *Jane Austen: A Study of Her Artistic Development* (New York: Oxford University Press, 1965).

Lodge, David, *Language of Fiction* (London: Routledge & Kegan Paul, 1966).

Lovell, Terry, 'Jane Austen and the Gentry: A Study in Literature and Ideology', in *The Sociology of Literature*, ed. Diana Laurenson, Sociological Review Monographs No. 26 (University of Keele, 1978) pp. 15–37.

Luria, Gina, Review of *Charlotte Brontë: The Self Conceived*, by Helen Moglen, and *Jane Austen and the War of Ideas*, by Marilyn Butler, *Signs*, 4 (1978) 374–80.

———, Review of *The Female Imagination*, by Patricia Meyer Spacks, *Signs*, 1 (1976) 979–83.

MacCarthy, B. G., *The Later Women Novelists 1744–1818* (Dublin: Cork University Press, 1947).

MacDonald, Susan, 'Passivity and the Female Role in *Pride and Prejudice*', *Women and Literature*, 6 (1978) 35–46.

McKillop, Alan, 'The Context of *Sense and Sensibility*', *Rice Institute Pamphlets*, 44 (1957) 65–78.

McMaster, Juliet, *Jane Austen on Love* (University of Victoria, 1978).

Magee, William, 'The Happy Marriage: The Influence of Charlotte Smith on Jane Austen', *Studies in the Novel*, 7 (1975) 120–32.

Mansell, Darrel, *The Novels of Jane Austen* (London: Macmillan, 1973).

Measham, D.C., 'Sentiment and Sentimental Psychology in Jane Austen', *Renaissance and Modern Studies*, 16 (1972) 61–85.

Mews, Hazel, *Frail Vessels: Woman's Role in Women's Novels from Fanny Burney to George Eliot* (London: Athlone Press, 1969).

Miles, Rosalind, *The Fiction of Sex* (London: Vision Press, 1974).

Miller, John (ed.), *A World of Her Own: Writers and the Feminist Controversy* (Columbus: Charles E. Merrill, 1971).

Millett, Kate, *Sexual Politics* (New York: Doubleday, 1970).

Minter, David, 'Aesthetic Vision and the World of *Emma*', *NCF*, 21 (1966) 49–59.

Mitchell, Juliet, *Psychoanalysis and Feminism* (New York: Pantheon Books, 1974).

———, *Woman's Estate* (New York: Pantheon Books, 1971).

Moers, Ellen, *Literary Women* (New York: Doubleday, 1976).

Moler, Kenneth, *Jane Austen's Art of Allusion* (Lincoln: University of Nebraska Press, 1968).

———, '*Pride and Prejudice*: Jane Austen's "Patrician Hero" ', *SEL 1500–1900*, 7 (1967) 491–508.

Monaghan, David, 'Jane Austen and the Feminist Critics', *Room of One's Own*, 4 (1979) 34–9.

———, 'Jane Austen and the Position of Women', in *Jane Austen in a Social Context*, ed. David Monaghan (London: Macmillan, 1981) pp. 105–21.

———, 'Jane Austen and the Social Critics: Recent Trends', *English Studies in Canada*, 2 (1976) 280–7.

———, *Jane Austen: Structure and Social Vision* (London: Macmillan, 1980).

Morgan, Susan, *In the Meantime: Character and Perception in Jane Austen's Fiction* (University of Chicago Press, 1980).

Mudrick, Marvin, *Jane Austen: Irony as Defense and Discovery* (Princeton University Press, 1952).

———, 'Jane Austen's drawing-room', in *Jane Austen: Bicentenary Essays*, ed. John Halperin (Cambridge University Press, 1975) pp. 247–61.

Murray, Michele (ed.), *A House of Good Proportion* (New York: Simon & Schuster, 1973).

Myers, Sylvia, 'Womanhood in Jane Austen's Novels', *Novel*, 3 (1970) 225–32.

Nardin, Jane, 'Christianity and the Structure of *Persuasion*', *Renascence*, 30 (1977) 43–55.

———, *Those Elegant Decorums: The Concept of Propriety in Jane Austen's Novels* (Albany, NY: State University of New York Press, 1973).

Newton, Judith, *Women, Power, and Subversion: Social Strategies in British Fiction* (Athens, Ga.: University of Georgia Press, 1981).

O'Connor, Frank, 'Jane Austen: The Flight from Fancy', in *Discussions of Jane Austen*, ed. William Heath (Boston: Heath, 1961) pp. 65–74.

Odmark, John, *An Understanding of Jane Austen's Novels* (Oxford: Basil Blackwell, 1981).

Ortner, Sherry, 'Is Female to Male as Nature is to Culture?', in *Woman, Culture, and Society*, ed. Michelle Rosaldo and Louise Lamphere (Stanford University Press, 1974) pp. 72–80.

Ovesey, Lionel, 'Masculine Aspirations in Women: An Adaptational Analysis', *Psychiatry*, 19 (1956) 341–51.

Paris, Bernard, *Character and Conflict in Jane Austen's Novels* (Detroit, Mich.: Wayne State University Press, 1979).

———, ' "Creations inside a Creation": The Case of Emma Woodhouse', *Psychocultural Review*, 2 (1978) 119–38.

———, *A Psychological Approach to Fiction* (Bloomington, Ill.: Indiana University Press, 1974).

Payne, Harry (rev. art.), 'The Eighteenth-Century Family: An Elusive Object', *Eighteenth-Century Life*, 5 (1978) 48–61.

Polhemus, Robert, *Comic Faith: The Great Tradition from Austen to Joyce* (University of Chicago Press, 1980).

Quinlan, Maurice, *Victorian Prelude* (New York: Columbia University Press, 1941).

Rackin, Donald, 'Jane Austen's Anatomy of Persuasion', in *The English Novel in the Nineteenth Century*, ed. George Goodin (Urbana, Ill.: University of Illinois Press, 1974) pp. 52–80.

Rees, Joan, *Jane Austen, Woman and Writer* (New York: St Martin's Press, 1976).

Reik, Theodore, *Psychology of Sex Relations* (New York: Rinehart, 1945).

Rich, Adrienne, *Of Woman Born: Motherhood as Experience and Institution* (New York: Norton, 1976).

Richetti, John, 'The Portrayal of Women in Restoration and Eighteenth-Century English Literature', in *What Manner of Woman*, ed. Marlene Springer (New York University Press, 1977) pp. 65–97.

Roberts, Warren, *Jane Austen and the French Revolution* (New York: St Martin's Press, 1979).

Robinson, Lillian S., 'Why Marry Mr. Collins?', in *Sex, Class, and Culture* (Bloomington, Ind.: Indiana University Press, 1978) pp. 178–99.

Rockwell, Joan, *Facts in Fiction* (London: Routledge & Kegan Paul, 1974).

Rogers, Katherine, 'Inhibitions on Eighteenth-Century Women Novelists: Elizabeth Inchbald and Charlotte Smith', *Eighteenth-Century Studies*, 11 (1977) 63–78.

———, 'Richardson's Empathy with Women', in *The Authority of Experience*, ed. Arlyn Diamond and Lee Edwards (Amherst, Mass.: University of Massachusetts Press, 1977) pp. 118–36.

Rosaldo, Michelle, 'Woman, Culture, and Society: A Theoretical Overview', in *Woman, Culture, and Society*, ed. Michelle Rosaldo and Louise Lamphere (Stanford University Press, 1974) pp. 17–42.

Rowbotham, Sheila, *Hidden from History: 300 Years of Women's Oppression and the Fight Against It* (London: Pluto Press, 1973).

———, *Women, Resistance and Revolution* (New York: Pantheon Books, 1972).

Ryals, Clyde, 'Being and Doing in *Mansfield Park*', *Archiv*, 206 (1970) 345–60.

Ryle, Gilbert, 'Jane Austen and the Moralists', in *Critical Essays on Jane Austen*, ed. B. C. Southam (London: Routledge & Kegan Paul, 1968) pp. 106–22.

Sacks, Karen, 'Engels Revisited: Women, the Organization of Production, and Private Property', in *Woman, Culture, and Society*, ed. Michelle Rosaldo and Louise Lamphere (Stanford University Press, 1974) pp. 207–22.

Sampson, Ronald, *The Psychology of Power* (New York: Pantheon Books, 1966).

Schnorrenberg, Barbara, with Jean Hunter, 'The Eighteenth-Century Englishwoman', in *The Women of England: From Anglo-Saxon Times to the Present*, ed. Barbara Kanner (Hamden, Conn.: Archon Books, 1979) pp. 183–228.

Schochet, Gordon, *Patriarchalism in Political Thought* (New York: Basic Books, 1975).

Schorer, Mark, 'The Humiliation of Emma Woodhouse', in *Jane Austen: A Collection of Essays*, ed. Ian Watt (Englewood Cliffs, NJ: Prentice-Hall, 1963) pp. 98–111.

———, 'Pride Unprejudiced', *Kenyon Review*, 18 (1956) 72–91.

Schreiner, Olive, *The Letters of Olive Schreiner 1876–1920*, ed. S. C. Cronwright-Schreiner (Boston: Little, Brown, 1924).

Seidenberg, Robert, 'For the Future – Equity?', in *Psychoanalysis and Women*, ed. Jean Baker Miller (New York: Brunner/Mazel, 1973) pp. 333–53.

Sherman, Julia, *On the Psychology of Women* (Springfield, Ill.: Charles C. Thomas, 1971).

Sherry, James, '*Pride and Prejudice*: The Limits of Society', *SEL 1500–1900*, 19 (1979) 609–22.

Sherry, Norman, *Jane Austen* (London: Evans Brothers, 1966).

Shorter, E., *The Making of the Modern Family* (New York: Basic Books, 1975).

Showalter, Elaine, 'Literary Criticism', *Signs*, 1 (1975) 435–60.

———, *A Literature of Their Own: British Women Novelists from Brontë to Lessing* (Princeton University Press, 1977).

Siefert, Susan, *The Dilemma of the Talented Heroine* (Montreal: Eden Press, 1978).

Southam, B. C., *Jane Austen's Literary Manuscripts* (London: Oxford University Press, 1964).

———, '*Sanditon*: the Seventh Novel', in *Jane Austen's Achievement*, ed. Juliet McMaster (New York: Barnes & Noble, 1976) pp. 1–26.

Spacks, Patricia Meyer, *The Female Imagination* (New York: Knopf, 1975).

———, *Imagining A Self: Autobiography and Novel in Eighteenth-Century England* (Cambridge: Harvard University Press, 1976).

————, 'Muted Discord: Generational Conflict in Jane Austen', in *Jane Austen in a Social Context*, ed. David Monaghan (London: Macmillan, 1981) pp. 159–79.

————, 'Women's Stories, Women's Selves', *Hudson Review*, 30 (1977) 29–46.

Spence, Janet and Robert Helmreich, *Masculinity & Femininity* (Austin: University of Texas Press, 1978).

Staves, Susan, '*Evelina*; or, Female Difficulties', *MP*, 73 (1976) 368–81.

Steeves, Edna, 'Pre-Feminism in Some Eighteenth-Century Novels', *Texas Quarterly*, 16 (1973) 48–57.

Steeves, Harrison, *Before Jane Austen* (New York: Holt, Rinehart & Winston, 1965).

Stewart, Grace, *A New Mythos: The Novel of the Artist as Heroine 1877–1977* (St Albans, Vt: Eden Press, 1977).

Stewart, J. I. M., 'Tradition and Miss Austen', in *Critical Essays on Jane Austen*, ed. B. C. Southam (London: Routledge & Kegan Paul, 1968) pp. 123–35.

Stone, Donald, 'Victorian Feminism and the Nineteenth-Century Novel', *Women's Studies*, 1 (1972) 69–72.

Stone, Lawrence, *The Family, Sex and Marriage in England 1500–1800* (New York: Harper & Row, 1977).

Sulloway, Alison, 'Emma Woodhouse and *A Vindication of the Rights of Women*', *Wordsworth Circle*, 7 (1976) 320–32.

Tave, Stuart, 'Jane Austen and one of her contemporaries', in *Jane Austen: Bicentenary Essays*, ed. John Halperin (Cambridge University Press, 1975) pp. 61–74.

————, *Some Words of Jane Austen* (University of Chicago Press, 1973).

Tayler, Irene and Gina Luria, 'Gender and Genre: Women in British Romantic Literature', in *What Manner of Woman*, ed. Marlene Springer (New York University Press, 1977) pp. 98–123.

Ten Harmsel, Henrietta, *Jane Austen: A Study in Fictional Conventions* (The Hague: Mouton, 1964).

Thompson, Clara, 'Cultural Pressures in the Psychology of Women', in *Psychoanalysis and Women*, ed. Jean Baker Miller (New York: Brunner/Mazel, 1973) pp. 49–64.

Thomson, Patricia, *The Victorian Heroine: A Changing Ideal, 1837–1873* (London: Oxford University Press, 1956).

Todd, Janet, 'Female Friendship in Jane Austen's Novels', *Journal of the Rutgers University Library*, 39 (1977) 29–43.

————, *Women's Friendship in Literature* (New York: Columbia University Press, 1980).

Trilling, Lionel, *The Opposing Self* (New York: Viking, 1959).

Trumbach, Randolph, *The Rise of the Egalitarian Family* (New York: Academic Press, 1978).

Van Ghent, Dorothy, *The English Novel: Form and Function* (New York: Harper, 1961).

Vigman, Fred, *Beauty's Triumph: or The Superiority of the Fair Sex Invincibly Proved* (Boston, Mass.: Christopher Publishing House, 1966).

Wagner, Geoffrey, *Five for Freedom: A Study of Feminism in Fiction* (Rutherford, NJ: Fairleigh Dickinson University Press, 1973).

Walling, William, 'The Glorious Anxiety of Motion: Jane Austen's *Persuasion*', *Wordsworth Circle*, 7 (1976) 333–41.

Watt, Ian, 'On *Sense and Sensibility*', in *Jane Austen: A Collection of Essays*, ed. Ian

Watt (New York: Harper & Row, 1961) pp. 41–51.

———, 'Serious Reflections on *The Rise of the Novel*', *Novel*, 1 (1968) 205–18.

Whitten, Benjamin, *Jane Austen's Comedy of Feeling* (Ankara: Hacettepe University Publications, 1974).

Wiesenfarth, Joseph, '*Emma*: point counter point', in *Jane Austen: Bicentenary Essays*, ed. John Halperin (Cambridge University Press, 1975) pp. 207–20.

———, *The Errand of Form* (New York: Fordham University Press, 1967).

Wilson, Angus, 'Evil in the English Novel', *Kenyon Review*, 29 (1967) 167–94.

———, 'The Neighbourhood of Tombuctoo: Conflicts in Jane Austen's Novels', in *Critical Essays on Jane Austen*, ed. B. C. Southam (London: Routledge & Kegan Paul, 1968) pp. 182–200.

Wilson, Mona, *Jane Austen and Some Contemporaries* (London: Cresset Press, 1938).

Wright, Andrew, *Jane Austen's Novels: A Study in Structure* (New York: Oxford University Press, 1953).

Yeazell, Ruth, 'Fictional Heroines and Feminist Critics', *Novel*, 8 (1974) 29–38.

Zeman, Anthea, *Presumptuous Girls: Women and Their World in the Serious Woman's Novel* (London: Weidenfeld & Nicolson, 1977).

Zietlow, Paul, 'Luck and Fortuitous Circumstance in *Persuasion*: Two Interpretations' *ELH*, 32 (1965) 179–95.

Zimmerman, Everett, 'Jane Austen and *Mansfield Park*: A Discrimination of Ironies', *Studies in the Novel*, 1 (1969) 347–56.

Index